AMERICAN INDIAN

CULTURE AND RESEARCH

JOURNAL

VOLUME 34
NUMBER 2
2010

American Indian Studies Center
University of California, Los Angeles
3220 Campbell Hall, Box 951548
Los Angeles, California 90095-1548

AMERICAN INDIAN CULTURE AND RESEARCH JOURNAL
Volume 34, Number 2 (2010)

The *American Indian Culture and Research Journal* is a scholarly quarterly providing an interdisciplinary forum for significant contributions to the advancement of knowledge about American Indians. Authors are requested to submit manuscripts.

STAFF

Guest Editor: Robert Alexander Innes

Acting Editor: Pamela Grieman

Senior Editor: Christine A. T. Dunn

Book Review Editor: Christine A. T. Dunn

Graphic Designer: William Morosi

Editorial Assistant: Amanda Pluskett-Turley

Sales & Subscriptions: Amanda Patrick

SUBSCRIPTION RATES

$40.00/year for individuals ($70.00/two years)—print only

$60.00/year for foreign individuals ($110.00/two years)—print only

PRINT AND ONLINE

$195.00/year for individuals

$245.00/year for institutions and departments ($450.00/two years)

$215.00/year for foreign individuals

$265.00/year for foreign institutions, departments, etc. ($490.00/two years)

$15.00 per single issue/back issue, plus postage

Online access is available at http://aisc.metapress.com/

Make checks payable to: Regents of the University of California

Mail to:

UCLA American Indian Studies Center Publications
3220 Campbell Hall, Box 951548
Los Angeles, CA 90095-1548

e-mail: sales@aisc.ucla.edu • fax: (310) 206-7060

Visit the American Indian Studies Center publications Web site at http://www.books.aisc.ucla.edu/

The *American Indian Culture and Research Journal* is a member of the Conference of Historical Journals. Articles in the *American Indian Culture and Research Journal* are indexed in *Academic OneFile, America: History and Life, Anthropological Literature, Article First, Arts & Humanities/Current Contents, Arts & Humanities Citation Index/ISI Web of Knowledge, Bibliography of Native North Americans, Current Index to Journals in Education* (ERIC), *Expanded Academic, Expanded Academic ASAP, Historical Abstracts, Humanities International Complete, IBZ (International Bibliography of Periodical Literature in the Humanities and Social Sciences), Journal of American History, Linguistics and Language Behavior Abstracts, MLA International Bibliography, Periodicals Index Online* (prior to 1995), *PAIS International, Social Sciences Citation Index/ISI Web of Knowledge,* and the *Sociological Abstracts.* The journal is available on microfilm through *University Microfilms.* Book reviews are indexed in *Book Review Index* and *International Bibliography of Book Reviews of Scholarly Literature in the Humanities and Social Sciences* (IBR).

 The *American Indian Culture and Research Journal* is printed on recycled paper.

Notice to Contributors

MANUSCRIPT SUBMISSION

1. Submit four (4) copies of the manuscript to: Editor, *American Indian Culture and Research Journal*, American Indian Studies Center, UCLA, 3220 Campbell Hall, Box 951548, Los Angeles, CA 90095-1548.

2. Because all manuscripts are evaluated by at least three anonymous referees, please keep identifying material out of the manuscript. Attach a cover page giving authorship, institutional affiliation, and acknowledgments.

3. All copy must be *typed, double-spaced* (including indented material and endnotes) on 8½ × 11 inch white paper. All margins must be at least one inch. After an article is accepted, the author will be asked to submit a CD containing the article. Manuscripts should be written in Microsoft Word. CDs will not be returned to authors.

4. The *Journal* requires that tables, endnotes, and format conform to *The Chicago Manual of Style*, 15th edition (Chicago and London: University of Chicago Press, 2003). Special attention should be given to Chapter 17. Do not use footnotes or any variation of the author-date system. Submissions that do not conform to our style format may be returned for retyping.

5. Copies of manuscripts submitted for review will not be returned to authors. Do not submit original artwork for review. Original artwork will be requested upon acceptance for publication.

6. The review process is ordinarily completed within three months. If processing is delayed beyond that point, authors will be notified.

7. Manuscripts accepted for publication in the *American Indian Culture and Research Journal* are subject to stylistic editing. Page proofs are sent to authors. **All authors and reviewers are required to assign copyright to the Regents of the University of California**.

MULTIPLE SUBMISSION POLICY: The *American Indian Culture and Research Journal* regards submission of a manuscript to one professional journal while that manscript is under review by any other journal as unacceptable. It is further assumed by the *American Indian Culture and Research Journal* that work submitted for review has not been previously published and is not scheduled for publication elsewhere. If other published or submitted papers exist that are based on the same or closely related data sets, such papers should be noted and referenced in a cover letter to the editor, and their relation to the submitted paper should be explained briefly.

Contents

Volume 34, Number 2

Special Edition:
New Interpretations of Native Cultural Preservation, Revitalization, and Persistence

Articles

Reviews

Introduction: Native Studies and Native Cultural Preservation, Revitalization, and Persistence

ROBERT ALEXANDER INNES

At a recent conference, Frances Widdowson presented a critical assessment of Native studies' academic credibility.[1] She asserts in her paper that Native studies rejects the notion of objectivity in favor of subjective truths, and that the "subjective theories and methodologies" offered by Native studies "cannot have universal applicability."[2] She describes indigenous theories and methods as being based on Native spiritual knowledge and asserts that because "no 'spiritual world' has been shown to exist," these theories and methods are not valid.[3] She states that arguments for self-determination, which she maintains are based on indigenous theories and methods, are also invalid. Widdowson goes on to say that, "'indigenous theories and methodologies' isolate aboriginal people, both as subjects of study and as political scientists, from everyone else in society." One negative result as Widdowson sees it is that "aboriginal peoples will never be exposed to the challenging ideas needed for intellectual progress. They also will be limited to undertaking research within the field of Native Studies."[4] Widdowson concludes that "the linkage between the use of Native Studies' approaches and aboriginal liberation is not self-evident; in fact promoting 'indigenous theories and methodologies,'" she claims, "acts to obscure the causes of aboriginal dependency and entrench native marginalization."[5] In essence, Widdowson's belief is that Native studies, with its emphasis on cultural preservation, revitalization, and persistence, plays a significant role in the current deplorable state of Native peoples.

Widdowson's assertions are significant, as I have found only one other person who has provided a critique of Native studies. Wilcomb Washburn's 1975 article outlines his critique of Native studies, which was basically a defense of the discipline of history.[6] In his article, Washburn questioned the academic capabilities of Native scholars and the viability of Native studies as a stand-alone discipline. However, two years later in 1977, Russell Thornton noted that "no systemic critique of American Indian Studies as a discipline is to be found in the literature." This is not to say that no criticisms existed, but, as Thornton states, "criticisms . . . often occurred only less formally, in everyday discourse of the academic system, by faculty, by administrators, by students."[7] The informal nature of the criticisms directed toward Native studies is confirmed in the literature of the last thirty years. Many Native studies scholars point out that the lack of academic credibility continues to be a major criticism of the discipline. Whereas none of these scholars actually cite these criticisms; they, like Thornton, just note that they exist.[8] Widdowson is a Canadian political scientist, and therefore her views are not widely known outside of Canada. Most of the contributors to this issue probably have not heard of her. Nonetheless, the kinds of criticism of Native studies she has articulated are widely known by Native studies scholars throughout North America. Significantly, Widdowson's criticisms are representative of all the criticisms that haunt the hallways of academia.

The criticisms of Native studies made by Widdowson and others reflect a lack of knowledge and understanding of Native studies. Broadly speaking, there are three main goals that scholars within the discipline of Native studies strive to achieve:

1. To access, understand, and convey Native cultural perspective(s).
2. To conduct research that benefits Native people and/or communities.
3. To employ research methods and theories that will achieve these goals.

These goals are informed by my experience as a student, researcher, and faculty member in Native studies since 1992 and by the many discussions I have had over the years with colleagues. My articulation of these goals is not meant to be definitive. I understand that Native studies is a diverse discipline, and not all Native studies scholars may agree that these are disciplinary goals. Nonetheless, these goals provide a launching point, a framework, to initiate discussions about disciplinary characteristics that act to unify disparate research topics, such as those addressed in the articles in this issue.

The eight articles presented all offer convincing arguments for Native cultural preservation, revitalization, and persistence in a way that conforms to the stated disciplinary goals and provides a counterpoint to the informal criticisms of many scholars and the explicit assertions of Widdowson leveled against Native studies. The authors in this issue were contacted to contribute an article that addresses cultural preservation, revitalization, or preservation in some way. At the heart of this project is the attempt to outline Native communities' various efforts to preserve their cultures and explain how the Native cultural values and principles inform Native peoples' actions. *Community* is broadly defined to refer to specific indigenous communities at the microlevel, such as a reservation or reserve, a tribal level, the pan-indigenous level, or to individuals or groups of individuals.

The authors' approaches to their research are illustrative of the aims of Native studies research and highlight their status as Native studies scholars. What becomes apparent from the articles presented is that in order to come to grips with Native cultural understandings, it is crucial to become familiar with certain central Native cultural concepts. Though the articles cover a diverse range of topics, through the use of various form of stories the authors convey the importance of maintaining kinship roles and responsibilities. What follows is a brief discussion of each of the disciplinary aims of Native studies. This discussion will not only serve to highlight Widdowson's mischaracterization of the discipline but also provides the context to understand how the authors in this special issue are engaged in Native cultural preservation, revitalization, and persistence in a way that adheres to the goals of Native studies.

ACCESSING, UNDERSTANDING, AND CONVEYING NATIVE CULTURAL PERSPECTIVES

Unlike Widdowson, Native studies scholars believe that Native cultural preservation, revitalization, and persistence can assist us in gaining a new and better understanding of historical and contemporary events that have and continue to impact Native people. Many Native studies scholars' expressions of Native culture can provide solutions to the current socioeconomic situations plaguing many Native communities. Therefore, being able to access, understand, and convey Native cultural perspectives is critical to Native studies and Native communities. Native studies scholars know that for Native people to maintain their separate identities, they must maintain their separate cultures. They know that Native culture, like Native people, is not simply an artifact from the distant past but a living, contemporary culture.

Contemporary Native communities are complex, with a diverse range of cultural expressions. Some communities continue to adhere to traditional cultural practices, such as traditional ceremonies, high Native-language retention rates, and traditional subsistence. Yet in other communities traditional practices are almost nonexistent. Some communities combine a mixture of traditional and nontraditional cultural practices. Though reservations and reserves are still important places for Native people, the reality is that the majority of Native people in North America reside in urban centers, creating some tensions and cultural differences between city Indians and reserve Indians. Differences even exist between Native urban communities. Some cities, such as Toronto, Los Angeles, and San Francisco, have drawn Native people from various geographical regions, while other cities, such as Minneapolis, Winnipeg, and Saskatoon, have drawn Native people from a relatively close proximity.

Native studies scholars have awareness and appreciation of the diversity of contemporary Native cultures. Whether through interpretations of historical documents or interviews with living people, the greater understanding of Native culture will increase the level of accuracy in conveying Native perspectives. Native studies scholars do not have to adhere to the cultural values embedded within Native communities. However, because Native studies scholars attempt to access the Native perspective, it is essential that they have at least some basic understanding of that perspective. This does not mean that a Native studies scholar has to be Native. Being Native does not automatically mean a person understands the Native cultural perspective, especially, say, if the person was raised alienated from a Native community and has never been socialized to Native culture as an adult. However, scholars, Native or non-Native, can learn Native culture. Certainly, the more intimate knowledge of the culture, the better. A person not raised in a Native community may initially be at a disadvantage in conveying a Native perspective than someone raised in a Native community. As a person becomes better acquainted with Native culture, his or her skill in interpreting Native cultural perspectives will improve.

Even with the range of cultural expressions there are cultural charac-teristics that are shared among most Native people. No matter whether they live on the Arctic tundra, in the desert of the Southwest, or in major North American cities; practice traditional or Christian ceremonies; or maintain traplines or Web sites, the ways in which Native people interact with each other are uncannily similar. Kinship relations, for example, have been and continue to be a central component of Native cultures. Not surprisingly, all the authors in this issue invoke the notion of kinship to varying degrees. The emphasis on kinship by many Native studies scholars highlights the role that kinship can play in Native cultural preservation, revitalization, and persis-tence and underscores the importance of being able to access, understand, and convey Native cultural perspectives.

CONDUCTING BENEFICIAL RESEARCH

The ultimate aim of Native studies is to bring positive change to Native people and their communities through research. Native studies is an ethical endeavor that seeks to provide research that benefits Native people, not just the researcher. The benefit can be something tangible such as leading to a multimillion-dollar land claim, improved governance, or a water supply, but it can also be something less pragmatic such as providing a community's history from its perspective in print for the first time. Whatever the benefit, Native studies scholars should have an idea of what the benefit is prior to conducting the research—the benefit should be a part of the initial research plan; it should not occur by chance after the research. This does not mean that there may be other unforeseen benefits, just that researchers should have an idea of the potential benefit of their research to the community prior to conducting the research.

In order for Native studies research to benefit the community, the onus is on Native studies scholars to gain the credibility in the Native and academic communities. Native studies research reflects the aims, aspirations, and perspectives of Native communities. Therefore, Native studies scholars should have a connection to a Native community. Depending on the specific research, researchers should make contact with the potential research community and discuss the research objectives, and develop research protocols that reflect the community and the research needs. A relationship between the researcher and the research community will encourage community confidence in the researcher and facilitate the researcher's understanding of the community's cultural perspective.

That Native studies scholars have a level of responsibility to the Native community does not mean they relinquish their academic responsibility or their academic freedom. Native studies scholars must produce sound scholarly research that withstands academic rigor. Research that is not well founded will be less likely to improve Native peoples' lives. Presenting the voices and perspectives of the Native community should not silence researchers' own voices and perspectives. Widdowson, in her response to Vine Deloria Jr.'s call for anthropologists to develop linkages with Native communities, derisively remarks, "So, anthropological research should proceed only if findings support the political agenda of the tribe being studied and sufficient bribes are offered to the aboriginal leadership to obtain their cooperation."[9] Creating linkages between researchers and the Native community does not mean that the Native community has to agree with all of the researcher's interpretations or recommendations. Because Native studies is a critical investigation of the Native experience with the aim of leading to positive change for Native people, there are research contexts that demand a critical analysis and an honest assessment of the shortcomings found within Native communities. Native studies has to guard against simply becoming a mouthpiece for Native governments, organizations, or individuals. Jace Weaver recently addressed this issue: "Commitment to Native community does not mean wallowing in victimhood and guilt. Nor does it mean presenting the most 'Indian' side of everything, in the face of contrary evidence. And it certainly does not mean surrendering our research to tribal councils. It means service to Native peoples. But it also means being committed to truth, accuracy, and academic freedom. Without these, all the words in the world are worthless to us as scholars and ultimately to those for whom we purport to advocate."[10] Identifying shortcomings and providing possible solutions could be of great benefit to Native communities.

RESEARCH METHODS AND THEORIES

In her critique of Native studies, Widdowson asserts that "one of the main distinctive characteristics of aboriginal methodologies . . . is that they do not strive for objectivity."[11] For Widdowson, what is most concerning is that the methods and theories employed by Native studies scholars are based on indigenous knowledge. She cites the Royal Commission on Aboriginal Peoples, which notes that the difference between Aboriginal and non-Aboriginal conceptions of history is that Aboriginal people see history as cyclical, while non-Aboriginal people see it as linear, in order to support her criticism that Aboriginal people conceptualize history crossing "the boundaries between the physical and spiritual."[12] She asserts that one of the assumptions of Native studies methods and theories is "the existence of a 'spiritual reality.'" However, as she maintains, because this reality does not exist, "it does not make sense to claim that there are methods and theories that can access this realm and increase human understanding."[13]

There are two main problems with Widdowson's contention that indigenous knowledge is the basis of Native studies methods and theories. First, she mistakenly conflates traditional worldviews of community members with Native studies theories and methods. Widdowson characterizes Native studies scholars as being more concerned with indigenous subjectivities than with truth claims. Her inability to distinguish between indigenous knowledge and Native studies' approaches to research led her to point out apparent contradictions when Native studies scholars make truth claims. She misses the fact that Native communities are complex entities, and that Native studies, generally speaking, is the objective analysis of Native subjectivities.

The second problem with Widdowson's assertion is that she assumes there is agreement on how to incorporate indigenous knowledge into research, and that all Native studies scholars utilize indigenous knowledge. In recent years there has been much discussion regarding how and to what degree indigenous knowledge can be incorporated into academic research. However, we are at the formative stages of this project. This is reflected in the fact that a definition of the term *indigenous knowledge* has not yet been universally agreed upon. By insisting that indigenous knowledge is synonymous with Native studies methods and theories, Widdowson reveals her specific lack of understanding that Native studies scholars utilize a multitude of methods and theories and her general lack of knowledge about the discipline.

Some Native studies scholars have argued that Native studies will not become a distinct discipline until it develops its own theories and methods based on indigenous knowledge.[14] Such scholars are working on ways to incorporate indigenous methods and theories into their academic research activities.[15] Certainly this is one approach that Native studies scholars can deploy to engage in cultural preservation, revitalization, and persistence in order to present Native cultural perspectives beneficial to Native communities.

However, I contend that Native studies *is* a distinct discipline predicated on improving Native people's lives and communities. As individuals, how we view the world is influenced by our life experiences. Many Native studies scholars have experienced the direct negative impact of colonization or have become conscious of the impact that colonization has had on Native people. This awareness has propelled Native studies scholars to seek positive change and is foundational to the discipline's goals. Therefore, Native studies scholars ask questions that require accessing, understanding, and conveying Native cultural perspectives that will result in research that benefits Native communities. The specific research questions that are asked dictate the specific methods and theories employed in research projects. A limited number of ways are available to gather data—administer a survey, interview and/or observe people, or collect written documents—depending on the research. Developing an ethical research relationship is more important than how the data is collected. An unlimited number of ways a researcher can interpret and theorize the data exists, shaped and influenced by the researcher's personal and academic experiences. What is significant about the goals of the discipline as outlined is that they allow for various disciplinary approaches. Though Native studies is multi- and interdisciplinary by nature, Native studies scholars are not obliged to employ multi- or interdisciplinary approaches. Some of the authors in this issue use many disciplinary approaches, while others use one. Some use traditional academic methods and theories, while others incorporate indigenous methods and theories.

The topics covered in this issue are varied. Yet what ties these diverse studies together is the authors' implicit desire to fulfill the goals of the discipline. In "Some Elements of American Indian Pedagogy from an Anishinaabe Perspective," Lawrence W. Gross anchors his American Indian pedagogy in the cultural understandings located in Anishinaabe stories that serve to guide students through an unconventional (to some of the students) university learning experience that emphasizes self-confidence and acceptance and encourages self-learning. Sheilah E. Nicholas's "Language, Epistemology, and Cultural Identity: 'Hopiqatsit Aw Unangvakiwyungwa' ('They Have Their Heart in the Hopi Way of Life')" argues that even though there has been a significant language shift from Hopi to English among young Hopi, Hopi cultural understandings found in traditional Hopi stories have been passed on to the younger Hopi, which is evidenced by their actions that conform to Hopi cultural beliefs. In "A Reading of Eekwol's 'Apprentice to the Mystery' as an Expression of Cree Youth's Cultural Role and Responsibility," Gail A. MacKay examines how traditional Plains Cree cultural understandings are conveyed through a story in a contemporary hip hop song to Native youth. Keavy Martin's "Is an Inuit Literary History Possible?" provides a compelling argument that traditional Inuit stories comprise an Inuit literary history, and that this history supports the notion of Inuit nationhood. In my article, "Elder Brother, the Law of the People, and Contemporary Kinship Practices of Cowessess First Nation Members: Reconceptualizing Kinship in American Indian Studies Research," I contend that contemporary members of the Cowessess First Nation have maintained aspects of their traditional kinship practices conveyed through their traditional Elder Brothers' stories. Theresa McCarthy's "Dę´:Ni:S Nisahsgaodę?: Haudenosaunee Clans and the Reconstruction of Traditional Haudenosaunee Identity, Citizenship, and Nationhood" applies stories of the origins and purpose of clans to explain how contemporary members of the Iroquois Confederacy are attempting to reinvigorate the sociopolitical dimensions of their clan system and thereby revitalize the integrity of the clans. Heidi Kiiwetinepinesiik Stark's "Respect, Responsibility, and Renewal: The Foundations of Anishinaabe Treaty Making with the United States and Canada" outlines the principles of respect, responsibility, and renewal found in the Anishinaabe story, "The Woman Who Married a Beaver," which shed light on the intent of the Anishinaabe treaty relationships with the US and Canadian governments. Sharon Milholland discusses how the traditional Navajo philosophies contained in their stories guide their views of land management, and how these views are incommensurate with the US government land-management laws and policies, in "In the Eyes of the Beholder: Understanding and Resolving Incompatible Ideologies and Languages in US Environmental and Cultural Laws in Relationship to Navajo Sacred Lands"; it further offers potential strategies to integrate the two disparate views.

This issue presents evidence to affirm the importance of relating the central role of Native stories and kinship to Native studies. All the articles present ways in which issues of cultural preservation, revitalization, and persistence can convey Native cultural understandings to the benefits of Native people and communities. This is what makes them Native studies scholars and gives hope for the future of the discipline of Native studies. I would like to thank all the contributors who not only agreed to submit their works, but also met, with short notice, the initial deadline. I would also like to thank the editors of the *American Indian Culture and Research Journal* and anonymous peer reviewers whose assistance greatly strengthened the contributions.

NOTES

1. Frances Widdowson, "Native Studies and Canadian Political Science: The Implications of 'Decolonizing the Discipline.'" Paper prepared for the Annual Meeting of the Canadian Political Science Association, Vancouver, BC, 4–6 June 2008.

2. Ibid., 12.

3. Ibid., 5.

4. Ibid., 12.

5. Ibid., 3.

6. Wilcomb Washburn, "American Indian Studies: A Status Report," *American Quarterly* 27, no. 3 (1975): 263–74.

7. Russell Thornton, "American Indian Studies as a Academic Discipline," *Journal of Ethnic Studies* 5, no. 3 (1977): 3.

8. This does not mean there have been no criticisms. E.g., Keith Windschuttle in *The Killing of History: How Literary Critics and Social Theorists Are Murdering Our Past* (New York: The Free Press, 1997) was very critical of the way in which cultural studies, including Native studies, have impacted traditional disciplines. However, other than Washburn (cited in n. 6), no specific critique of Native studies has been cited by the following authors: Clara Sue Kidwell, "Native American Studies: Academic Concerns and Community Service," *American Indian Cultural and Research Journal* 1, no. 1–2 (1978): 4–9; Terry P. Wilson, "Custer Would Never Have Believed It: Native American Studies in the Academia," *American Indian Quarterly* 5 (1979): 207–27; Patrick Morris, "Native American Studies: A Personal Reflection," *Wicazo Sa Review* 2, no. 2 (1986): 9–16; M. Annette Jaimes, "American Indian Studies: Toward an Indigenous Model," *American Indian Culture and Research Journal* 11, no. 3 (1987): 1–16; William Willard and Mary Kay Downing, "American Indian Studies and Inter-Cultural Education," *Wicazo Sa Review* 7, no. 2 (1991): 1–8; Elizabeth Cook-Lynn, "Who Stole Native American Studies?" *Wicazo Sa Review* 12, no. 1 (1997): 9–28; Mary Katherine Duffie and Ben Chavis, "American Indian Studies and Its Evolution in Academia," *The Social Science Journal* 34, no. 4 (1997): 435–45; Winona Stevenson, "Ethnic Assimilates Indigenous: A Study of Intellectual Neocolonialism," *Wicazo Sa Review* 13, no. 1 (1998): 33–51; Jack Forbes, "Intellectual Self-Determination and Sovereignty: Implications for Native Studies and Native Intellectuals," *Wicazo Sa Review* 13, no. 1 (1998): 11–23; Elizabeth Cook-Lynn, "American Indian Studies: An Overview Keynote Address at the Native Studies Conferences, Yale University, February 5, 1998," *Wicazo Sa Review* 14, no. 2 (1999): 14–24; Winona Wheeler, "Thoughts on the Responsibilities for Indigenous/ Native Studies," *Canadian Journal of Native Studies* 21, no. 1 (2001): 97–104; Duane Champagne, "In Search of Theory and Method in American Indian Studies," *American Indian Quarterly* 31, no. 3 (2007): 353–71; Jace Weaver, "More Light Than Heat: The Current State of Native American Studies," *American Indian Quarterly* 31, no. 2 (2007):

233–55; Chris Andersen, "Critical Indigenous Studies: From Difference to Density," *Cultural Studies Review* 15, no. 2 (2009): 80–100; Clara Sue Kidwell, "American Indian Studies Intellectual Navel Gazing or Academic Discipline?" *American Indian Quarterly* 33, no. 1 (2009): 2–17.

     9. Frances Widdowson and Albert Howard, *Disrobing the Aboriginal Industry: The Deception behind Indigenous Cultural Preservation* (Kingston, ON: McGill-Queens University Press, 2008), 68.

     10. Weaver, "More Light Than Heat," 239.

     11. Widdowson, "Native Studies and Canadian Political Science," 5.

     12. Ibid., 4.

     13. Ibid., 5.

     14. See, e.g., Jaimes, "American Indian Studies: Toward an Indigenous Model"; Duffie and Chavis, "American Indian Studies and Its Evolution in Academia"; and Champagne, "In Search of Theory and Method in American Indian Studies."

     15. Two recent examples are Shawn Wilson, *Research as Ceremony: Indigenous Research Methods* (Halifax, NS, and Winnipeg, MB: Fernwood Publishing, 2008); and Margaret Kovach, *Indigenous Methodologies: Characteristics, Conversations, and Contexts* (Toronto: University of Toronto Press, 2009).

AMERICAN INDIAN CULTURE AND RESEARCH JOURNAL 34:2 (2010) 11–26

Some Elements of American Indian Pedagogy from an Anishinaabe Perspective

LAWRENCE W. GROSS

In 2005 I published an article discussing the teaching method we used for an introduction to American Indian studies course at Iowa State University.[1] As might be expected, since the publication of that article my career and teaching have continued to develop. I am no longer at Iowa State but have moved to the Department of Native American Studies at Montana State University—Bozeman. Under these circumstances, a pedagogy based on American Indian approaches has become that much more appropriate. Additionally, I have more years worked with the teaching method in question, and as a result, I have refined the technique some, although the basic approach remains intact. In my previous piece, I did not delineate the elements that go into an American Indian pedagogy. I will address that issue here. Because I am most familiar with Anishinaabe culture, I will primarily limit my remarks to that nation.

My article about teaching American Indian studies explained a blended teaching method we used at Iowa State University that drew from American Indian pedagogical approaches as well as methods traditional to the academy. I discussed the history of the teaching method and the theory informing the technique; briefly outlined some elements of American Indian pedagogy and the logistics of the class; and ended with some observations on the effectiveness of the technique.

For this article, it is important to have an understanding of the course assignments. Students are required to write a four- to five-page paper about their family, community, and place and about their interest in and/or knowledge of the course topic and how it developed. Students are encouraged to talk with their family members in order to get material. The material from the paper is given in an oral presentation. Students are informed they will all receive an A for the oral presentation. The idea is to allow students to be the complete authority in the classroom when they do their respective

Lawrence Gross is enrolled on the White Earth Reservation as a member of the Minnesota Chippewa tribe. He is an assistant professor in the Department of Native American Studies at Montana State University—Bozeman.

11

presentations. Additionally, every week, except for the last week of class, students have to write a one- to two-paragraph participation paper about ideas generated from the readings and lectures. Students suggest their own grade. This gives them the freedom to discuss their reaction to the class material openly and honestly. I adjust the grades up or down depending on the degree to which students provide detailed evidence that they did the reading. Thus, it is mandatory for them to provide page numbers and/or quotations for the readings. Finally, the students expand the first paper into a ten-page research paper by adding a five- to six-page research component. The research portion follows the dictates for a paper of this type, with requirements for a thesis, theme, or topic, and proper use of citations and references.

As far as Anishinaabe pedagogy is concerned, two important earlier writers are Francis Densmore and M. Inez Hilger. Densmore spent time among the Anishinaabeg in northern Minnesota in the late nineteenth and early twentieth centuries, and she wrote extensively about her experiences. One of her more important works is *Chippewa Customs*.[2] Although she does discuss the life cycle of the Anishinaabeg, she does not include a great deal of information about Anishinaabe pedagogy.[3] Much the same can be said for Hilger's *Chippewa Child Life and Its Cultural Background*.[4] Hilger also worked among the Anishinaabeg in northern Minnesota but at a later date than Densmore. Most of Hilger's observations were made in the 1930s and 1940s. She includes a section on training children, but, like Densmore, her writing does not address the philosophies informing Anishinaabe pedagogy.[5] Although her work provides valuable ethnographic information, the work is more descriptive in nature and of little help in getting to the heart of Anishinaabe teaching methods.

I find Roger Spielmann to be one of the more astute observers of Anishinaabe culture. Spielmann spent some time with the Pikogan and Winneway Anishinaabe communities in Canada during the 1980s and 1990s. He wrote about his experiences in *"You're So Fat!": Exploring Ojibwe Discourse.*[6] His comments on teaching and learning are worthy of note:

> It seems to me that the foundation for traditional teachings is the belief that true learning is flexible and open-ended, that change is a permanent part of life, and that absolute knowledge is not the goal of the quest. What can be learned is the capacity to pay attention to all the details which may influence the outcome of a particular course of action, a capacity learned as much by the way one lives as by what one hears. . . .
>
> From the perspective of the elders in the communities of Pikogan and Winneway, teachers are those who can demonstrate the relation-ship between philosophy and practice. It is important to remember that one's way of life is a model for what one is trying to transmit. Who do people in a community seek out for advice, prayer, guidance, instruction, and so forth? Different people in a community have different powers and different ways of gaining knowledge, and there-fore, have different responsibilities to those around them.

> The elders at Pikogan taught me in subtle ways that everyone is at times a teacher and at times a learner, from children, strong dreamers, interpreters, visionaries, and skilled hunters to storytellers, orators, and ethnohistorians. Traditional education prepared Aboriginal children to become fully functioning members of their communities and nations. . . . This form of education is practical, life-long, and integrated into the fabric of community and society.[7]

I especially appreciate the way Spielmann provides a very accurate explanation of the dynamics involved in Anishinaabe learning. However, his book centers on the nature of discourse in the culture rather than pedagogy. So even though his remarks are insightful, they are too limited to give us a fuller picture of Anishinaabe pedagogy.

These three authors are the major commentators on Anishinaabe pedagogy. As can be seen, it is difficult, if not impossible, to understand Anishinaabe pedagogy from these works. Rather than relying on secondary sources, my remarks will be informed by my own exposure to Anishinaabe culture. In that regard, I would like to say that I make no apologies for writing as an Anishinaabe. I am a member of the White Earth Nation in Minnesota and proud of it. To pretend that I am some kind of disinterested academic or curious outsider would do a disservice to my identity as an Anishinaabe and to the Anishinaabe people. By the same token, I must humbly state that I cannot claim as great a familiarity with the culture as I would like. For example, I am still working on my Anishinaabe language skills. However, I have spent enough time among my people to develop an adequate sense of the culture. As much as the following delineates some Anishinaabe elements of American Indian pedagogy, they also represent my own thinking and experience.

At least nineteen elements go into Anishinaabe pedagogy. They include:
1. Maintaining a sense of family.
2. Maintaining a sense of community.
3. Maintaining a sense of place, especially in seeing the land as a teacher.
4. Oral tradition.
5. Storytelling.
6. Relationships.
7. Balance.
8. Uniting past, present, and future: that is, acknowledging the past to imagine a better future to work toward in the present.
9. Remaining open to mystery.
10. Observation.
11. Visioning/creativity/imagination.
12. Preserving a positive self-identity.
13. Developing forgiveness.
14. Pragmatism.
15. Training to task mastery as opposed to grading level of task achievement.
16. Accretive thinking.
17. Recognition of the complex nature of truth.
18. Respect for people outside one's culture.
19. Humor.

Some of these considerations describe Anishinaabe ways of knowing, or Anishinaabe epistemology. Others describe Anishinaabe ways of being in the world. To put it in simple terms, these elements outline how the Anishinaabeg think and act. In that regard, it might seem that I am not discussing pedagogy. However, if pedagogy is imagined as training individuals in the ways of thinking and being of a given culture, then it would make sense to apply those very ways of knowing and being to pedagogical practices. I would argue that these elements do constitute as least some of the pedagogical aspects of Anishinaabe culture, and I will discuss these elements, explaining how I see them acting in Anishinaabe culture and giving examples of how I bring the given element into the university setting.

Maintaining a sense of family and community are closely related and do not require a great deal of analysis. For me, one of the most important defining characteristics of Anishinaabe identity has to do with families. As I tell my students, in order to ascertain whether someone is American Indian, ask the individual to name his or her Indian relatives. From my experience, those Anishinaabeg who are vested in their communities have a very strong sense of who their family members are and can easily start naming relatives going out several degrees, such as second and third cousins. The knowledge of relatives stretches back in time as well. Some families maintain stories going back many generations, and I have heard stories involving my great-great-grandfather. Thus, it is common for the Anishinaabeg to immerse their children in stories related to their families.

It is interesting how family stories can also provide a continuing sense of connection between people. For example, my grandmother took care of an old Anishinaabe gentleman by the name of Billy Hill. Not long ago, when I was an independent researcher living in Bemidji, Minnesota, the then-president of Leech Lake Tribal College, Leah Carpenter, invited my wife and me to the free Monday lunches for the students at the college. Later, one of my aunts told me that one of Leah Carpenter's great-grandfathers was none other than Billy Hill, which I relayed to Dr. Carpenter at the earliest opportunity. With family connections spanning the generations like this, one almost feels as if one is living a Louise Erdrich novel.

Another aspect of maintaining a sense of family is the clan system. As is well-known, traditional society was clan-based, and although Anishinaabe clans have been under assault for a number of years, my experience in Anishinaabe communities indicates that the importance of clans is starting to make a comeback. For example, the Anishinaabeg are taught to give their clan when introducing themselves. It is true that the functional meaning of clan identity for the Anishinaabeg has not recovered fully. I have not heard of individuals practicing exogamy, for example. However, Anishinaabe culture continues to evolve, and I suspect clan practices will grow as an important component of Anishinaabe life. Maintaining a sense of family is still important for the Anishinaabeg. I will discuss my classroom practices for this and maintaining a sense of community after introducing the role of place in Anishinaabe society.

Community can be defined in a number of ways for the Anishinaabeg, from the village level, to the reservation, and on up to the nation as a whole.

Most Anishinaabeg have a historical sense of what communities their families originate from, including those Anishinaabeg who no longer live on a reservation. As part of introducing themselves, the Anishinaabeg are taught to relate their reservation of origin. This notion of introductions is not just a social matter. It is very serious because giving one's name, clan, and reservation is part of praying, at least in the way I was taught. At the start of prayers one is to announce to the *manidoog*, or spirits, one's Indian name, clan, and reservation, preferably in the Anishinaabe language. I cannot discuss certain aspects of prayers. However, because spiritual growth and learning are an important part of traditional Anishinaabe practices, it should be evident that knowing one's family and community form the foundation of all Anishinaabe education.

Maintaining a sense of place relates to knowing the land. This aspect of Anishinaabe teaching is closely related to observation. For now, suffice it to say that it is important to maintain a close connection to the land. One of my cousins, who will remain anonymous, told me about how he was taught the watercourses on White Earth Reservation by Thomas Shingobe, an old, respected elder in the community. The Anishinaabeg have close relations with water, and one cannot understand Anishinaabe culture without understanding water. For example, many years ago, a causeway was built across Rice Lake on the White Earth Reservation in order to accommodate Minnesota State highway 200. The elders in the community expressed concern that the causeway would interrupt the flow of water necessary for the wild rice. To this day, people still talk about how those elders were correct, and how the causeway has had a negative impact on the water flow, and thus the wild rice, in the lake.

This example speaks to the importance of the land being a teacher. I maintain that the land teaches human beings how to live on that particular land. Through years of observation and direct experience, the Anishinaabe elders developed a sense for how water moves through their territory. They developed an understanding of how to live on the land. Examples of this can still be found. On the Fond du Lac Reservation, an effort was made to clear the movement of water through the reservation in order to maximize the wild rice crop.[8] In this sense, the land is a teacher, and the Anishinaabeg are taught to learn from the land.

I use these three elements in my college teaching by having the students write an essay about their identity in terms of family, community, and place. Two things are worth mentioning, however. First, as the years have gone by, I have come to appreciate this assignment much more. It helps me make a connection with the students on a personal basis. I find I am a more effective teacher by knowing at least something about the background of each individual student. Second, I find that students have a difficult time relating to maintaining a sense of place, especially students from urban areas, whereas, quite often, the students from Montana and other rural states can understand this aspect of the assignment readily enough. I have read a number of essays since I have been at Montana State in which students from rural areas talk about spending hours just sitting in one place absorbing the surroundings.

Urban students do not understand this part of the assignment nearly as well. Of late, I have taken to using a suggestion from my colleague at the University of Wyoming, Christopher Russell, who employs the same teaching technique and with whom I used to work at Iowa State University. He tells students to think about a place they go to in their mind to feel a sense of peace or to think of the place where they would like to be buried when they die. For urban students it might also help to tell them to think about the human infrastructure of their place, the buildings, roads, and bridges, as well as the parks and other natural areas. How do those factors combined lend feeling to maintaining a sense of place, even in an urban area? Is there any place they like to go just to get away from it all?

In discussing the oral tradition and storytelling with my students, I generally follow the conventions of Anishinaabe culture. Oral tradition relates to the sacred stories and important myths and legends of the people. These primarily concern Bebaamosed, the One Who Walks Around, otherwise known as Wenaboozhoo. The Anishinaabe tradition is a bit different from other American Indian societies in which the telling of legends is reserved for a special group of people. It is also different from scripture-based traditions. For scripture-based traditions, it is doubtful many people know the scriptures by heart and probably could not relate them orally. For the Anishinaabeg, people are encouraged to learn and tell the ancestral legends, especially those involving Wenaboozhoo. What this means is that each Anishinaabe individual carries a corpus of sacred stories within him- or herself. The corpus will vary from person to person. Nonetheless, for the Anishinaabeg, the sacred stories are not written on paper but in the hearts of the people.

Storytelling involves narratives about everything else, but most are personal stories about oneself and one's family, including one's ancestors. As Christopher Vecsey explains, the Anishinaabeg of old were great storytellers and could commence telling stories in the fall, not quit until spring, and never repeat the same tale twice.[9] The Anishinaabeg still relish storytelling, and Jim Northrup's short story "The Odyssey" provides a good example of this.[10] The story talks about three Indians driving from the Fond du Lac Reservation to St. Cloud, Minnesota, in a van to pick up some furniture: "The monotony of the trip was broken by more stories. By the time they got to St. Cloud, the back of the truck was full of them and their embellished outcomes."[11] Although it is a work of fiction, the piece gives a good sense of the current-day storytelling tradition of the Anishinaabeg. From my experience, it is also true that the Anishinaabeg encourage their children to become storytellers. The ability to tell stories, both the old legends and modern tales, is actually considered an important teaching goal for the Anishinaabeg.

Much like the assignment in which students write about their identity in terms of family, community, and place, I have also come to value the role of storytelling in my class, especially the oral presentations about the material in the autobiographical essay. As I tell students, everyone is going to encounter problems in life. At those times, it is important to tell one's story instead of spiraling down into a self-destructive cycle. Lately, with the economic problems the world faces as a result of the recession that started in 2007, I have noticed an uptick in the number of news stories about shootings. Oftentimes, the stories involve individuals who had a hard time coping with financial stress. The affected individuals take out their problems on their families or coworkers. I suspect part of the problem is that these individuals either did not know how to tell their stories or refrained from telling them. Doing so might help mitigate some of these troubling acts. I encourage students to learn how to tell their own stories, to give them the skills necessary to deal with hard times like these.

We say "Gakina indinawemaaganag" (all my relations) in Anishinaabe-mowin, the Anishinaabe language. As A. Irving Hallowell has pointed out, Anishinaabe conceptions of relationships extend beyond the human realm to include other-than-humans.[12] Forming relationships is part of learning to maintain a sense of place. Continuous observation helps the Anishinaabeg develop a relationship with the land and all the other beings with whom we share Anishinaabeaki, the Anishinaabe land. However, the relationship extends into other areas. As Hallowell noted, a sense that the animals can communicate with human beings exists. As one of my teachers puts it, the animals speak Anishinaabemowin and will never speak English. When I asked him if he meant that the animals literally speak Anishinaabemowin, he said, "Yes." Animals can come to individuals in spiritual ways; I will not go into detail about this out of respect for the spiritual life of the Anishinaabeg. It should also be noted that relationships are something that take work. Again, without going into details, we have ceremonies in which we take care of our relatives, human and nonhuman, remembering that nonhuman relatives can include such animate beings as drums and songs. The Anishinaabeg are taught to nurture their relationship with other beings.

In the classroom setting, the importance of relationships mainly involves getting to know the students on an individual basis through their auto-biographical essays on family, community, and place and through their oral presentations of the same material to the entire class. One thing I have noticed is that getting to know the students on an individual basis helps develop trust. I have been known to go off the course syllabus if I have something of importance to discuss with the students. Generally, the students tolerate this, especially because we have found that some of our best learning occurs during these course digressions.

It is vitally important for the individual to maintain balance in life and in society in general. For the Anishinaabeg, maintaining balance is closely related to *mino-bimaadiziwin*, or a good life. I have discussed the concept of *bimaadiziwin* in another article, so I will not go into detail here.[13] Some aspects of a good life include rising and going to bed with the sun and following other practices in order to help maintain health and well-being. The importance of balance manifests itself in other ways in Anishinaabe life. For example, it is important to keep one's desires in check in order to avoid overexploitation of natural resources. In his column, "Fond du Lac Follies," Northrup talks about harvesting natural resources. When relating how much wild rice they harvested or maple syrup they made, he has often written, "enough for a Shinnob, not enough for a Chimook," or enough for an Anishinaabe but not enough for a white man.[14] This stress on conserving natural resources is aimed at maintaining a balance between human beings and the natural world.

Instances in which the Anishinaabeg do not honor balance are telling. Recently, the Red Lake Nation has exercised its sovereignty over Upper Red Lake, cutting off non-Indians from fishing in the lake. The results have not been so encouraging and point to the fact that Indians can violate their ideals as well. It turns out that the Anishinaabeg have been overfishing the lake, and so the stock of fish has dropped precipitously. The elders' reaction has been intriguing. Their view is that the Anishinaabeg are not following ceremonies in harvesting the fish, and because of that the fish are not sacrificing themselves anymore. The elders teach that if the Anishinaabeg started fishing in a spiritual manner again, human desire would be held in check, and, as a result, the fish would be willing to offer themselves to the people again.

In the classroom, balance entails maintaining a sense of equality between the instructor and the students as much as possible. Much of this approach relates to the co-construction of knowledge as presented by William Tierney in his book on Native Americans in the academy.[15] Allowing the students to tell their own story and listening to their voices in the weekly participation papers they have to write about the readings and lectures opens up new avenues for learning. I commonly read short excerpts from the participation papers in class, responding to the students' comments and questions. Maintaining that balance helps me to be a better teacher and gives me ideas that find their way into my research.

Of all the elements listed, uniting the past, present, and future seems to be the one that best resonates with my students, who primarily are non-Native. The idea is to acknowledge the past in order to imagine a better future to work toward in the present. This means that we do not get stuck in the past, dwell in the past, and play the blame game. Also, this approach is proactive in nature. It is more than simply saying that those who do not learn from the mistakes of history are bound to repeat them. That is a negative approach, pointing out what not to do. Instead, we look for positive ideas that can be drawn from history in order to create a better world for all people. Usually, at the end of the semester I will ask the students for their ideas regarding how they can create a better future for Indian people and for their families, communities, and places. Hopefully, their ideas will one day find expression as their lives and careers continue to develop.

Remaining open to mystery speaks as much to an approach to knowledge as it does to keeping an open mind to the wonders of the universe, recognizing that human beings cannot know the answer to everything and do not need to know the answer to everything that exists. This does not mean that knowledge cannot be pursued. Certainly it should be. However, it is also recognized that human beings will never know everything. Two conclusions result from that observation. First, there are times and ways in which knowledge presents itself in the most surprising and unexpected ways. How and why that occurs remains a mystery, and the process cannot be controlled or reduced to a formula. It certainly cannot be shaped into a method such as the scientific method. Second, simply put, it also means that the mysteries of life are to be savored and not solved.

How can one practice remaining open to mystery? According to my elders in the Anishinaabe community, it is through developing the power of observation. I believe this stress on the power of observation can be found in other Native cultures as well. In the case of the Anishinaabeg, I have often heard elders discuss the importance of paying attention to the smallest details. We are encouraged to observe the behavior of ants, leaves in the trees, songs of the birds, and so forth, and work to discern what our observations can tell us. In science it is recognized that serendipitous discoveries come to those who are prepared to recognize them. The same can be said of remaining open to mystery. Observation is the method that prepares the individual for those times when the mystery of life reveals something of importance.

Both remaining open to mystery and observation find their expression in my college teaching in the form of visioning/creativity/imagination, which can be seen as an extension of remaining open to mystery and observation. It might be seen as observation in a different vein. However, a couple of important points need to be made. First, when it comes to the academic setting, we are not encouraging students to go on vision quests or anything of the sort. Instead, the notion of visioning is used as a heuristic device to lead us into the area of creativity and imagination. Again, among the Anishinaabeg, I find the degree to which teachers encourage people to exercise their creative mind interesting. In my case, I am working with a recognized spiritual leader in our community. One of the first things he had me do was make a warrior's pipe out of pipestone. Pipestone is sacred, and I had never worked with it before. A warrior's pipe has a fairly complex design as well, with an axe blade beneath the bowl part of the pipe. The directions I received from my teacher were vague at best, and I was more or less thrown into the project. About two months later, I had my pipe, much to my surprise and my teacher's delight. A large part of this exercise, as my teacher related to me, was to get me to learn how to work with my hands. He sees it as being very important to Anishinaabe identity to be able to work with one's hands. In the case of the Anishinaabeg, creativity and imagination are based in the creative arts, much more so than in the so-called life of the mind. Still, the stress on imagination and creativity can certainly be said to form an important component of the pedagogical approach of the Anishinaabe people. As might be expected, in the classroom setting, I encourage my students to exercise their own creativity and imagination. Knowing that they are free to take control of the topic and carry it to areas of their own choosing is an empowering experience for the students. I believe they create better work all around in having the freedom to explore the course topic on their own.

My experience making the warrior's pipe under my teacher's limited supervision also allows me to talk about forgiveness and developing a positive self-identity. It seemed that, for my teacher, the more important aspect of my making a warrior's pipe was not to have a pipe in the end but to have a learning experience. Several times it looked as if I would wind up ruining the pipe, and I did put a rather large crack in it. Fortunately, my teacher wanted to have a flaw in the pipe, a wound, as it were, that would represent, or stand in for, the wounds suffered by veterans. We discussed the possibility that I might wind up wrecking the whole project. His reaction was that if such an event came to pass, we would simply bury the pipe in the woods and forget about it. Fortunately, the crack is now almost indiscernible, the pipe is functional, and it turned out almost exactly the way my teacher wanted it.

This sense of forgiveness and willingness to give people a second chance seems to have been a large part of traditional child-rearing techniques. I have yet to come across a Native culture that believed in and practiced corporal punishment as part of their standard cultural practices.[16] Instead, the emphasis always seemed to be on positive reinforcement, rewarding good behavior, and always, as much as possible, being gentle with children, not speaking to them in a harsh voice or an angry tone. Unfortunately, as is well-known, the boarding-school era introduced violence into our domestic cultures so physical punishment is now more common among Native people. However, if we concentrate on traditional child-rearing practices, it is clear that instilling a positive self-identity and practicing forgiveness should be important components of American Indian pedagogy.

Making the warrior's pipe is also an example of the pragmatic teaching approach of the Anishinaabeg. Although one of my teacher's goals is to teach me to work with my hands, he also encourages me to learn other practical skills of various sorts. For example, he wants me to take up archery, a skill set from the old days. Interestingly enough, he is also teaching me different songs. This might not seem like a practical skill. However, songs have life and power in Anishinaabe thinking. Learning songs becomes a very important task, one not to be taken lightly. For my college teaching, I concentrate on making the class as practical as possible for the students. Thus, I encourage them to write research papers that will be of practical value to them in their lives and careers. Having the students include a section in their autobiographical essays about their interest in Indians and how it developed often provides a gateway for their later research in the class.

Training to task mastery as opposed to grading one's level of task achievement can be illustrated by the work I did making the warrior's pipe. The important point in making the pipe was not to win an award or to be judged or graded on my degree of competence. Making mistakes was acceptable. The important point was that I learn how to make a pipe.

Accretive thinking is a process whereby the same topic is circled back to and discussed again. A useful image is to picture an upward spiral. Accretion comes from geology and refers to the building up of layers. In accretive thinking, as the topic is repeated, additional layers of meaning are added. This seems to be a common technique among elders. I have noticed that elders have a tendency to repeat themselves. When that happens, it is imperative for students not to roll their eyes and think, "There he (or she) goes again." Instead, it is better to think about the context in which the topic was raised before and to consider what has been learned in the meantime that adds to one's understanding of the subject. Additionally, if a person is really smart, he or she will consider when and how the topic might come up again and then think about what one might know in the future that will add to his or her knowledge. This is how to build up layers of meaning and add to the depth of one's knowledge. It is also a way to encourage intellectual engagement with the topic so that one more deeply considers the complexity of the matter. Also, the accretive approach recognizes the limitations and idiosyncrasies of human beings. In most cases, people need to hear the same thing, sometimes many times, before there is that "aha" moment when they truly understand the teaching on a deeper, intuitive level.

I mainly use this method in discussing genocide in my survey course on American Indians. Rather than teach a unit on genocide, I return to the topic in different ways throughout the semester. By the end of the course, students have developed a greater appreciation for the hardships endured by American Indian people. I use this method in my American Indian religions class to stress the importance of relationships. Rather than have one unit on the topic, I discuss the role and function of relationships in the religious life of American Indians. By the end of the semester, I have dissuaded most of the students from their romantic notions about Indians being close to nature and instead have instilled them with a sense of the hard work and satisfaction that can come from maintaining healthy spiritual relationships with the Creator, spirits, other-than-humans, and human beings.

As far as I can tell, American Indians in general as well as the Anishinaabeg are not interested in truth with a capital "T." Instead, there is a recognition that multiple truths can exist, and the existence of multiple truths is an acceptable state of affairs. This approach to the truth finds expression in at least two forms. First, on the individual level, the Anishinaabeg, along with other American Indians, have their own take on epistemology. I have heard elders and others explain that what one individual experiences the Creator has put there for that person, and that two people can encounter the seemingly same event and have completely different experiences. One of my teachers told me a story about two Indians at a powwow who looked up and saw some eagles, which they pointed out to each other. Two white men standing behind them looked up, too. One white man said, "Some Indians. They can't even tell buzzards from eagles." My teacher's commentary was that those white men did not know what the Indians saw. Instead of insulting the Indians, they should have been asking themselves why they saw buzzards when the Indians saw eagles.

The second manner in which the recognition of the complex nature of truth manifests itself in Native American cultures involves accepting that different groups live by different truths. I have noticed that when Native Americans get together, they exchange information about their respective beliefs and practices. I have yet to hear a traditional Indian tell another, "Well, if you believe in that, you're going to hell." Instead, an interest in learning from each other exists. This sentiment is expressed in a probably apocryphal story about an anthropologist visiting a Native village. He was told that a certain spot in that village was the center of the world. They then went to visit another Indian village, where one of the Indians said a certain spot in their village was the center of the world, to which the Indian from the first village agreed. While returning to the first village, the anthropologist asked the first Indian how he could agree with the Indian in the second village that their spot was the center of the world when he said a spot in his own village was the center of the world. The Indian replied, "Well, when we're in our village, our spot is the center of the world. When we're in their village, their spot is the center of the world." Effectively, this means that Native Americans acknowledge that systems are true within their own respective systems. In that sense, truth exists. However, there is also recognition that the truth will probably not prevail outside of its given system. Note that this includes religious truths.

The notion that the complex nature of truth includes religious truths is obviously foreign to the Judeo-Christian-Islamic worldview, in which each respective branch claims exclusive privilege to the one, valid religious truth. From my understanding of Native American cultures, it is not necessary and can even be dangerous to proclaim one truth for all people in all times. The Native American point of view, including the Anishinaabeg, is that the Creator placed different people in different areas and gave them instructions—religious beliefs and practices—for living on that land. Thus, the religious beliefs and practices of the Anishinaabeg are appropriate for the Anishinaabeg, but not, for example, their Dakota neighbors, who live in a different area. Further, it would be damaging and dangerous for the Anishinaabeg to insist that the Dakota live by the religious truths and practices of the Anishinaabeg. The result would be social disruption and damage to the land. It is better to allow people to live by the religious truths and practices given to them by the Creator.

This does not mean that people cannot learn from each other, or even exchange beliefs and practices. When Native Americans get together, they often exchange information regarding their respective beliefs and practices. Sometimes, one group will even take up a practice from another. This is the case with the Anishinaabeg. Currently, some Anishinaabeg practice the Big Drum ceremony. I have been to some of these ceremonies. Interestingly enough, the keepers of the ceremony often point out that it was a gift to the Anishinaabeg from the Dakota. The way the Anishinaabeg tell it, a Dakota woman had a dream about the Big Drum ceremony and presented the ceremony to the Anishinaabeg. These are some of the kinds of teachings and practices connected with the recognition of the complex nature of truth. Suffice it to say, the Anishinaabeg, along with other Native Americans, are interested in emphasizing the complex nature of truth as part of a teaching strategy.

Respect for people outside one's culture is closely related to the recognition of the complex nature of truth and does not require nearly as extensive an explanation. Because the Anishinaabeg accept that the truth is complicated and that people should be allowed to live by the truths revealed to them by the Creator, it follows as a natural consequence that the Anishinaabeg have, as one of their ideals, respect for people outside their culture. This is not always the case in reality but is certainly an ideal toward which the Anishinaabeg strive and which they work to express. For example, the Anishinaabeg sweat lodge is built with twelve poles. Two poles go in each of the four cardinal directions for a total of eight poles. This results in a square at the top of the lodge. The remaining four poles make an X between the cardinal points and, therefore, make an X in the square at the top of the lodge. On the four branches of the X the Anishinaabeg tie different colored cloth to represent the four races: red, white, yellow, and black. We are taught that when we are in the sweat lodge we should pray for all people, including the whites. I have heard elders say that it does not make sense to pray only for the Anishinaabeg or to pray for all the races except the whites. Those elders strongly emphasize the need to pray for all people because it is one way of teaching respect.

In our classes, recognition of the complex nature of truth and respect for people outside one's culture mainly find expression in the oral presentations. Each student tells his or her own story, and, in so doing, the students learn to respect each other and value each other's input. Especially when it comes to class discussions, students can feel free to speak from their individual experience and know that their input will be valued. They speak their truth as they know it. The oral presentations are very important in that they help move the class from being a collection of strangers to a group of colleagues learning together.

I have written about humor in relation to Anishinaabe culture elsewhere.[17] For this article, I am interested in how my teachers not only use humor in their own teaching but also how they expect me to use humor; so the humor cuts both ways. Additionally, the more ribald the humor, the better, it seems. As might be expected, a lot of teasing goes back and forth. This is not to say that there is nothing but humor. Obviously, there is a serious side to teaching. However, the use of humor is highly encouraged in the Anishinaabe teaching environment. I try to bring the Anishinaabe sense of humor into the class-room. I exercise quite a bit of self-deprecating humor but also like to tease the students. It is important to exercise prudence in using humor in this regard. It is easy for students to take the instructor as a fool if he or she plays one in class. To avoid this, I make sure the material presented in class has depth, and that I lecture on it with conviction. When it comes to teasing, it is important to know the students and keep the teasing within reasonable limits.

These elements of Anishinaabe pedagogy are used to develop an Anishinaabe human being, fully capable of functioning in the society and world of the people. Many of the elements listed can be found in other Native cultures. In that regard, the specifics would focus on the particulars of Anishinaabe culture, such as the sacred stories and other items indigenous to the nation. In bringing these elements into the classroom, the idea is not to try to turn non-Native students into Indians but to use these elements to help inform my own teaching and bring diversity to the academy. The elements discussed and the approach I explained in my earlier work on teaching American Indian studies has been successful, and the students report that they enjoy being exposed to a different teaching method. Over the years, however, my thoughts on teaching have continued to develop, and so I would like to say a few words about where my teaching currently stands.

In my paper, "Teaching American Indian Studies to Reflect American Indian Ways of Knowing and to Interrupt Cycles of Genocide," I included a definition of *genocide* drawn from the work of Ward Churchill. Looking back on it now, it would have been better to use the definition of *genocide* found in the United Nations Convention on the Prevention and Punishment of the Crime of Genocide.[18] I appreciate Churchill's detailed definition of *genocide*. However, the United Nations Convention has the status of an international agreement, which the Churchill definition does not. In light of those circumstances, I ask readers to refer to the United Nations Convention on genocide when consulting my article on teaching American Indian studies.

When it comes to teaching my classes, I have made a few changes in the logistics on the first assignment and the student's interest in the topic and how it developed. In the past, I would allow students to rewrite the paper as many times as they desired up to a final deadline. However, I found that the students were not paying enough attention to my suggestions for improving their papers. To get their attention I now allow three rewrites of the paper up to the final deadline. I insist that footnotes and sources be formatted correctly and that the paper have a minimum of writing errors. For example, in order to earn an A grade, a paper must have two or fewer writing errors on any given page, three for a B, four for a C, and so forth. Although it might seem like a lot of work, after grading the first draft, subsequent grading goes rather quickly, and I rarely get more than four or five rewrites for any given class period. Using this approach, I am able to practice forgiveness and give the students a second chance. In writing an essay that truly deserves a high grade, this approach also helps the students develop a positive self-identity. Knowing that their story will be validated also contributes to the student's positive self-identity.

Unfortunately, one thing I have learned over the years is that students are not sure how to approach this type of essay. Most have never encountered an assignment like this before. In order to help them out, I collect electronic versions of good examples of this assignment. I have the students e-mail me a copy. After editing and adding comments, the paper is ready for distribution. I send the students several examples with different styles of writing, so they have a better sense of what I look for in the assignment. I find that this helps make the first draft stronger and speeds up the entire process of rewriting the papers.

One of the biggest challenges I have faced is working with first-generation college students. Students who are first-generation college students usually say so in their oral presentations. Quite often, these are student athletes, but first-generation students can come from any rank within the student population. In my experience, first-generation college students have the hardest time with writing assignments. To assist these individuals, I am instituting a process whereby I will require first-generation students to sign up for consultation on the first assignment. Other students are invited to seek help as well. However, because of the unique status of first-generation college students, I am particularly interested in seeing that they get the help they need in order to succeed. The number of first-generation college students I have in any given class is limited. As such, I do not anticipate being overwhelmed with this approach to helping them.

It could be said that many of the features of American Indian pedagogy are common to people around the world. This is not too surprising in that humans have a generally limited number of responses to dealing with the challenges of life, including educating people. However, the particular constellation of elements in American Indian pedagogy also makes the approach unique. For example, the lack of punishment is striking and certainly stands in contrast to current Western and Asian approaches to learning. As we continue to develop an American Indian pedagogy, we should continue to consider what kind of human beings we want to create and how we can best help people succeed and express their full, individual humanity. In that regard, I would like to finish with what I think is at the root of American Indian pedagogy. If I may put it this way, the Creator has given each of us different talents and tasks to complete in this world. It is important for each of us to develop our own vision in life so that we may most fully express our talents and best succeed in our tasks. It is vitally important that we do not follow somebody else's dream or somebody else's dream for us. Having others impose their dreams on other individuals is, in effect, playing God, or interfering with those individuals' mission in life. It is incumbent on individuals to become most fully the person they are. Individuals should not fully develop their talents just for themselves, but do so for the benefit of their family, community, and place. Turning the analysis around, it becomes important for the community to encourage the development of strong individuals so the community as a whole may become strong.[19] In a very real way this is how we can use indigenous cultures, in this case, American Indian pedagogy, to understand indigenous people utilizing an approach developed from within the culture and to create a better future not just for Native people but also for all humanity.

NOTES

1. Lawrence W. Gross, "Teaching American Indian Studies to Reflect American Indian Ways of Knowing and to Interrupt Cycles of Genocide," *Wicazo Sa Review* 20, no. 2 (2005): 187–234.

2. Frances Densmore, *Chippewa Customs*, Bureau of American Ethnology Bulletin 86 (Washington, DC: Government Printing Office, 1929).

3. Ibid., 48–72.

4. M. Inez Hilger, *Chippewa Child Life and Its Cultural Background* (St. Paul: Minnesota Historical Society Press, 1992). Originally published as *Chippewa Child Life and Its Cultural Background*, Bureau of American Ethnology Bulletin 146 (Washington, DC: Government Printing Office, 1951).

5. Ibid., 55–60.

6. Roger Spielmann, *"You're So Fat!": Exploring Ojibwe Discourse* (Toronto: University of Toronto Press, 1998).

7. Ibid., 91–92.

8. Jim Northrup, "Fond du Lac Follies," *The Circle*, 14 October 1994; 16 September 2001; 14 September 2003.

9. Christopher Vecsey, *Traditional Ojibwa Religion and Its Historical Changes* (Philadelphia: American Philosophical Society, 1983), 84.

10. Jim Northrup, "The Odyssey," in *Walking the Rez Road* (Stillwater, MN: Voyageur Press, 1993), 55–59.

11. Ibid., 57.

12. A. Irving Hallowell, "Ojibwa Ontology, Behavior, and World View," in *Culture in History: Essays in Honor of Paul Radin*, ed. Stanley Diamond (New York: Columbia University Press, 1960), 19–52.

13. Lawrence W. Gross, "*Bimaadiziwin*, or the 'Good Life,' as a Unifying Concept of Anishinaabe Religion," *American Indian Culture and Research Journal* 26, no. 1 (2002): 15–32.

14. Jim Northrup, "Fond du Lac Follies," *The Circle*, 24 May 1990; 21 October 1990; 16 May 1998; 20 April 2000; 22 May 2004; 21 May 2005; 16 October 2005.

15. William G. Tierney, *Official Encouragement, Institutional Discouragement: Minorities in Academe—The Native American Experience* (Norwood, NJ: Ablex Publishing, 1992).

16. Hilger, *Chippewa Child Life*, 59. She does cite instances of corporal punishment among the Anishinaabeg. However, other Anishinaabeg stated that people who hit their children are not real Indians. Remembering that Hilger made her observations in the 1930s and 1940s, I suspect the use of corporal punishment she discusses may have been introduced into the culture by Euro-Americans. In any event, it is clear corporal punishment was not accepted as a standard cultural practice among the Anishinaabeg. Spielmann's observations are closer to my own in this regard when he states, "In Pikogan parents rarely spanked or severely reprimanded their children. Children are disciplined, for sure, but in subtle ways." See Spielmann, "*You're So Fat!*" 39. In my own family, my great-grandmother raised thirteen children and did not hit them. My grandmother raised twelve children and did not hit them. My own mother raised nine children, and she never once yelled at us or hit us. I suspect my own family's practices are closer to the traditional practices of the Anishinaabeg than the instances of corporal punishment Hilger discusses.

17. Lawrence W. Gross, "The Comic Vision of Anishinaabe Culture and Religion," *American Indian Quarterly* 26, no. 3 (2003): 436–59; Lawrence Gross, "Silence as the Root of American Indian Humor: Further Meditations on the Comic Vision of Anishinaabe Culture and Religion," *American Indian Culture and Research Journal* 31, no. 2 (2007): 69–85.

18. "Convention on the Prevention and Punishment of the Crime of Genocide," The Human Rights Web, http://www.hrweb.org/legal/genocide.html (accessed 16 March 2010).

19. I am pleased Spielmann shares my assessment of Anishinaabe pedagogy. See Spielmann, "*You're So Fat!*" 39.

AMERICAN INDIAN CULTURE AND RESEARCH JOURNAL 34:2 (2010) 27–46

Elder Brother, the Law of the People, and Contemporary Kinship Practices of Cowessess First Nation Members: Reconceptualizing Kinship in American Indian Studies Research

ROBERT ALEXANDER INNES

INTRODUCTION

Raymond DeMallie has argued that kinship studies are a significant but often ignored area of research within American Indian studies (AIS), suggesting that AIS scholars' aversion to kinship research has been due to the latter's close association with anthropology. According to DeMallie, kinship studies, with their evolutionary and cultural relativist theories, abstract taxonomies, and endless charts, seem far removed from and irrelevant to AIS scholars and Native communities. Yet, in pointing to examples of the negative impact of kinship breakdown on the Grassy Narrows Ojibwe and the possibility for positive change with the revitalization of the Pine Ridge Lakota kinship unit, or *tiyoshpaye*, DeMallie stated that kinship is "fundamental to every aspect of Native American Studies." Accordingly, he challenged AIS scholars "to explore the richness of the Native American social heritage and find creative ways to build on it for the future."[1]

Few researchers have pursued kinship studies of Native North American people since the 1970s. Instead, researchers have focused on international indigenous people and applied unique approaches to kinship research. Exploring the relationship between gender and kinship or the link between economics and kinship are examples of approaches taken by researchers of international indigenous people.[2] Though few researchers have explored kinship within a Native American context, recent studies of Native American

Robert Alexander Innes is a member of Cowessess First Nation and an assistant professor in the Department of Native Studies at the University of Saskatchewan.

identity construction have examined the persistence of distinct cultural identity within contemporary Native American communities, identities that are closely linked to kinship.[3] These studies suggest that ethnic identity is a fluid process. These innovative approaches to kinship research of indigenous people worldwide provide AIS scholars with exciting possibilities for undertaking similar research on Aboriginal people. These studies further point to a need for answering DeMallie's call for more kinship studies in a Native North American context. However, to date no studies like these have been conducted in Canada. How Cowessess First Nation band members have constructed their identities over time, and the link between their identities and notions of kinship, is of prime interest to my study.

In my research I take up DeMallie's challenge by examining the importance of kinship relations in the maintenance and affirmation of individual and collective identity for members of the Cowessess First Nation, located in southeastern Saskatchewan. Specifically, the study examines how Cowessess band members' continued adherence to principles of traditional law regulating kinship has undermined the imposition of the Indian Act's definitions of *Indian* by acknowledging kinship relations to band members who either had not been federally recognized as Indians prior to 1985 or were urban members disconnected from the reserve. This acknowledgment defies the general perception that First Nations people have internalized the legal definition of *Indian* and in the process rendered traditional kinship meaningless. It also questions the accepted idea that conflict is the only possible outcome of any relationship between "old" members and "newly recognized" Indians. The importance of kinship to Cowessess band members blurs the boundaries (as defined by the Indian Act) among status Indians, Bill C-31s, Métis, and nonstatus Indians, thus highlighting the artificiality of those boundaries.

I argue that the attitude of older Cowessess band members toward new members stems from kinship practices that are historically rooted in the traditional law of the people that predates the reserve era and that have persisted since at least the nineteenth century. In the prereserve era, Aboriginal bands in the northern plains were relatively small, kin-based communities that relied on the unity of their members for survival. Band membership was fluid, flexible, and inclusive. There were a variety of ways that individuals or groups of people could become members of a band, but what was of particular importance was that these new members assumed some sort of kinship role with its associated responsibilities. For Cowessess people, these roles were behaviors that were carefully encoded in the traditional stories of the Cree trickster/transformer, or our Elder Brother. Elder Brother stories were "the law of the people" that outlined, among other things, the peoples' social interaction including the incorporation of individuals into a band. Incorporating new band members served to strengthen social, economic, and military alliances with other bands of the same cultural group. However, many bands in the northern plains were multicultural in nature, so the creation and maintenance of alliances cut across cultural and linguistic lines.

The Cowessess First Nation is an example of a multicultural band because its prereserve composition comprises five major cultural groups: the Plains

Cree, Saulteaux, Assiniboine, Métis, and English half-breeds. The total membership of the contemporary band is 3,724, with nearly 80 percent living off reserve. This represents the third largest of seventy-five First Nations in Saskatchewan and the largest in southern Saskatchewan. Band members live throughout the province and in every province and territory in the country, particularly in major urban centers such as Winnipeg, Calgary, Edmonton, Vancouver, Toronto, and Ottawa. However, nearly 1,800 band members reside in the provincial capital of Regina, approximately one and one-half hour drive west of the reserve.[4] Band members have also relocated to several foreign countries. Many of these off-reserve members are men and their wives (and descendants) who first left the reserve in the 1950s. A significant number are also C-31s—that is, women who left the reserve to find employment and/or married nonstatus Indians, and therefore lost their status—who regained their status and had their children's status reinstated.

My study describes how kinship for contemporary Cowessess First Nation band members, in spite of the historical, scholarly, and legal classifications of Aboriginal peoples created and imposed by outsiders, persists to define community identity and interaction based on principles outlined in the Elder Brother stories. Classifying Aboriginal people has had profound impacts on the ways that non-Aboriginal people view Aboriginal people and on how some Aboriginal people view themselves. Cowessess members' interpretations become of great significance in order to understand how contemporary First Nations put into practice their beliefs about kinship roles and responsibilities and demonstrate that these practices and beliefs are rooted in historical cultural values. In addition, this practice confounds the tribally specific histories that tend to extrapolate relations at the band level to relations at the tribal level and, therefore, presents a distorted view of historic Aboriginal societies as distinctly bounded entities.

The first section of this article provides a brief history of the legislation that has defined *Indian* in Canadian law and of the challenges to these definitions that eventually led to the 1985 implementation of Bill C-31, which amended the Indian Act's membership code. The second section outlines the notion of the law of the people conveyed through stories of Elder Brother. The third section links the values found within the stories to kinship patterns practiced by Cowessess members in the early reserve period to the mid-twentieth century. Finally, the last section discusses the findings of interviews with twenty-seven Cowessess band members that show their continued adherence to aspects of their traditional kinship expectations.

LEGAL DEFINITIONS OF *INDIAN*

The legislative history regulating Canadian First Nations is one of an imposition of a legal standard to determine who would be federally recognized as Indian. This standard has created an artificial boundary between peoples where none previously existed and has created tension and conflict, as various interests debate where that boundary should be drawn. In 1850, prior to the creation of Canada, the colonial government passed two pieces of legislation that marked the first attempt to define in law who was an Indian.[5] Although the colonial government's objective was ostensibly to establish who could live on First Nations' lands, the acts were really "designed to reinforce the rights of settlers to the entire land by restricting Indians to specific territories within it."[6] The acts, as John Tobias states, "established the precedent that non-Indians determined who was an Indian and that Indians would have no say in the matter."[7]

In 1876, the Canadian government passed An Act to Amend and Consolidate the Laws Respecting Indians, better known by its short title, the Indian Act, 1876. Consisting of one hundred sections, the Indian Act had far-ranging implications on all aspects of First Nations' life including the management of reserve land and resources, the operations and scope of power of band councils, the ways that courts dealt with non-Christian Indians, and alcohol use, and it described the "privileges of Indians." Like the earlier legislation, the Indian Act attempted to redefine kinship patterns of First Nations people by outlining whom the Canadian government would acknowledge as Indian.[8]

The Indian Act underwent many extensive amendments through 1927, with minor amendments in the 1930s, and a major revision in 1951 that sought primarily to accelerate the assimilation process but was also used to control and punish those First Nations individuals who were perceived as undermining federal goals. The effect of these definitions was that some aspects of the traditional kinship patterns were disrupted while others, such as the incorporation of non-Indian men, were made illegal. Women who married non-Indians and their children were legally excluded from band membership and Indian status, a clear violation of traditional kinship systems for many First Nations groups. Section 12(1)(b) of the amended Indian Act of 1952 reinforced the attack of the kinship patterns, as it stated that a "woman who is married to a person who is not an Indian was not entitled to be registered as an Indian."[9] The sexual discrimination of the Indian Act was entrenched in Canadian law until the 1970s, when some First Nations women challenged this membership criterion and sparked a response from on-reserve band members and First Nations leadership.

In the early 1970s, two First Nations women, Jeanette Corbiere Lavell, an Ojibwe originally from Wikwemikong First Nation, and Yvonne Bedard, from the Six Nations Reserve in southern Ontario, launched court actions that claimed that section 12(1)(b) violated the Canadian Bill of Rights based on gender. Both women had lost their Indian status after they married non-Indian men. In 1973, the Supreme Court of Canada ruled against the women asserting that section 12(1)(b) did not breach the Bill of Rights as this section was applied equally to all status Indian women.[10] However, in 1977, Sandra Lovelace, a Maliseet woman from New Brunswick, brought her case to the United Nations Human Rights Committee claiming that Canada had violated the International Covenant on Civil and Political Rights on the grounds of sexual discrimination by preventing her recognition of federal Indian status when she married a non-Indian. The United Nations committee ruled that it could not adjudicate Lovelace's case based on sexual discrimination as she had married prior to Canada signing the covenant. It did, however, closely examine whether the Indian Act contravened Article 27 of the covenant, which states, "In those states in which ethnic, religious, or linguistic minorities exist, persons belonging to such minorities shall not be denied the right, in community with other members of their group, to enjoy their own culture, to profess and practice their own religion, or to use their own language." The committee ruled that because Lovelace could no longer live in her community, Canada had breached Article 27 of the International Covenant on Civil and Political Rights by denying her right to access the culture of her community.[11] This ruling was an important factor that compelled the Canadian government to proceed to make changes to the Indian Act.

In 1985, when the Canadian government passed Bill C-31 to amend the membership code of the Indian Act, many First Nations leaders expressed their displeasure. The amendment allowed for those people who had lost their federally recognized Indian status, many of who were women who lost their status upon marrying non-Indians, to regain their status and pass on their status to their children. Comments made in the news media and in parliamentary hearings about the amendment highlight the tension it caused in many communities due to the complex definitions of federal Indian status and band membership, which engendered issues of cultural authenticity, governance, and government funding for First Nations.[12] These issues influenced individual and collective responses to the new members.

STORY OF ELDER BROTHER AND THE WOLVES

Historically, the Elder Brother stories played a crucial role in detailing the prescribed social interactions of the people. Elder Maria Campbell has said that the Elder Brother stories contained the law of the people.[13] The legal systems of precontact Aboriginal peoples, as James Zion points out, "were based upon the idea of maintaining harmony in the family, the camp, and the community."[14] The failure to follow prescribed regulations could, according to what happens to Elder Brother in the stories, result in severe negative consequences. Conversely, adhering to the positive behavior Elder Brother displays was seen as the ideal that all should attain. An understanding of the stories facilitates an understanding for the incorporation of members into the Cowessess band in the pre- and postreserve periods. The stories are also helpful in gaining insight into contemporary peoples' ability to maintain certain aspects of their kinship roles and responsibilities.

Traditionally, stories, and especially trickster/transformer stories, acted to impart the philosophical ideals upon which Aboriginal societies should function.[15] As Robert Williams Jr. notes, "The stories socialized children and reminded adults of their roles and place within the universe. . . . Indians have long practiced the belief that stories have the power to sustain the many important connections of tribal life."[16] The telling of trickster stories, such as those of Elder Brother, was a means by which to convey Aboriginal philosophical meanings to the people. Elder Brother is a spirit being who has many human characteristics. He can be generous and kind, yet he can also be selfish and cruel. In a story, if he was kind, he usually met with success; if he was cruel, he often met a disastrous and sometimes humorous end. His adventures and misadventures acted to guide the peoples' social interactions, and because of this he is highly regarded. As Basil Johnston states about the esteem the Ojibwe have of Nanabush, "For his attributes, strong and weak, the Anishnabeg came to love and understand Nanabush. They saw in him themselves. In his conduct was reflected the characters of men and women, young and old. From Nanabush, although he was a paradox, physical and spirit being, doing good and unable to attain it, the Anishnabeg learned."[17]

Elder Brother stories conveyed Cowessess traditional law to its people. These stories functioned as a legal institution. Though this institution was unlike those in other parts of the world, it functioned in the same way. As Zion and Robert Yazzie explain, "When a legal institution articulates a norm or validates a custom, that is 'law.'"[18] The Elder Brother stories explained the rules for expected normative behavior. These ideals were enshrined in the peoples' notion of themselves, with each retelling of Elder Brother stories and with each act that could be attributed to these stories.

A number of legal scholars have linked traditional narratives, whether stories, songs, or prayers, of Aboriginal peoples to their traditional legal system.[19] For example, Williams points out that "stories are told in tribal life to educate and direct young ones, to maintain the cohesiveness of the group, and to pass on traditional knowledge about the Creator, the seasons, the earth, plants, life, death, and every other subject that is important to the perpetuation of the tribe."[20] John Borrows states that the traditional tribal customary principles "are enunciated in the rich stories, ceremonies, and traditions within First Nations. Stories express the law in Aboriginal communities, since they represent the accumulated wisdom and experience of First Nations conflict resolution."[21] Donald Auger asserts that "the knowledge gained by individuals from story-telling was that of relationships and the importance of maintaining balance and harmony."[22] Stories act to connect our "normative system to our social constructions of reality and to our vision of what the world might be."[23] Robert Cover explains the connection between narratives and law:

> No set of legal institutions or prescriptions exists apart from the narratives that locate it and give it meaning. For every constitution there is an epic, for each Decalogue a scripture. Once understood in the context of the narratives that give it meaning, law becomes not merely a system of rules to be observed, but a world in which we live . . . in this normative world, law and narrative are inseparably related . . . every narrative is insistent in its demand for its prescriptive point, its moral.[24]

The Elder Brother stories reflect the moral normative behaviors that Cowessess band members were expected to follow. Through these stories, "their sense of justice and fairness" were prompted.

In 1913, anthropologist Alanson Skinner collected Elder Brother stories from a number of elders from Cowessess that set the parameters by which Cowessess people were expected to act. The following is a condensed excerpt from a story of Elder Brother and a group of wolves. In the story, Elder Brother is adopted by the wolves and then assumes the accepted kinship roles and responsibilities.

> One night some wolves heard Elder Brother singing. The oldest says "I believe that is my eldest brother. He has a good song . . . watch for him, and run and say to him, 'My uncle, what are you saying?'" When the wolves met up with Elder Brother, they told him that their father wanted to meet him. The father asked his elder brother what his song meant. Elder Brother told him and then decided that he would stay with the wolves for a while. Some time later, Elder Brother decided he wanted to leave, but he wanted one of his nephews to go with him. The old wolf allowed his youngest son to leave.
>
> After a dream, Elder Brother addressed the young wolf, "My nephew, never go along the lake-shore. Do not run on the beach." Later, the young wolf was thirsty. Forgetting Elder Brother's instructions, he went to the lake and drank some water. He suddenly became crazy. Elder Brother realized his nephew had gone missing and knew that the White-Lynx had taken him. He tracked White-Lynx and listening to the Sun, shot at his shadow. He was successful on the attempt, but he did not kill him. The White one, though injured escaped. Elder Brother met up with old toad, who was on her way with her medicines to heal White-Lynx. Elder Brother killed and skinned her and put on her skin. He went to White-Lynx, now as the old toad. When he arrived the people said, "Oh, our old grandma is coming again." As the toad, Elder Brother entered the White-Lynx's lodge. Upon entering, he saw the skin of his nephew hanging on a pole. He then saw White-Lynx with an arrow in his side. He had a pipe be filled and then asked everyone to leave. "Now, shut the door. I shall smoke and take out the arrow now, but don't let any one look in." When this was done, Elder Brother walked up to White-Lynx and grabbed the arrow in his hand and pushed it into the Lynx's heart as hard as he could. He then grabbed his nephew's skin and fled, tearing off the toad skin. Once Elder Brother had ensured that he had lost his pursuers, he brought him back to life.[25]

The story outlines a number of prescribed behaviors required in the maintenance of respectful kinship relations with Cowessess people. It highlights the value of inclusion by the facts that although Elder Brother was not related to the wolves, he was adopted into the pack and considered a relative; the younger wolves were expected to address and treat him as an older relative; and he assumed the roles and responsibilities expected of a relative. In the same way he was adopted by the wolves, Elder Brother is permitted to adopt a younger wolf that Elder Brother calls nephew. However, it is when Elder Brother and the young wolf were on their travels that the kinship roles and responsibilities become more explicit. Elder Brother is responsible for the well-being of the young wolf. When the young wolf goes to the water against the instructions of Elder Brother, the listeners learn that there are negative consequences for not heeding the words of elders. In searching for and rescuing his nephew, Elder Brother fulfilled his responsibility not only to the young wolf but also to his other relative, the old wolf. By entering the White-Lynx's village, Elder Brother exhibits characteristics, such as bravery, daring, and ingenuity, that are important for young males to internalize. These were central tenets of the warrior societies, whose primary duty was to protect and provide for the people. From his story, the kinship obligations for Cowessess people were made clear. The people understood that for the society to be self-perpetuating, it was incumbent that members adhere to the principles of Elder Brother stories.

Elder Brother stories help to explain traditional kinship practices of the prereserve and early reserve periods, when Cowessess people easily incorporated others into their band, including the adoption of white children. However, the assimilation policies of the Canadian government sought to undermine the law of the people, including regulations guiding kinship practices. These attempts were in many respects successful. Yet for many Cowessess people the notions of kinship as epitomized in Elder Brother's behavior continue to exist, demonstrating that the ideals of the traditional law of the people are still implicitly central principles guiding band members' social interactions. The extent to which current Cowessess band members tell Elder Brother stories or even know about them is not certain. However, what is apparent is that the values that are encoded in these stories have persisted from prereserve and early reserve periods to the present.

THE MULTICULTURAL ETHOS OF THE COWESSESS BAND

In the early reserve period, Louis O'Soup, an important First Nations political leader for nearly forty years, typified the multicultural ethos of the Cowessess band. He was a Cowessess headman during the signing of Treaty Four in 1874, and he later became chief of the band and was notable for lobbying for treaty rights and the economic and social improvement of First Nations people. Though most historians have identified O'Soup as Saulteaux, he was of mixed ancestry. O'Soup's father was Ojibwe/Métis, his mother was Assiniboine, and his wife was Nez Perce.

The Cowessess band continued the prereserve practice of accepting new members into the band well into the reserve period. Sometime during the 1890s, for example, two men, Wapamouse (also spelled Wapahmoose) and Patrick Redwood, transferred into the band. Wapamouse was a descendant of Chief Wahpemoosetoosis, who had signed Treaty Four, and Redwood was a carpenter. Both men married Cowessess women and transferred their band membership to Cowessess from their original bands. Cowessess families adopted a number of Euro-Canadian children. For example, O'Soup, who suffered the loss of three daughters, adopted a boy of Irish descent. The boy's parents had apparently deserted him, and he was left with the priest at the

Qu'Appelle Industrial School, where the adoption was arranged.[26] According to Janice Acoose, O'Soup adopted her paternal grandmother, Madeline, also of Irish descent.[27] Madeline later married the famous Saulteaux long-distance runner Paul Acoose from the neighboring Sakimay First Nation.[28] According to band elders, a number of Cowessess families traveled to Winnipeg around 1905 and adopted up to seven white children, including Mariah Lerat, the mother of Harold Lerat. Harold Lerat is a band elder who in his recently published book confirmed that Gus Pelletier and Annie Two Voice had adopted his mother.[29]

The band also accepted individuals who had either elected to give up their Indian status voluntarily or had transferred to other bands but later decided to reapply to be treaty Indians and band members.[30] For example, Harold Lerat's grandfather's brother, Pierre Lerat, who had married a Métis woman named Cecile Desjarlais, enfranchised and was given $160 in Métis scrip. He later requested to be a treaty Indian and was allowed back, but with his annuity payments withheld until the scrip money was paid back.[31] Many Métis and half-breeds who had married Cowessess band members applied to be let in to treaty. "Even though there were bureaucrats that did not agree with allowing half-breeds into treaty, the deal ended up that if the half-breeds came back into treaty, their annual treaty money for all members of the family would be held back until the amount paid to them in scrip was recovered."[32]

In the late 1890s, O'Soup transferred to the Pine Creek Indian Reserve near Lake Winnipegosis and lived with Chief Gambler's band.[33] In 1907, he applied to be allowed back at Cowessess. A vote was held in which his application was defeated seventeen to eight. Another vote was passed unanimously in favor of not allowing any more transfers into the band. However, when O'Soup again applied to be allowed back onto the reserve the next year, only one person out of twenty-nine voted against his return.[34] Although there was some animosity against allowing new members into the band, the band nevertheless continued the cultural practice of inclusion from prereserve times.

According to the Department of Indian Affairs records, Cowessess people continued their long-standing relationship with the Métis, especially with those living in the Métis community of Marieval, well into the postwar years. One elder who was interviewed said that some of her relatives married men from the "Métis side"—referring to the fact that Marieval was on the north side of the Qu'Appelle River, which was the border of the reserve: "My aunts married Métis people. We used to go visit them. My mother and them were close. . . . You see the Métis lived over here on the other side of the [Qu'Appelle] River." One World War II veteran, who grew up in Marieval, described their relations with the Cowessess people during the 1930s as being very close. People from Marieval, he said, would go to the reserve to play baseball, attend church, and join community dances.[35] The persistence of intermarriage between these communities facilitated their close relations. This particular veteran had married a Cowessess woman, and his mother was from Cowessess. The close relationship between Cowessess people and the Métis was facilitated by the fact that the Roman Catholic Church was located on the reserve because many people from both sides of the river were Catholic and faithfully attended mass and other church functions.

The presence of the Roman Catholic Church on Cowessess also acted as a unifying factor with the non-Aboriginal population, as French Canadians and eastern European immigrants attended the church. A possible explanation for the multiethnic nature of the parishioners was the existence of the Ku Klux Klan, which flourished in 1920s Saskatchewan and targeted French Canadian and eastern European immigrants because they did not speak English and were Catholic.[36] With a few notable exceptions, the presence of the newcomers was well received by Cowessess people. In 1921, however, a petition was submitted to the priests to create a separate parish for the Indians and Métis parishioners due to the racist attitudes of some French Canadians. This never occurred, and in 1934 the priests indicated that 5 Polish, 7 French, 34 Métis, and 107 Indian families attended the church on Cowessess.[37] One Cowessess member mentioned that many French Canadian, German, and Métis are buried in the Cowessess cemetery.

CONTEMPORARY VIEWS OF KINSHIP

In Cowessess First Nation, unlike many other First Nations, little animosity was directed toward new members. Cowessess band members' responses to the amendments reflect the principles of the Elder Brother stories, as many have maintained kinship practices and innovated new ones. The central practices that act to maintain family connections included ways that fulfill responsibilities to family members and community such as family gatherings, in which members, especially children, are reminded of their family histories and their relations; the role of elders in socialization that act to link the past, present, and future; strategies by urban members, for example, living in close proximity to each other; and the way some members defined *family* that ignores biological, racial, and legal classifications imposed by others.

I interviewed twenty-seven Cowessess members living on- and off-reserve about their views of Bill C-31, specifically whether they believed the new membership code to be beneficial for Cowessess. Most felt that allowing relatives to regain their Indian status and secure band membership was good for the band. None of the band members interviewed exhibited the level of animosity toward any individual new member that has reportedly occurred on other First Nations. This is not to say, however, that all participants agreed with all aspects of Bill C-31. Nonetheless, the views of Cowessess people about C-31s demonstrate that the law of the people still resonates with band members.

Many of those interviewed understood why others lost their status. People either voluntarily enfranchised because they believed that they would be better able to provide for their family or because women had married nonstatus Indians. Many recalled the factors that led their families, or people they knew, to lose their status. One respondent outlined the circumstances surrounding his family becoming enfranchised:

> At one point our Indian status was taken away from us because our dad thought that we would never ever come back to what he thought was a racist [situation and a] lack of opportunity area to live. And that's

the reason—they were basically looking for other ways to live and to survive. And so they moved off the reserve. Um, there's always been a policy of the Canadian government to assimilate us, to reduce our treaty rights and all that kind of stuff. But back then, you know, there were a number of injustices being done that were very calculating and callous in the way the government treated us. Any women who married a non-Indian man lost her status. For four hundred dollars a head you could sign your family off the reserve and all your rights and benefits as an Indian. And so we did that. My dad did that to us. And so we became at the end of the process in '85, we were then reclassified Bill-C31s because we reapplied to become status Indians. The fact that they took our status away from us made our bodies no less Indian than we ever were. Our bloodline shows that we are very strongly attached to, to Cowessess and that never changes. So it's only the government and the way they, their policies dictate who is and who isn't an Indian. That really is the legal side of how we view our people, but then there's the real view, can't take Indianness away from you, you know.

This longtime reserve resident, now living in the urban area, outlined the impact that Bill C-31 had on the band:

Well, Cowessess, we always had a big membership. We always knew that we don't know most of our people. I guess we always knew it [Bill C-31] was going to inflate our population, but it probably increased by five to six hundred. The law came in '85, I think, but it wasn't until the beginning of the nineties that Cowessess membership starting increasing really fast. I think the Bill C-31 registrations are done now, at least for what it was intended. But our population probably increases about a hundred every year. We are probably thirty-two hundred now. When I started working for Cowessess eleven years ago, it was probably twenty-two hundred, and then it just jumped. It was all of the applications from Bill C-31. They said it would increase the membership list, and then they said there would be less [funds available for the band from the federal government] going around. But there wasn't enough room for people to stay here [to move back to the reserve; there is a chronic housing and land shortage] anyway.

The divisiveness of Bill C-31 was also reflected in the reaction of the Cowessess First Nation's band council to the implementation of the new amendment. During a band council meeting that I attended in 2003, one counselor proudly proclaimed, "We accepted all C-31s into the band." Another man who was a counselor when Bill C-31 was introduced said that he was originally against the bill because it meant that there might be more new members living on the reserve than "original" members. He also noted that "a lot of these people went out and came back, and a lot of them, I don't know how many, but there were a few who volunteered, then came back again, which I don't think is right." He was particularly against the idea of those who had voluntarily enfranchised being reinstated, rather than just those women who had lost their status through marriage. Twenty years after the passage of the bill, he seemed to have softened his position. When asked if he thought that allowing the Bill C-31s back into the band was a positive or negative experience, he stated, "I think that's a good thing, then you get to know the people." Then he added, perhaps half-jokingly because he was in his seventies and had been married for many years, "I could have married my cousin and never know it." The disagreement of the council over Bill C-31 reflected the opinions of the band as a whole. These feelings did not go unnoticed by some Bill C-31 members. One Bill C-31 member was quoted in a special online issue of *Windspeaker*, a national Aboriginal newspaper, concerning Bill C-31. He noted that, "If it were up to the bands, I think they would be a bit more discriminatory and I don't think I would have got my status if my band had the choice of choosing who would be a member."[38] However, there is no indication of why he believed the band would not have allowed him to return.

Though Cowessess accepted all their Bill C-31 members, it was not an explicit endorsement of the bill. Cowessess, like most Saskatchewan First Nations, did not implement their own membership codes within the allowed two years after the bill was passed and, therefore, were compelled to follow the code of the Indian Act. If Cowessess had implemented its own membership code, it could have been more inclusive or exclusive than the Indian Act.

Though there were some notable disagreements, the responses of longstanding band members to C-31s were generally positive. However, it must be kept in mind that a significant number of participants were C-31s or had relatives who were C-31s. For example, one reserve resident related how her family was always physically and emotionally close. When she was young, her immediate and extended family lived in a cluster of homes near each other. As they grew older, her family would "have lots of family gatherings. We lived together, we moved to the city together, but now that we are getting older we are settling down back at home and closer together." For her, Bill C-31 had positive ramifications for her relatives. She believed of Bill C-31 that, "Oh, it was a good thing for me because I had a first cousin that signed off the reserve, and with Bill C-31 they got some of their treaty rights back." For this woman, Bill C-31 meant that her close relatives were able to access treaty benefits, including the right to reside on the reserve near her, therefore allowing her to maintain her close familial bonds.

The attitudes of several band members who were interviewed are reflected in the views of these two well-respected community members, who noted that Bill C-31 did not go far enough:

> I don't deny the women getting their status back because I don't think it was right that they lost it when an Indian married a white man, and when an Indian married a white woman she gained status. It wasn't right for the woman to lose her status. They draw the line on Bill C-31, so when a woman got her status back she was a Bill C-31 and her children, but not her grandchildren would get their status. Which I don't think is right.

> I think it's unfair for the non-Indian women that married Indian men. They became band members and they enjoy benefits that Indian men have, but after '85 these white women, they can't acquire the status of their husbands anymore. So you have families on the reserve who enjoy all of the benefits from being a status Indian on the reserve, and then you have another family with a white woman who enjoys no status, so if something happened to her husband they have nothing.

The first respondent refers to the fact that the children of those reinstated did not receive full status. That is, a reinstated person can pass status to their children, but the children cannot pass on their status on to their own children unless they marry another status Indian.[39] The second respondent refers to a situation in which a white spouse, in this case a woman, marries a band member and resides on the reserve. According to the 1985 amendment to the Indian Act, she would not be entitled to any band membership benefits, no matter how long she lived on the reserve. This woman would have to leave the reserve if her husband should die before her. For this respondent, this undermines cultural kinship practices of Cowessess people. Housing issues, including inheritance of houses, fall under land management. The Cowessess Lands Management Act, which failed ratification, had planned to allow nonmember spouses to continue to live on the reserve after the passing of their member spouse. That these two prominent band members expressed disappointment that all individuals who were considered relatives were not included in Bill C-31 suggests that Cowessess people have retained inclusive notions of kinship held by earlier generations of Cowessess people. It also counters the opposition to Bill C-31 put forth by many First Nations leaders.

This following respondent pointed out that Bill C-31 does not take into account all the possible ways in which people have lost their status.

> Well, I will tell you one thing—it almost creates an imbalance between who is Indian and who is not Indian. It upsets me because my ex, I knew her family before I knew her. I was raised with her family but she was taken away and raised in the white world when she was very young. So I didn't know her. We are not related. They had a big family, too, but a lot of their grandkids got taken away. Some of them lost their status. My ex and her sisters were all raised in different homes and one of them lost her status. Some of her sister's kids have status and some don't. Her sister then passed away and orphaned her son. So now what I have is my kids and their first cousin. Their first cousin comes from the same background, an Indian mom and an Indian dad, but he doesn't have status. So now we have two kids, first cousins. My kids have status, but [the cousin] doesn't have status. So he can't count on the reserve when he goes up for school [postsecondary funding]. My daughter is going to school with funding but he can't.

I asked, "So, do they see each other differently?"

No, I don't think so. Like, on the reserve there [are] a lot of kids that were raised on Cowessess that aren't Cowessess band members. And that's so unfair, especially when these are our kids [children of Cowessess band members]. I think that it is in a sense very unfair for families to have one [with status] and one not to have. I think that they miss out on a lot of benefits that they could be entitled to. So that is one way of breaking down the community, cutting them off, then they don't have the support of their community.

His explanation is noteworthy for a number of reasons. First, although it is unclear why his nephew was not eligible to be reinstated, he did highlight a perceived shortcoming of Bill C-31 that not all relatives are necessarily eligible to gain their Indian status. Second, the kinship relationship among him, his children, and his nephew was not altered regardless of legal definitions of *Indian*. Additionally, his narrative pointed to the fact that his nephew's case is not an isolated one. As he noted, there were a number of children raised on the reserve who were not band members, which implies that he believed that there were many people who should be eligible for band membership and Indian status.

One person whom I interviewed was a C-31 who felt that he and other C-31s were discriminated against after regaining status. This person noted that he had had a hard time gaining access to housing since he returned to the reserve. However, he later said that the chief and council often favored their own families, whereas his family was small, with few relatives on the reserve and no family members on the band council.

Another person claimed that some band members were still not in favor of Bill C-31:

There were certain members that didn't like the C-31s. All it was, they were giving the Indian women her rights back that lost her status and her first children. I didn't see anything wrong with that. Where people started to have a problem was where they started coming back and wanting land from other people. That's where there was a problem because there wasn't very much land to be taken and from a Bill C-31 who never knew very much about living on a reserve in the first place.

The notions held by some Cowessess members that Bill C-31 members did not have the requisite knowledge or experience about living on a reserve is somewhat perplexing. Although it is true that there are many C-31s, especially the children of reinstated people, who never lived on the reserve, many C-31s were actually born and raised on the reserve. In addition, many who had lost their status continued for years to visit their relatives on the reserve. However, what really makes this notion puzzling for Cowessess band members is that because there have been Cowessess people migrating to urban areas for more than fifty years, there are at least two generations of families who never lost their status but have never lived on the reserve. In effect, there are many C-31s who would have more knowledge and experience about living on the reserve than some long-standing members.

The following research participant explains the difference between Cowessess people's views about C-31s and other First Nation's views and highlights the traditional view of kinship evinced by many Cowessess members.

> It never really made that much of a difference. . . . Other reserves were different than Cowessess [in their treatment of C-31s] where most of their members [other reserves' band members] stay on the reserve, and for them bringing in people who are Bill C-31s created a quite a bit of jealousy. So many [other bands] made a rule that Bill C-31s weren't band members. Cowessess did not do that probably because we are more open than that. In that most of our people live off the reserve. Our people have been marrying other people for a long time, white people included, for generations by now. In that sense, it's [including Bill C-31 people as band members] not anything new. We're a small reserve—they are all Indians. On our reserve, eighty percent of our people leave and marry other people. So in that sense, when Bill C-31 came along you had almost two extremes. Where one was very strict about who were Indians, and the other extreme, maybe people wanted to be inclusive of who their members bring in. So Cowessess would be more on the other extreme of being more accepting. There are some [Cowessess] people who have a hard view of membership, but not the majority.

His explanation acknowledges the historic exogamous marriage practice of Cowessess people, a practice that continues to the present day. It also recognizes the fact that Cowessess people understand that this marriage practice is an accepted cultural trait.

A further example of the inclusionary practices of the contemporary Cowessess First Nation is illustrated by the relationship between the band and its urban members. In response to the large number of band members residing in Regina, Cowessess established an urban office and an urban councilor. The urban office offers a number of programs and services for its Regina members and publishes a newsletter to inform urban members of the important issues, programs, and events. The January 2008 newsletter announced the formation of a youth drum group. The drum group reflects contemporary Cowessess kinship values. The announcement stated that in order to join the group a person had to be a male youth between thirteen and seventeen years old. A youth, according to the announcement, "should be a Cowessess community member, meaning a Band Member or a child of a Band Member." This notion of who is considered a community member is in direct contrast to the definition imposed by the Canadian government through the Indian Act. Also, urban members in Regina were able to vote in band elections prior to the 1999 Supreme Court decision in the *Corbiere* case, which stated that urban band members of all Canadian First Nations have the right to vote in band elections.[40] This is not to say that no tensions exist between urban and reserve residents, but that in general there has been and continues to be a conscious effort to maintain the ties with urban members.

CONCLUSION

The views of a majority of Cowessess band members' about Bill C-31 and the creation of new members mirrors the values embedded in the Elder Brother stories that convey the traditional law of the people. Though some viewed Bill C-31 as having a negative impact on the band, most saw it as being positive for the band. Many mentioned that they were happy that their relatives were able to regain their status. Many respondents' views were consistent with the United Nations Human Rights Committee decision in *Lovelace*. Many felt, for example, that Bill C-31 did not go far enough because there were C-31 band members who were unable to pass on their status to their children, and therefore the children would be denied access to the culture of their community. In addition, others stated that they felt it was important that those members who were alienated from the reserve be reunited. For those Bill C-31 band members, many mentioned that since their reinstatement they felt a connection to their homeland—a place from where they or their ancestors originated. They also spoke about the importance of attending family reunions held on the reserve. In addition, many of the urban members talked about how they passed on family histories and genealogies in order to ensure that their children understood who they were and from where they came. Though most band members spoke positively about C-31s, it should be noted that the interviews took place nearly twenty years after the passage of Bill C-31, and time may have softened some Cowessess people's view regarding the legislation and the people who had regained their status. However, these interviews demonstrate, in part, that the level of resistance to, and the resentment of, Bill C-31 as expressed by many First Nations leaders was not as evident for most Cowessess First Nation band members.

Kinship ties have been, and continue to be, in DeMallie's words, "funda-mental" to members of the Cowessess First Nation. I have attempted to link the traditional "law of the people" to contemporary Cowessess band members' interactions in a way to answer DeMallie's challenge for American Indian studies scholars to apply kinship in a relevant and creative manner. The "law of the people" prescribed the expected normative behavior for Cowessess band members, including regulating kinship patterns, and was conveyed through the stories of Elder Brother. With the implementation of the Indian Act, the traditional "law of the people" was undermined as band membership became much more rigid because specific guidelines and procedures were required in order to gain and retain membership. Nevertheless, some First Nations, such as Cowessess, were able to preserve certain aspects of their historically inclusive membership practices within the confines of the restrictive measures imposed by the Indian Act, which allowed them to sustain the band's multicultural nature and has served as a mechanism for the physical, mental, and emotional survival of its members. The contemporary kinship patterns ensure that band members' collective identity as Cowessess people also survives. Cowessess peoples' attitudes are shaped within the context of family/kinship connections, not by externally defined tribal or cultural affiliations. A person's family name places that person within the familial reserve context. This is not to say that cultural affiliation is totally ignored, but that it is not the primary identifier that connects people, not in the way that family/kinship does. For Cowessess, family/kinship ties are of greater importance for identity than place of residence, gender, cultural affiliation, or notions of race. As Cowessess Elder Harold Lerat states, the inclusive attitude of most band members in the past and in the present shows that "whether Indian, Metis, or white, it didn't matter," demonstrating that the principles of the law of the people and Elder Brother still resonate with and guide interactions of Cowessess First Nation band members.

NOTES

1. Raymond DeMallie, "Kinship: The Foundation for Native American Society," in *Studying Native America: Problems and Prospects*, ed. Russell Thornton (Madison: University of Wisconsin, 1998), 350.

2. Thomas Hakansson, "The Detachability of Women: Gender and Kinship in Processes of Socioeconomic Change among the Gusil of Kenya," *American Ethnologist* 21, no. 3 (1994): 516–38; Kevin Birth, "'Most of Us Are Family Some of the Time': Interracial Unions and Transracial Kinship in Eastern Trinidad," *American Ethnologist* 24, no. 3 (1997): 585–601; Cornelia Ann Kammerer, "Descent, Alliance, and Political Order among Akha," *American Ethnologist* 25, no. 4 (1998): 659–75; Edward Lowe, "A Widow, a Child, and Two Languages: Exploring Kinship and Attachment in Chuuk," *American Anthropologist* 104, no. 1 (2002): 123–37; Soo Ho Choi, "Land Is Thicker Than Blood: Revisiting 'Kinship Paternalism' in a Peasant Village in South Korea," *Journal of Anthropological Research* 56 (2000): 349–63; Doug Jones, "Group Nepotism and Human Kinship," *Current Anthropology* 42, no. 5 (2000): 779; Diane Austin-Broos, "Places, Practices, and Things: The Articulation of Arrente Kinship with Welfare and Work," *American Ethnologist* 30, no. 1 (2003): 118.

3. Loretta Fowler, *Shared Symbols, Contested Meanings: Gros Ventre Culture and History, 1778–1984* (Ithaca, NY, and London: Cornell University Press, 1987); Alexandra Harmon, *Indians in the Making: Ethnic Relations and Indians Identities around Puget Sound* (Los Angeles: University of California Press, 1998); Martha Knack, *Boundaries Between: Southern Paiute, 1775–1995* (Lincoln: University of Nebraska Press, 2001).

4. The population is as of December 2008. See Department of Indian Affairs and Northern Development Web site, http://pse5-esd5.ainc-inac.gc.ca/fnp/Main/Search/FNRegPopulation.aspx?BAND_NUMBER=361&lang=eng (accessed 7 June 2010). The Regina population is not official but is an estimate of some of the band members to whom I have spoken. For further information on the band's composition see Robert Alexander Innes, "The Importance of Family Ties to Members of Cowessess First Nation" (PhD diss., University of Arizona, 2007). However, according to the Cities and Environment Unit, Dalhousie University, which is involved in community planning with Cowessess, there are 1,000 band members residing in Regina, representing 11% of the total First Nation population in that city.

5. The acts were *An Act for the Better Protection of the Lands and Property of Indians in Lower Canada* and *An Act for the Protection of the Indian in Upper Canada from Imposition, and the Property Occupied or Enjoyed by them from Trespassing and Injury.* For more information about these acts see Diedre A. Desmarais, "The Native Women's Association's Struggle to Secure Gender Equality Rights within the Canadian Constitution"

(master's thesis, University of Regina, 1998); Harpa K. Isfeld, "Who and What Is a Canadian Indian? The Impact of Bill C-31 upon Demographic and Epidemiologic Measure of Registered Indian Population of Manitoba" (master's thesis, University of Manitoba, 1997); Kathleen Jamieson, "Sex Discrimination and the Indian Act," in *Arduous Journey: Canadian Indians and Decolonization*, ed. J. Rick Ponting (Toronto: McClelland and Stewart, 1986), 112–36; Bonita Lawrence, *"Real" Indians and Others: Mixed-Blood Urban Native Peoples and Indigenous Nationhood* (Vancouver: University of British Columbia Press, 1999); J. R. Miller, *Skyscrapers Hide the Heavens: A History of Indian-White Relations in Canada* (Toronto: University of Toronto Press, 2000); Jennifer Lynn Shade, "Traditional Methods of Determining Tribal Membership" (master's thesis, University of Victoria, 2002); John Tobias, "Protection, Civilization, Assimilation: An Outline History of Canada's Indian Policy," in *As Long as the Sun Shines and Water Flows: A Reader in Canadian Native Studies*, ed. Ian A. L. Getty and Antoine S. Lussier (Vancouver: University of British Columbia Press, 1983), 39–55.

    6. Lawrence, *"Real" Indians and Others*, 51. See also Jamieson, "Sex Discrimination and the Indian Act."

    7. Tobias, "Protection, Civilization, Assimilation," 41–42.

    8. Sharon Venne, *Indian Acts and Amendments 1868–1975: An Indexed Collection* (Saskatoon: University of Saskatchewan, Native Law Centre, 1981), 24.

    9. Ibid., 361–62.

    10. *Attorney-General of Canada v. Lavell* [1974] S.C.R. 1349.

    11. *Sandra Lovelace v. Canada*, Communication No. R.6/24 U.N. Doc. Supp. No. 40 (A/36/40) at 166 [1981].

    12. Earl Fowler, "FSI Opposes Marriage Law," *Saskatoon StarPhoenix*, 14 September 1981, A3; Earl Fowler, "Legislation Would Restore Rights of Indian Women," *Saskatoon StarPhoenix*, 23 January 1984, A3; Canada. *Standing Committee on Indian Affairs and Northern Development: Respecting Bill C-31, An Act to Amend the Indian Act Minutes of Proceedings and Evidence.* Ottawa, 1985; Canadian Press, "Indian Leaders Warns Gov't That Plan Will Meet Resistance," *Regina Leader Post*, 20 October 1985, A14; Deanna Wuttunee, "Indian Act Amendments—Bill C-31," *Windspeaker*, July 1985, 13; Earl Fowler, "Indian Chiefs: Male Chauvinist Label Unfair," *Saskatoon StarPhoenix*, 16 November 1985, A6; Brian Maracle, host, "Native Women Fight for Equal Rights," *Our Native Land* radio program, Canadian Broadcasting Corporation (original broadcast 2 March 1985), http://archives.cbc.ca/society/native_issues/clips/16040/ (accessed 16 February 2006); Earl Fowler, "Indian Will Fight Band Status Issue," *Saskatoon StarPhoenix*, 14 May 1987, A8; Earl Fowler, "Indian Act Changes Will Deprive Many of Benefits: Eramus," *Saskatoon StarPhoenix*, 7 February 1987, A3; Earl Fowler, "Most Indian Bands Will Reject Reinstated Members," *Saskatoon StarPhoenix*, 18 June 1987, A7; Canada. *Standing Committee on Aboriginal Affairs and Northern Development. C-31 Fifth Report.* Ottawa: House of Commons, 1988; Canadian Press, "Sask. Bands Must Enact Laws to Fight Bill C-31: Ahenakew," *Saskatoon StarPhoenix*, 28 January 1988, A7; Marg Ommenney, "Bureaucracy Thwarts Native Women's Rights, Groups Says," *Saskatchewan StarPhoenix*, 27 February 1988, A8; Darren Schuettler, "Indian Act Changes Bring New Problems for Native Women," *Western Producer*, 14 January 1991, 51.

    13. Maria Campbell, personal communication.

    14. James Zion, "Harmony among the People: Torts and Indian Courts," *Montana Law Review* 45 (1984): 265.

15. Basil Johnston, *Ojibway Heritage* (Toronto: McClelland and Stewart, 1990).

16. Robert Williams Jr., *Linking Arms Together: American Indian Treaty Visions of Love and Peace* (New York: Oxford University Press, 1997), 84.

17. Johnston, *Ojibway Heritage*, 20.

18. James Zion and Robert Yazzie, "Indigenous Law in North American in the Wake of Conquest," *Boston College of International and Comparative Law Review* 20 (1997): 74.

19. Donald J. Auger, "The Northern Ojibwe and Their Family Law" (DJur, York University, 2001); Christina Zuni Cruz, "Tribal Law as Indigenous Social Reality and Separate Consciousness: [Re]incorporating Customs and Traditions into Tribal Law," *Tribal Law Journal* 1, no. 1 (2001): 1–27; William, *Linking Arms Together*; Robert Yazzie, "Life Comes from It: Navajo Justice Concepts," *New Mexico Law Review* 24 (1994): 175–90; Zion and Yazzie, "Indigenous Law."

20. Williams, *Linking Arms Together*, 84.

21. John Borrows, *Recovering Canada: The Resurgence of Indigenous Law* (Toronto: University of Toronto Press, 2002), 14.

22. Auger, "The Northern Ojibwe," 124.

23. Robert Cover, "Forward: Nomos and Narrative," *Harvard Law Review* 97, no. 4 (1983): 10.

24. Ibid., 4–5.

25. Alson Skinner, "Plains Cree Tales," *Journal of American Folklore* 29, no. 113 (1916): 345–46.

26. Sarah Carter, "O'Soup, Louis," in *Dictionary of Canadian Biography Online*, http://www.biographical.ca/EN?ShowBio.asp?BOLD=41754&query=cowessess (accessed 4 March 2006).

27. Janice Acoose, *Iskwewak—kah'ki yaw ni wakomakanak: Neither Indian Princesses nor Easy Squaws* (Toronto: Women's Press, 1995), 7

28. Barbara Ziemen, "Run for Acoose," *Saskatchewan Indian* 12, no. 7 (1982): 59–63.

29. Harold Lerat, *Treaty Promises, Indian Reality: Life on a Reserve* (Saskatoon, SK: Purich Publishing, 2005).

30. Enfranchisement, as Patrick Macklem notes, was the "administrative process that provide incentives to [primarily] Indian men to trade their [Indian] status for the right to vote and hold property." *Indigenous Difference and the Constitution of Canada* (Toronto: University of Toronto Press, 2001), 228. Any First Nations person deemed capable of assuming the responsibilities of citizenship was no longer considered a ward of the government.

31. Lerat, *Treaty Promises*.

32. Ibid., 91.

33. Carter, "O'Soup, Louis."

34. Lerat, *Treaty Promises*.

35. Robert Alexander Innes, "The Socio-Political Influence of the Second World War Saskatchewan Aboriginal Veterans, 1945–1960" (master's thesis, University of Saskatchewan, 2000).

36. Martin Robin, *Shades of Right: Nativist and Facist Politics in Canada, 1920–1940* (Toronto: University of Toronto Press, 1992); Julian Sher, *White Hoods: Canada's Ku Klux Klan* (Vancouver, BC: New Star Books, 1983).

37. Lerat, *Treaty Promises*.

38. *Windspeaker: Classroom Edition*, Premiere Edition, March, nd, http://www
.ammsa.com/classroom/CLASSIC-31.html (accessed 23 March 2006).

39. On March 11, 2010, the Canadian government introduced Bill C-3, which
will amend the Indian Act to allow children of reinstated persons to pass on their
Indian status to their children. See Parliament of Canada, http://www2.parl.gc.ca/
HousePublications/Publication.aspx?DocId=4470443&Language=E&Mode=1&Parl
=40&Ses=3.

40. *Corbiere v. Canada* (Minister of Indian and Northern Affairs) [1999] 2 S.C.R.

AMERICAN INDIAN CULTURE AND RESEARCH JOURNAL 34:2 (2010) 47–65

A Reading of Eekwol's "Apprentice to the Mystery" as an Expression of Cree Youth's Cultural Role and Responsibility

GAIL A. MACKAY

On a chilly Toronto evening in November 2005, an envelope was opened in a darkened auditorium, and the words spoken reached out across the land to Muskoday First Nation in Saskatchewan.[1] No doubt Lindsay Knight's family was watching the televised Canadian Aboriginal Music Awards that night and would have felt elated to hear her being honored with the award for Best Rap or Hip Hop Album. The poetry of a young Cree woman reverberated with her contemporary listening audience and connected them to current, historical, and timeless realities.

Knight, who goes by the name Eekwol in her professional work, presented the album *Apprentice to the Mystery*, which can be read as an expression of youth's role and responsibility in Cree culture. This article lays out an appreciation of her artistic and critical contribution by first establishing an understanding of the social context of Cree youth in Saskatchewan, then highlighting relevant points of Cree history, social structure, and values that orient an interpretation of youth's role and responsibility. The article turns to close readings of two tracks from the album and interprets the poet's critical social commentary grounded in Cree and Anishinaabe values and experience.

At the outset of this exploration, some clarification about identifiers and identity should be made. The terms *Aboriginal, indigenous*, and *Native*, though nuanced, are used interchangeably in this writing to identify descendants of the original inhabitants of the territory that is now bounded by Canadian borders. These terms as they are used here include people who are status Indians (federally recognized), nonstatus Indians, Métis, and Inuit. The term *Aboriginal*, drawn from the definition of *Aboriginal peoples* in the Canadian Constitution 1982, Section 35 (02), is used in government and academic

Gail MacKay is a PhD student at the University of Saskatchewan, has a masters of education in Indian and Northern Education, and is a sessional instructor at First Nations University of Canada and the University of Saskatchewan. Her research focuses on Native youth, gender, language, and literature.

writing. The term *indigenous* calls attention to people's ancestral belonging to the land that transcends colonial history. *Native* is also a term that avoids the restrictions of legal definitions. Of these three, *indigenous* and *Native* are more commonly used by individuals to self-identify and make reference to an "inclusive we." The term *First Nations* is a self-naming term that identifies individuals previously identified as Indians, the sociopolitical collectives previously identified as bands, and their reserved lands.[2]

The identities of indigenous peoples of the northern plains in Saskatchewan are more complex than can be characterized by single tribal names. This complexity is in part due to the shared cultural kinship patterns of the Cree, Saulteaux (a dialect of Anishinaabe), Métis, Assiniboine, Dakota, and Lakota.[3] It is also due to historical, military, political, and, more importantly, social alliances that made it possible for them to understand each other's languages, participate in each other's ceremonies, intermarry, and build multicultural bands.[4] During the past century, multilingual ability has declined with each generation, and increasingly there is a tendency to narrow the indigenous identity to a single tribal identity.[5] The risk of permitting this to go unchallenged is to disregard the rich multicultural heritage of mixed bands and to develop tunnel vision when isolating and simplifying an understanding of cultural practices and philosophies.

Muskoday First Nation, like many First Nations in southern Saskatchewan, has a multicultural heritage. "Ancestors of Muskoday First Nation . . . were from St. Peters Reserve, a Saulteaux reserve near Selkirk Manitoba," and they traveled in the 1800s to the present location of the reserve prior to signing Treaty Six.[6] Muskoday First Nation is commonly identified as a Cree First Nation, and its Web site shows that the languages spoken are Cree and English.[7] Saulteaux cultural heritage is harmonious with Cree cultural values, but it is also a living part of people's ceremonial life and teaching.[8] This topic is explained in more detail in the section on Cree history, social structure, and values of youth.

SOCIAL CONTEXT OF CREE YOUTH IN SASKATCHEWAN

Statistics that describe Aboriginal youth's lives in Saskatchewan show trends of low income and low education attainment, unemployment and poverty, core housing needs, mobility and homelessness, and exploitation and alienation. Youth age range is variously set to be between fifteen and twenty-five years, thirteen and twenty-nine years, and eighteen and twenty-four years by Statistics Canada, national Aboriginal organizations, and federal programs, respectively.[9] The Canadian Council on Social Development examined the growing poverty rates of Aboriginal children in urban areas and reported in 2003 that 52 percent of all Aboriginal children were poor, and that the Aboriginal population was young. In 2001 one-third of the national Aboriginal population was aged fourteen years or younger.[10] During the last thirty years or more, there has been a significant shift of Aboriginal population from reserves to the cities. Examples are the Cowessess First Nation in which 80 percent of band members live off reserve and Muskoday First Nation in which, of the approximately twelve hundred band members, more than six hundred live off reserve. Mobility patterns are noted in numerous research reports that indicate Aboriginal people change residence at a higher rate than non-Aboriginal people. Norris and Jantzen refer to this urban-rural mobility as "churn" and argue that it is motivated by people moving to maintain family and cultural relationships.[11]

Statistics from the 1996 and 2001 censuses provide the following statistical snapshot of Aboriginal people in Saskatchewan in the time frame that Eekwol was writing and recording her album. Although the 2006 census indicates some improvements, the trends have remained the same.[12] In Saskatoon, where 9.1 percent of the city population was Aboriginal, 37 percent of that population was between the ages of fifteen and thirty-four years and was likely caring for the 38 percent of the population between the ages of zero and fourteen years. The scope of social and economic disparity is indicated by the 1996 census statistics for Saskatoon:

- 22.5 percent of the poor population in Saskatoon was Aboriginal.
- 64.9 percent of the Aboriginal identity population lived in poverty.
- 51.3 percent of the Aboriginal population earned less than $10,000.
- 55 percent of Aboriginal youth lived below the low-income cutoff.
- 25.1 percent of the Aboriginal population was unemployed (3.7 times the rate of the non-Aboriginal population).
- 45 percent of Aboriginal youth had jobs.
- 48.1 percent of the adult Aboriginal population had less than grade twelve education.
- 10.8 percent of the Aboriginal population was a lone parent.[13]

Add to this the fact that Aboriginal people have been the victims of violent crimes at a disproportionate rate. In 1997, for example, 42 percent of victims in Prince Albert and Regina were Aboriginal compared to their 10 percent proportion of the population in these Saskatchewan cities.[14] Aboriginal children were disproportionately represented among the sexually exploited children in Saskatchewan.[15] First Nations women between the ages of twenty-five and forty-four years were five times more likely than other women of the same age to die as the result of violence.[16] These numbers reckon an implicit contemporary orthodoxy of social and economic marginalization for many Aboriginal youth in Saskatchewan. Not surprisingly the atmosphere is racially charged: Aboriginal youth feel judgment and suspicion directed toward them, and Aboriginal and non-Aboriginal parents fear for the safety of their children. Real estate agents steer clients to neighborhoods away from the concentration of Native residents. In news media and social policy reports we can hear the calls from the mainstream middle class for the judicial system to subdue and for the social welfare system to rescue Aboriginal youth. This is reality. The following section describes the historical and social foundation of youth's resistance.

CREE HISTORY, SOCIAL STRUCTURE, AND VALUES OF YOUTH

David Mandelbaum's *The Plains Cree* provides a history of the Plains Cree and situates their origin in the forested area between Lake Superior and Hudson's Bay. His account of the Woodland Cree's western expansion as a consequence of the fur trade is challenged by contemporary historians' and archaeologists' interpretations, but this debate does not concern the discussion here except to note the geographic distribution of strong linguistic similarities of the various dialects of Cree spoken in parkland, plains, and woodlands territories from British Columbia through Alberta and Saskatchewan, through to the woodland territories of Manitoba, Ontario, and Quebec. Likewise, there are strong dialectic similarities between Anishinaabe (a sister language to Cree) and Cree's dialects, which are spoken in Saskatchewan, Montana, North Dakota, Manitoba, Minnesota, Wisconsin, Michigan, and Ontario.[17] Mandelbaum states that it is known from fur traders' reports that as early as 1730, Plains Cree hunted buffalo and fought against the Blackfoot for hunting territory, revenge, and prestige. The Plains Cree bands suffered in the 1800s due to smallpox epidemics, the decimation of the buffalo, and the intrusion of the Canadian state. It was in a dire shortage of food that Cree, Saulteaux, and Assiniboine bands signed treaties Four and Six in Saskatchewan in 1874 and 1876.[18]

In the pretreaty era, the Plains Cree organized themselves in small mobile bands of people related through kinship ties. The chief's authority relied upon his persuasive oratory and respect given him for his demonstrated virtues of bravery, wisdom, kindness, and generosity. No one was obliged to follow his leadership and could choose to leave the band to join another band at any time. There were social organizations of the Worthy Young Men Society and the Warrior Society. A man's membership in these societies was by invitation, based on recognition of his achievements and abilities to serve the well-being of the band. Membership carried status and responsibilities for protection and provisioning. Following the signing of the treaty, the Plains Cree settled on lands they reserved for themselves. The Indian Act was Canadian federal legislation passed in 1876 that consolidated all previous legislations dealing with Indians and Indian lands. From 1885 to1920, the Indian Act was routinely amended and increasingly used to control every aspect of Indians' lives. Among the most destructive to Cree society were the amendments that controlled the political leadership of the band and the socialization of children. The Christian churches functioned as colonial agents by administering the residential schools that the Indian Act required Indian children to attend.

Fundamental to the political and social organization of the Cree is the principle of personal autonomy. Under the stresses of colonial oppression this ethic of autonomy was transformed in Cree people's minds to be a vice. Cree leaders perceive this transformation as the undoing of the integrity of Cree communal life. In the biography of John Tootoosis, the authors recount their interviews with the remarkable leader of the Federation of Saskatchewan Indians and report his dismay at some Cree people's acceptance of the categories of "good Indians" and "trouble-makers." In this culturally oppressed view, "good Indians" were those who were compliant and obedient; "trouble-makers" were those who questioned the authority of Indian agents, laws passed into the Indian Act, and the Canadian government's reneging on treaty promises.[19] In a similar vein, Reverend Edward Ahenakew, from Atahkakoop First Nation, wrote a condemnation of the harm inflicted by the residential schools in *Voices of the Plains Cree*: "for those who do live, who do survive and who graduate from the school at the age of eighteen, during every day of their training they have acted under orders. Nothing they did was without supervision. . . . They never needed to use their own mind and wills. They came to think that it would be wrong if they went their own way. Now discipline and expediency in life are good, but will and initiative are better."[20] This value of autonomy, well documented in Cree and Anishinaabe sources, is integral to the fulfillment of youth's responsibility in their stage of life.

The Plains Cree and Anishinaabe have strong parallels in history, territory, language, and culture. Archaeologists collected, during the 1960s and 1970s, a large volume of Blackduck pottery, a Late Woodland ware (ca. 0–AD 1600), in the vicinity of Muskoday Reserve.[21] This discovery supports the understanding that Cree and Anishinaabe people have had a long history of sharing territory. In more recent history, Plains Cree and Saulteaux bands together signed Treaty Four and Treaty Six with the Crown. Tanner recorded the ways that Plains Cree and Ojibway shared material culture, such as the horse, fishing, maple and box-elder sugar, and ceremonies, such as the Sun Dance and the Midewewin, at the beginning of the nineteenth century.[22] Saskatchewan First Nations such as Cowessess, Gordon, Muskowekwan, Pasqua, Piapot, Poundmaker, Sakimay, Saulteaux, and Whitebear were known as mixed bands because there were sufficient numbers of Cree and Saulteaux families constituting the community.[23] Consequently, intermarriages occurred, which facilitated further cultural sharing and blending. The languages are mutually intelligible, though fluent speakers say that it takes two or three days of immersion to be able to converse with each other.

Linguistic similarities between Cree and Anishinaabe correspond to a shared philosophy of life. An example to illustrate this is in the Plains Cree word *mino-pimatisiwin* and the Anishinaabe word *bimaadiziwin* to refer to the idea of "the good life." Michael Hart, a social worker at Fisher River Cree First Nation in Manitoba, uses the concept of *mino-pimatisiwin* as a model for helping Aboriginal people in his practice. He defines the term as meaning a life of personal healing, learning, and growth: the good life.[24] The ethic of personal autonomy and the principle of *mino-pimatisiwin* provide insight into cultural understanding of youth's role and responsibility. Lawrence Gross explains the philosophical significance of the concept *bimaadiziwin* in Anishinaabe philosophy.

> The teaching of *bimaadiziwin* operates at many levels. On a simple day-to-day basis, it suggests such actions as rising with the sun and retiring with the same. Further, *bimaadiziwin* governs human relations as well, stressing the type of conduct appropriate between individuals, and the manner in which social life is to be conducted. *Bimaadiziwin* also

covers the relationship with the broader environment. So, for example, it teaches the necessity of respecting all life, from the smallest insects on up. *Bimaadiziwin*, however, does not exist as a definitive body of law. Instead it is left up to the individual to develop wherever it can be found. This makes the term quite complex, and it can serve as a religious blessing, moral teaching, value system, and life goal.[25]

The idea of personal autonomy being foundational to a person's finding their identity and purpose in life is reinforced by the guidance Cree elders give parents about parenting.

The *Kisewatotatowin Aboriginal Parenting Handbook* was produced under the guidance of Northern Plains Cree elders in Saskatoon. The term *Kisewatotatowin* means, "having and giving great love, caring, generosity, patience, trust and respect to your child, your family, your community, your nation and the universe."[26] The handbook describes the stages of adolescence and adulthood. Adolescents are called *Okayak*, the young people, and undergo training in order to learn the necessary survival skills and competencies needed to fulfill their role as adult men and women. The parenting handbook counsels parents on how to cope with the physical, intellectual, and emotional changes teenagers undergo in this stage. Included in the advice is the direction to involve the whole family in decisions and to allow the youth to make mistakes in action, reaction, and judgment during this time of experiment and newfound freedom. Adolescence is the time when the youth should be working with an elder and helping with ceremonies. The man's role is to protect and the woman's role is to bring warmth and protection to the home.

The Northern Plains Cree philosophy of guiding an adolescent's growth is harmonious with the traditional Anishinaabe teachings about the cycle of life. Basil Johnston explains that in the stages of life, which is a journey over four hills, "the second hill is that of youth. It is a time in life when the young begin to bloom in spirit and flourish in physical power and stature. What is striking is that youth encompasses many ages. There are those very young, hardly out of infancy: there are those who are much older. But no one proceeds to the next stage until he has received a vision. Until that time, a man or woman remains a youth."[27] Johnston explains that in times past, a girl's passage to womanhood occurred at about twelve years of age with the onset of menarche. He provides insight that goes beyond Mandelbaum's interpretation of women's defiling nature, but Johnston also is male and so does not carry women's teachings. He notes that a girl may have a vision bestowed upon her, or she may choose to seek a vision. Her community and family supported her determination. Johnston's explanation of the significant experience of youth is an important foundation to understanding youth's role and responsibility during this stage of life. The relevance of this Anishinaabe cultural information to Eekwol's youth rhetoric is strengthened by the reality of cultural blending that is occurring in cities, which reveals that Aboriginal people are adapting and using what is useful to the survival of an indigenous way of relating to the world. An example of this is Mohawk, Cree, and Anishinaabe women in Toronto who prepare their daughters and nieces for womanhood by holding a yearlong puberty ritual that is drawn from the Anishinaabe berry fast ritual.[28]

Johnston's monograph expands on the ideas of autonomy as central to a youth's self-actualization. The quotation conveys the depth and subtlety of the experience:

> from the moment a youth begins to understand, his training and prep-aration begins and continues until the vision comes to him. Between the ages of twelve and fourteen he ought to begin to seek his vision. Because no one knows when the state of readiness of body and spirit is attained, the teaching and preparation continues. In some cases the state of fitness comes readily and early, in other instances, much later in life. But the teaching and instruction end only at the vision.
>
> For youth, the struggle in the moral order consists of the prepara-tion, seeking, and attainment of the vision. What makes the search difficult is that the vision is not to be sought outside of oneself; nor is it to be found outside of one's being. Rather it must be sought within one's inner substance and found therein. . . . Since it will be found within a person's inner self, the search must be conducted alone, without the assistance or guidance of others. There are no signs to mark the trail; there are no trails set by others to encourage the seeker.[29]

Johnston explains that in this stage between childhood and adulthood, the youth is autonomous in awareness, exploration, interpretation, and fulfill-ment of his purpose revealed to him in vision.

> In and through vision a person may see, hear, sense or even feel his first self, his incorporeal substance. By vision he will discover that his nature demands growth in order to attain fullness and power. From the moment of the enlightenment the seeker has a purpose. From the moment of the coming the seeker is obliged to regulate his deeds, according to the vision. In a way a vision is discovery of self and what ought to be. Growth begins.
>
> . . . [W]hile the vision gives an insight into the quality of the inner being, what it is and what it ought to be, it can do no more than give some direction about the course of life. . . .
>
> With the vision, existence becomes living; the youth is no longer young. He has now a freedom, which only he and no other can exer-cise and fulfill. It is his own. Yet his freedom and independence must be consistent with his communities' laws and codes and with the great laws that govern the world. Through vision a person goes from youth to adulthood.[30]

Johnston's description in many instances recounts the interaction between adults and youth and between elders and youth. I believe this is a fundamental aspect of youth's self-realization. Though the adults do not guide or direct youth in their vision or self-discovery, the adults' roles as supporter and model are crucial. Without grounding or leadership, misguided youth adopt the identity of activists and revolutionaries but remain puppet-like in their posturing in camouflage and masks, counting coup by their number of arrests. The adults' leadership and elders' counsel together develop the understanding and skills needed to be a leader.

Cree elders Jim KaNipitehtew, Joe Douquette, and Peter Vandall give further insight into the role of elder in youth's education. In his speeches "Leading Our Children Astray" and "Counseling the Young," Elder Ka-Nipitehtew laments how youth have lost the ability to hear the elders' counsel because television, drugs, and the fast pace of modern life distract them. He says that people need to return to the old teachings because a time of great suffering lies ahead.[31] Elder Douquette speaks of "Cree Education" and says, "Long ago this land was so clean. As for these Crees of old, they had their own education, they knew it well, they taught their children: they told their children how young people should live, they warned them against everything."[32] Elders counseled youth and adults, giving guidance on the laws of the physical world and the codes of behavior guiding human interaction with the physical world and social world.[33] Elders' counsel does not dictate behavior, but rather by sharing the wisdom gained through a long life, it provides a warning that the listener is obliged to contemplate, comprehend, and act upon with his or her free will. Respect is a fundamental cultural attribute. A Cree youth from Cumberland House defined it as "listening to a person even if you don't believe what they are saying."[34] The benefit of that understanding is that one learns humility with the development of understanding and maturity. Thus, the balance between obedience and initiative is clear in Cree education of youth, in the guidance of youth seeking their vision, finding their purpose and identity. Eekwol's lyrics exemplify the dynamic of youth being guided by elders' counsel to uphold the great laws and follow the principle of living a good life, acting on a Cree understanding of personhood, and exercising personal autonomy.

EEKWOL'S POETRY EXPRESSES CREE YOUTH'S CULTURAL ROLE

Eekwol's song "Too Sick" is a narrative and lyrical representation of the harsh realities of a contemporary orthodoxy depicted by the statistics in the first section. The music video for the song, the ninth cut on the album, was aired on MuchMusic and MTV.[35] The phrase *too sick* in hip-hop vernacular translates as *very good* or *very bad* depending on the context. For some audiences, the video may have been the introduction to Eekwol's music. The music industry has slotted her as an Aboriginal female hip-hop emcee, and the subject matter of "Too Sick" appeals to the stereotyped expectations of a mainstream audience. The song begins with an idealized image of a warrior in sunshine; the goal was to raise a family traditionally. Shifts in time and perspective mark the transition and development of the story of love failing to overcome substance abuse and violence against women, murder, incarceration, and parent-child separation. To the non-Aboriginal audience, it is a grim but marketable contemporary Native story. However, I suggest an alternate reading to examine how Eekwol connects with her young Aboriginal female audience on issues of relationships, self-confidence, and self-preservation, and with her young Aboriginal male audience on the issues of male role loss and cultural preservation.

The shifts in time and perspective are the moments when the story advances but also the moments of critical decisions to be made by the players. The lyrics sung audibly, inviting fans to sing along, begin in the first person, contemplate the tender hope of love, and follow the fall into the hopelessness of intimate violence.

> When the sun stood high in my ancestors' eyes
> a warrior sat on the earth with a smile
> The rays reflected his frame shadowing his profile
> I was prepared to share my life with his mind and ability
> . . . . The goal's to raise a family traditionally[36]

Aboriginal youth are familiar with the images of a precontact idealized past. The contracted word *goal's* makes the verb tense ambiguous: it could be past, as in "the goal was," or present, as in "the goal is." The omission of the sound in the contraction serves the meter and poetic device of interfacing past and present. The first line of the following quotation emphatically draws the story into the present and, in the manner of girlfriends' conversational style, divulges personal reflection of events presenting points of entry where the young female listener in a female-gendered style of conversation would take a turn in order to relate a similar experience as a way of affirming the speaker.[37]

> Now in 2004 what remains are the traces of that history
> Blind as his compliments
> See commitments to me rolled off his tongue
> my perfection was the foundation of his words[38]

Following the confessional style of women's conversation, the following lines express the familiar psychological trait of women trying to save men from past emotional trauma, giving shelter in their love.

> I was the one
> His past was filled with loneliness and misery
> Years of violence and neglect plagued his memory
> Drunkenness informed his life
> Now we're two broken crutches in a tree of questions
> I asked he would confess them

But the story advances quickly in a familiar cycle of abuse from a honeymoon period, to a violent episode, to contrition and denial, and back to a honeymoon period.

He believed and I believed we were above it
F'k the past
he was safe with me and I loved it
but it leaked out a little as the pain came in trickles
I was caught in the middle of his pride and his riddles
He couldn't figure out
Shout him with a shout
And I tried to understand as he pushed me to get them out
I was quick to recoup
I took the falls
finding nice posters for the holes in the walls

At this point the song moves to the refrain that punctuates a shift in the plot development. The dynamic of the sick relationship is established. What seemed too good has turned too bad, and the contagion of violence is overwhelming. The two responses are to accept victimhood personally by blaming the situation on the loss of culture and to despair in a detached manner and devalue the woman's life to nothing. In the refrain, the woman is moving away from a personal reflection of her experience to seeing it from the perspective of others.

Too sick to stop the cycle hammer this nail into my head
living in the cost of a culture lost some say
I'm better off . . .
dead

Following this transition is a sample of a fiddle tune, which belongs to the music of a previous generation of youth. But it recalls the violence that attended the drinking parties of that generation too. Subtly, the visceral memory of violence is recalled for the Aboriginal listeners. The accompanying video images, framed through a car windshield and seen from the passenger's perspective, include a sequence of a bridge, city lights, and blurred car headlights traveling on a darkened country road and approaching a curve. Without judgment the poet connects the violence of the past to the present in the perspective of one who is not in control of the situation. But she does not totally absolve the new generation or the female victim of their responsibility in bringing forward the dysfunction wrought by alcohol and violence.

The next segment of the song is the one that appears on the video clip used to pitch the video to MTV programmers. It is a succinct episode of the dysfunctional relationships in a cycle of abuse. The lyrics speak specifically to young women. The speaker notes her culpability and being too sick to stop the cycle.

One for the road
so we dabbled with the drink
Said he needed to relax
didn't always want to think

I'll admit I was a part of it
It made him happy brought us closer
besides I'm not as pretty or as confident a person when I'm sober
Plus my connections in the world threatened him
didn't trust guys, said they're all into the medicine
but the parties were fulla the types he despises
saw the negative attention when he looked into my eyes
I guess I presented it to everyone
My slutty
intentions
and I sure as hell paid for it
seconds after it was mentioned
the glass hit my lip
felt the floor as I slipped
three or four tried to loosen his grip

At this point the song becomes a cautionary tale. The woman acknowledges the role of alcohol, jealousy, and her part in the dynamic of the relationship. Leading into the refrain flute music accompanies a male voice apologizing, "Oh man, I'm so sorry . . . Promise . . . Promise," and distances the listener from the situation. The emotion is detached in the fade-out of the apology and the repetition of the refrain. The repeated phrasing, however, suggests two readings of the line: "Some say I'm better off . . . dead." When following the lyric "I'm better off" and not anticipating the pause, the listener interprets the line to mean the woman is better off without the man and accepts the suggested possibility that she left the relationship. But the word *dead* follows a silent beat, and it leaves only the conclusion of desperation and murder.

Here, two-thirds of the way through the song, after the femicide, the refrain marks the poet's shift to the male experience. She switches to the second-person pronoun *you*, directs her words to the man, and draws the male listeners into the narrative. Words, not just sounds, are removed to keep the meter and give force to the poetic dual meaning. By using present and past tense in the line, and by alternating between devastating present and idealized dream, the poet fuses the context of the man waking up after a drunken blackout and being told of his crime of murder and the context of a generation of indigenous men struggling to fulfill their traditional male role.

Man, wake up, you're dreaming of the past
When you ever want or needed a role in the cast
The winter morning cold clean
When the hunt's as its best
You had no arrows
Took a knife
And stabbed your girl in the chest
No family to bring her home to where
they're already at rest
Carried on the tradition of alcohol and violence

The city stripped you clean of your culture, selves and dreams
The pen walls continue to remind you of your girl's screams

Looking to fulfill his male role in society, the man dreamed of the past traditional roles of warrior and hunter. But without the tools, and falling victim to
the city and cultural genocide, the man turns his energy to violence against
his woman and corrupts the indigenous traditional way of life. This final part
of the song presents a picture of a new icon of Indian men as prisoners and a
new tradition of alcohol and violence.

The line "no family to bring her home to where they're already at rest"
has particular resonance with the Aboriginal audience members who live and
die in the city and returns to the reserve to be buried in their home cemetery.
The alienation is situated in the places of the city and the penitentiary. Before
the song ends with the refrain being repeated three times, the lines spoken to
the man in prison describing the consequences may be interpreted as words
of warning to young men and women alike.

it was love no doubt, but how you drew it, it burned out
long ago when you should have
stopped the cycle from carrying through
now the son you created saw the things you do and
will probably pick up where you left off too
She wanted to save you so bad
should'a saved herself first
what could be the best thing you had
took a turn for the worst
but don't live off regret,
she's gone, move on
but don't forget

"Too Sick" may appeal to the mainstream because it represents a conclusion
already drawn, and in that light the song may be read as youthful melodrama.
However, considering the common experiences of a large portion of the
Aboriginal population, it is a song of warning for victims and a song of affirmation for survivors. It, like "Apprentro," carries a youth's voice of resistance
speaking directly to youth, reminding them of their power and responsibility
to challenge the status quo.

Eekwol's first lines of "Apprentro," the first track on the album *Apprentice
to the Mystery*, are

It's time for you to listen for a minute
'Cause this is where I share, share bits and pieces of my truth
What I know and don't know about life.[39]

The oppositional positioning of the audience in relation to the poet, and
the implied oppositional positioning of her truth to theirs, suggests that the
audience is comprised of people outside her world, people unfamiliar with

the social context of a young indigenous woman in Saskatchewan. But in the next lines wherein she uses the first-person plural pronoun she aligns herself with the audience:

> It's time to think back to remember who we were
> Whoever that may be
> Take back what we dream and say what we mean

The references are sufficiently vague to be applicable to a range of experiences possibly identified with by a colonized people defeated by subjugation, misunderstood youth railroaded by prejudice and condemnation, or, conceivably, survivors of addiction or abuse. In thirty seconds she deftly catches the ear of her listeners, and by using the tropes of the first-person pronoun and presenting experiences familiar to her audience, she earns the authority to speak from their perspective. She then proceeds in the first person to describe self-reflection, doubt, criticism, and determination with which her audience can sympathize.

> But I always feel like obstacles are stopping me
> And could it be that I'm tryin' not to see
> creating diversions convenient to me
> Running away, hurting my people, my family, those most important to me
> Well I can't do that anymore
> Because I'm guessing through experience and lessons
> And I'm stopping the cycle
> And sending the message
> And I'm trying everyday I walk this earth
> to stay away from what's bad for me

In the final lines of the introduction, accompanied by the music's crescendo, she asserts affirmation of their shared strengths and asserts power in an anthem of liberation.

> And the only way I can do that is by
> Recognizing the strengths we have
> Power in numbers, we got
> Power in spirit, I got
> Power in music, I got
> Power in my voice
> Hear it

The unique appeal to the Aboriginal youth audience is in the references that operate as hypertext, that link the listeners to inherited knowledge through associative retrieval.[40] Aboriginal youth, upon hearing these lines, would recognize that the strengths she alludes to are the cultural strengths of Aboriginal societies. "Power in numbers" relates not only to the current

Aboriginal baby boom but also to the cultural ethic of community support and cooperation. Community gatherings such as round dances, wakes, funerals, feasts, and powwows depend upon a large contingent of impromptu volunteers who work together to feed, care, and provide for everyone in attendance. Accomplishments are usually attributed to the efforts of many. Aboriginal youth would recognize the cultural belief of "power in spirit" that aids human beings in all their endeavors and is present in all living things.[41] Similarly they would recognize the cultural belief in "power in music" as supplication for divine help, and as a means of conjuring and healing. "Power in my voice" refers to the sacred nature of words carried by the life force of breath. These lines affirm youth's culturally based resistance to the orthodoxy of oppression.

A close reading of "Apprentro" provides examples of a Cree youth seeking vision and purpose. The song changes pace and beat following the introductory call for liberation, "Power in my voice, hear it." The next lines review the situation of Aboriginal societies in a postmodern world, critique people's complacency and abandonment of spiritual traditions, and enforce the prophecy of the tenuous opportunity to survive.

> Just bound by scraps of a tattered history
> The nnn-nation blind sided and
> shadowed the mystery
> Too many colonized minds falling through the cracks
> And now we're running out of time[42]

The use of the word *mystery* so early in the song and on the album is highlighted because it repeats a dominant concept in the album title, *Apprentice to the Mystery*. It alerts the listener of the great significance of this concept to the overall message of the work. The audience is ambiguous because the summary and caution may be interpreted to apply to an individual or a collective. This ambiguity is sustained into the next group of rhymes.

> Left lost off track
> Opportunity for sacrifice
> Climb the oppressor's ladder and
> And disrespect your ancestors' lives
> It's gone on for too long
> Question who's really strong or
> just a pawn, long arm of the government
> raise his magical wand it's on
> Make it official the pawn who'll never really belong

The first three lines have potent critical significance when they are referenced to an understanding of the qualities of a Cree leader. Compassion, generosity, sacrifice, and kindness guided ancestors' decisions to protect the earth for subsequent generations. All this is for naught if the Indian leaders, driven by greed and ambition, serve the interests of the oppressors. The poet calls upon the audience to expose the imposter for what he is and reveal that he will never really belong because he does not guide his actions by the laws sustained and transmitted by the ancestors. There is a slight pause and the caution to heed the wisdom of the elders is repeated twice with a pause in between stamping the message with emphasis.

> We need to maintain the knowledge and wisdom from the elders before it's all gone
> We need to maintain the knowledge and wisdom because it's going so fast.

Closely following this are her lines describing her own commitment, which is tempered with humility and avoidance of directing others to follow her example.

> So what I am doing is
> Observing the mystery
> Understanding the mystery
> Following the mystery
> Becoming the mystery
> I'm nothing without the mystery
> I know nothing about the mystery
> A tiny source of the force of this
> Universal history

These lines relate to the youth's responsibility of seeking a vision as Johnston describes it. The words *observing, understanding, following,* and *becoming* are hypertextual references to the Anishinaabe (and, I posit, also the Cree) vision quest to gain knowledge of the incorporeal nature of one's being that is part of a greater "something." To name it restricts it. *Mystery* is the preferred understanding of *manitou*, which in the past has been glossed as *spirit* or *God*. The poet is humble: "I'm nothing without the mystery." She does not interfere in others' quest to know more: "I know nothing about the mystery." She is not a guide. She is only an apprentice to her own mystery. She is "a tiny source of the force of this universal history."

CONCLUSION

Eekwol's poetry gives us a lasting impression of the performance of a Cree youth identity in a postmodern time. Her songs "Too Sick" and "Apprentro" are read as expressions of Cree youth fulfilling the role and responsibility of people in that stage of life: thinking critically, exercising their autonomy, acting consciously, and serving the well-being of the collective. The analysis of Eekwol's work as the expression of a young adult guided by her vision and the advice and teachings of her elders is based on the works of Johnston and the counseling texts of Duquette, Vandall, and Ka-Nipitehtew.[43] From a cultural foundation that respects youth, Eekwol's poetry presents a constructive and positive perspective and representation of youth.

Eekwol is masterful in connecting her audience to current, historic, and timeless realities. Her word-crafting keeps a beat, makes a memorable rhyme, and builds complexity of meaning. She deftly employs the second-person pronoun, contractions, omission of words and sounds, and colloquial phrasing to use ambiguity as a rhetorical device in order to connect the current with historic realities. Dual meanings engage the listeners to contemplate and comprehend the significance relevant to their own experience. As a means of politicizing youth's constructive resistance, Eekwol's hip-hop storytelling and rhymes reach youth's intellect and passion and challenge youth to act with their free will. Without judgment or condemnation she leads the listeners to reflect on their own responsibility for and contribution to *mino-pimatisiwin*, living a good life.

Her use of hypertextual references to indigenous people's social realities, cultural ethics, and beliefs is subtle enough that the sacred beliefs of the people are respected and protected, and the uninitiated do not feel excluded. The effect is to reach indigenous youth on a wavelength they know is just for them. This is their music. Its message interfaces their present reality with the timeless reality of their cultural teachings. It incites them to feel their power and act to change the way things are. It calls upon them to fulfill their role as indigenous youth.

NOTES

1. This paper is an expanded version of a paper written for Dr. Damián Baca in a graduate course at Michigan State University.

2. Identity is fluid, and the identifier may change to suit the connotation appropriate to the audience, context, or purpose. E.g., in an interview about gender and hip-hop, Eekwol identifies herself as "indigenous," the Aboriginal Peoples Choice Awards identify her as "First Nations" on its Web site, and a writer for *SAY Magazine* identifies her as a "Cree Member of Muskoday First Nation." *Eekwol on Gender*, A Libra Lemons Production, 2008, http://www.youtube.com/watch?v=VA3uRLZ_1zM (accessed 29 November 2009); Aboriginal People's Choice Awards, 2009, http://www.aboriginal-peopleschoice.com/3200C15_17T1037T16T1036T2T1.dhtm?eid1038=85 (accessed 29 November 2009); "Lindsay Knight, Recording Artist," *SAY Magazine*, http://www.saymag.com/canada/spokesppl/eekwol.html (accessed 29 November 2009).

3. Dene people are also an indigenous group in Saskatchewan. Their territories are in the Taiga region. Historically there was less cultural exchange with the other indigenous groups named here because they did not have the same degree of economic, political, or social alliances with those groups as those groups had with each other. Samuel Hearne, *A Journey from Prince of Wales Fort in Hudson's Bay to the Northern Ocean* (Edmonton, AB: M. G. Hurtig, [1791] 1971).

4. Ethnohistorians have examined the topic of multicultural bands on the northwestern plains. Patricia Albers, "Changing Patterns on Ethnicity in the Northeastern Plains," in *History, Power, and Identity: Ethnogenesis in the Americas, 1492–1992*, ed. Jonathon

Hill (Iowa City: University of Iowa Press, 1996), 90–188; Neal McLeod, "Plains Cree Identity: Borderlands, Ambiguous Genealogies and Narrative Irony," *Canadian Journal of Native Studies* 20, no. 2 (2000): 437–54; Regna Darnell, "Rethinking the Concepts of Band and Tribe, Community and Nation: An Accordion Model of Nomadic Native American Social Organization," in *Papers of the Twenty-Ninth Algonquian Conference*, ed. David Pentland (Winnipeg: University of Manitoba Press, 1998); Theodore Binnema, *Common Contested Ground: A Human and Environmental History of the Northwestern Plains* (Toronto: University of Toronto Press, 2004); Laura Peers, *The Ojibwa of Western Canada, 1780–1870* (Winnipeg: University of Manitoba Press, 1994); John Tanner, *The Falcon: A Narrative of the Captivity and Adventures of John Tanner* (New York: Penguin Books, 2000); Laura Peers and Jennifer S. H. Brown, "There Is No End to Relationship among the Indians: Ojibwa Families and Kinship in Historical Perspective," *The History of the Family: An International Quarterly* 4, no. 4 (1999): 529–55; Robert Alexander Innes, "Elder Brother, the Law of the People and Contemporary Kinship Practices of Cowessess First Nation Members: Reconceptualizing Kinship in American Indian Studies Research," *American Indian Culture and Research Journal* 34, no. 2 (2010): 27–41.

    5. McLeod, "Plains Cree Identity."

    6. Christian Thompson, "Muskoday First Nation," *The Encyclopedia of Saskatchewan*, 2006, http://esask.uregina.ca/entry/muskoday_first_nation.html (accessed 28 November 2009).

    7. Muskoday First Nation, *Official Home Page*, http://www.muskoday.ca/index.php?option=com_content&view=frontpage&Itemid=1 (accessed 29 November 2009).

    8. Acknowledging the Cree and Saulteaux heritage of the Muskoday First Nations answers why it is valid to make reference to Saulteaux cultural teachings in order to expand understanding of Cree philosophy of youth's role and responsibility. This is highlighted by the publication of Muskoday First Nation of Saulteaux traditional teachings. Diane Knight, *The Seven Fires Teachings of the Bear Clan as Recounted by Dr. Danny Musqua* (Muskoday First Nation, SK: Many Worlds Publishing, 2002).

    9. Standing Committee on Aboriginal Peoples, *Urban Aboriginal Youth: An Action Plan for Change* (Ottawa, ON: Standing Committee on Aboriginal Peoples, 2003).

    10. Canadian Council on Social Development, *Aboriginal Children in Poverty in Urban Communities: Social Exclusion and the Growing Racialization of Poverty in Canada* (Ottawa, ON: Canadian Council on Social Development, 2003).

    11. Mary Jane Norris and Lorna Jantzen, "Aboriginal Languages in Canada's Urban Areas: Characteristics Considerations and Implications," in *Not Strangers in These Parts*, ed. David Newhouse and Evelyn Peters (Ottawa, ON: Policy Research Initiative, 2003), 179–93.

    12. Saskatchewan Trends Monitor, "Sask Trends Provincial Aboriginal Representative Workforce Council June 2," http://www.sasktrends.ca/publications.html (accessed 27 November 2009).

    13. Statistics Canada, *Aboriginal Peoples Survey* (Ottawa, ON: Statistics Canada, 2000).

    14. Canadian Centre for Justice Statistics, *Police-Reported Aboriginal Crime in Saskatchewan* (Ottawa, ON: Canadian Centre for Justice Statistics, 2000).

    15. Department of Justice, *Report and Recommendations in Respect of Legislation, Policy and Practices Concerning Prostitution-Related Activities* (Ottawa, ON: Department of Justice, 1998).

16. Indian and Northern Affairs, *Aboriginal Women: A Demographic, Social and Economic Profile* (Ottawa, ON: Indian and Northern Affairs, 1998).

17. Dialects of Anishinaabe are known by various names in different regions and include *Saulteaux* in Saskatchewan and Manitoba; *Ojibwe* (also spelled *Ojibway* and *Ojibwa*) in Minnesota, Wisconsin, Ontario, and Michigan; *Chippewa* in North Dakota, Minnesota, Wisconsin, and Ontario; and *Pottawatomie* and *Odawa* (variously spelled) in Ontario. See M. Paul Lewis, ed., *Ethnologue: Languages of the World*, 16th ed. (Dallas, TX: SIL International, 2009), http://www.ethnologue.com/ (accessed 29 November 2009).

18. David M. Arnot, "The Five Treaties in Saskatchewan: A Historical Overview," *Expressions in Canadian Native Studies* (Saskatoon: University of Saskatchewan, 2000), 232–64.

19. Norma Sluman and Jean Goodwill, *John Tootoosis: Biography of a Cree Leader* (Ottawa, ON: Golden Dog Press, 1982).

20. Edward Ahenakew, *Voices of the Plains Cree* (Regina, SK: Canadian Plains Research Centre, 1995).

21. Doug Frey, Margaret Hanna, and David Hanna Meyer, "The Enigma of Saskatchewan Blackduck: Pottery from the Hanson (FgNi-50) and Honess (FgNi51) Sites," *Midcontinental Journal of Archeology* 24 (1999): 153–76.

22. Helen Hornbeck Tanner, *The Ojibway of Western Canada, 1780–1870* (St. Paul: Minnesota Historical Society Press, 1994).

23. Saskatchewan Indian Cultural Centre Heritage Site, "Our Languages," http://www.sicc.sk.ca/heritage/sils/ourlanguages/sitemap.html (accessed 14 April 2009).

24. Michael Hart, *Seeking Mino-Pimatisiwin: An Aboriginal Approach to Helping* (Halifax, NS: Fernwood, 2002).

25. Lawrence Gross, "*Bimaadiziwin*, or the Good Life, as a Unifying Concept of Anishinaabe Religion," *American Indian Culture and Research Journal* 26, no. 1 (2002): 15–32.

26. Allen Safarik, *Kisewatotatowin Aboriginal Parenting Handbook* (Saskatoon, SK: Health Canada, Health Promotion and Programs Branch, 1997).

27. Basil Johnston, *Ojibway Heritage: The Ceremonies, Rituals, Songs, Dances, Prayers and Legends of the Ojibway* (Toronto: McClelland and Stewart, 1998).

28. Kim Anderson, "Honouring the Blood of the People: Berry Fasting in the 21st Century," in *Expression in Canadian Native Studies*, ed. R. Innes, R. Laliberte, P. Setee, and J. Waldrum (Saskatoon: University of Saskatchewan Extension Division, 2000), 374–94.

29. Johnston, *Ojibway Heritage*.

30. Ibid.

31. Freda Ahenakew, *The Counseling Speeches of Jim Ka-Nipitehtew* (Winnipeg: University of Manitoba Press, 1988).

32. Freda Ahenakew, *Stories of the House People, told by Peter Vandall and Joe Duquette* (Winnipeg: University of Manitoba Press, 1987).

33. Johnston, *Ojibway Heritage*.

34. Gail MacKay, *Community Perceptions of a Cree Immersion Program at Cumberland House* (Saskatoon: University of Saskatchewan, 2001).

35. Eekwol, *Too Sick*, director Jim Morrison. Maverick Films. 2004. www.youtube.com/watch?v=0XuYikRUl7g (accessed 29 November 2009).

36. Eekwol, "Too Sick," *Apprentice to the Mystery* (Mils Productions, 2005).

37. Deborah Tannen, *You Just Don't Understand: Women and Men in Conversation* (New York: Ballentine, 1991).

38. This and the next 6 passages are from Eekwol, "Too Sick."

39. This and the next 3 passages are from Eekwol, "Apprentro," *Apprentice to the Mystery.*

40. Haas explains that hypertext is an element of American Indian rhetoric and examines "how American Indian communities have employed wampum belts as hypertextual technologies—as wampum belts have extended human memories of inherited knowledges through interconnected, nonlinear designs and associative storage and retrieval methods." Angela Haas, "Wampum as Hypertext: An American Indian Intellectual Tradition of Multimedia Theory and Practice," *Studies in American Indian Literatures* 19, no. 4 (2007): 77.

41. David T. Mandelbaum, *The Plains Cree: An Ethnographic, Historical and Comparative Study* (Regina, SK: Canadian Plains Research Centre, 1979).

42. This and the next 3 passages are from Eekwol, "Apprentro."

43. Ibid.

AMERICAN INDIAN CULTURE AND RESEARCH JOURNAL 34:2 (2010) 67–80

Is an Inuit Literary History Possible?

KEAVY MARTIN

My father had a short wave radio, and I remembered how my grandmother Jeannie enjoyed listening to the radio and twisting the dial for signals. Living in the bush there were not many radio programs to find. Once in a while, she would come across the BBC and sometimes they would play Greenlandic Inuit songs. Greenlanders are well known for their singing and they have beautiful songs. She would call us to gather around the radio, saying, "You have to listen to this. These are our relatives who live in faraway lands." And while we listened to these songs, she would tell us that even though they live in a distant place called Akukituk (Inuktitut for Greenland), we were all one people and that someday we were all going to get together.
—Mary Simon, *Inuit: One Future—One Arctic*

In 1921, the Greenlandic anthropologist Knud Rasmussen set out to travel twenty thousand miles by dog team across Inuit Nunaat—the Inuit homeland. During this three-year journey—the famous Fifth Thule Expedition—Rasmussen was struck by the similarities in the language and culture of Inuit communities across the entire Arctic. Considering the geographical and historical distance between groups of Inuit, Rasmussen observed that "it would be natural for the language and traditions of the various tribes to have lost all homogeneity. Yet the remarkable thing I found was that my Greenland dialect served to get me into complete understanding with all the tribes."[1] The Inuit people may have been composed of widespread regional groups, but their language and literary traditions told a different story. They spoke of a connection that surpassed geographical and historical distance.

This hypothesis was confirmed in 1977, when Inuit representatives from Alaska, Arctic Canada, and Greenland gathered in Barrow, Alaska, for the inaugural meeting of the Inuit Circumpolar Council (ICC).[2] Since the time of Rasmussen's journey, a great deal had changed in the North: the fur trade had collapsed, and southern administrations had significantly expanded

Keavy Martin is an assistant professor of Aboriginal literatures at the University of Alberta. She is currently at work on the book-length manuscript, *Stories in a New Skin: Approaches to Inuit Literature in Nunavut,* and is involved in a collaborative project to re-edit the prison writings of Anthony Apakark Thrasher.

their management of Arctic peoples and resources.[3] As Mary Simon, current president of the Inuit Tapiriit Kanatami explains, "As a means of insuring protection of Inuit culture and the Arctic's resources, [the delegates at Barrow] believed it necessary to establish a unified position on . . . issues that might affect their people and homelands."[4] The council laid down a series of resolutions, which began as follows:

> WHEREAS, the Inuit of Greenland, Alaska and Canada are *one indivisible people with a common language, culture, environment and concerns*; and
> WHEREAS, the Inuit of the circumpolar region declares the oneness of its culture, environment and land and the wholeness of the homeland and that it is only the boundaries of certain nation states that separate us; and
> WHEREAS, we have met in the first Inuit Circumpolar Conference held in Barrow, Alaska, from June 13–18, 1977, to discuss our communal aspirations and concerns; and
> WHEREAS, we wish to reaffirm our right to self-determination; and
> WHEREAS, there is a need for an international organization of Inuit to study, discuss, represent, lobby and protect our interests on the international level;
> NOW, THEREFORE, BE IT RESOLVED:
> 1. That the Inuit Circumpolar Conference is formed. . . .[5]

This approach seemed to mark a radical shift in Inuit self-perception, particularly as the assembled delegates agreed upon the use of the label *Inuit* to refer to their peoples as a whole.[6] As André Légaré points out, "the generic term 'Inuit' was used by [regional] groups only when they were confronted, in traditional times, with Indian groups or more recently, with Europeans."[7] For many residents of Arctic communities, the term *Inuit*, which can be translated as "the people," is not always the identity marker of choice. Alaskan Inuit are more commonly known as Yupiit, Alutiit, or Iñupiat, while residents of the Mackenzie Delta region are called Inuvialuit.[8] Even in areas where the term *Inuit* is employed, the more common and often more meaningful labels are the region-specific *-miut* appellations.[9] However, for the purposes of solidarity, the members of the ICC adopted an umbrella term. Michèle Therrien explains, "According to [the Inuit gathered at Barrow], [the ethnonym *Inuit*] could be used without undermining local designations. This choice was made in response to a situation where it seemed important to emphasize the unity, and not the disparity, of a large cultural group concerned with its future as a distinct society."[10] But for Michael Amarook, then-president of the Inuit Tapirisat of Canada, a change in Inuit self-conception was apparent: "For the first time in history," he said, "we have become one people."[11]

Inuit Nunaat extends across the entire Western hemisphere, but the borders of Russia, the United States, Canada, and Greenland segment it. Further divisions exist within the nation-states as well; in Canada alone, the self-governing Inuit political regions include the Inuvialuit Settlement Region (Northwest Territories), Nunavut, Nunavik (Northern Quebec), and

Nunatsiavut (Labrador). As one might expect, the literature of this territory is likewise varied and complex. I use the term *literature* in an inclusive sense to refer to any work of art in the medium of language—including storytelling and song—rather than in the strict sense that refers to letters and thus privileges written forms of expression. The texts that make up the Inuit literary corpus span thousands of years and a number of genres: they include the classic stories and songs of the oral tradition, more recent memoirs and life writing, elders' oral histories, and contemporary fiction, poetry, and film. Local contexts are highly important to these works, as the literature of each region takes on the particular flavors of its geography and political history.

Lands and literatures are closely connected, and the fate of one tends to be inevitably reflected in the other. Just as southern prospectors and administrators have made forays into Arctic territory, Inuit intellectual culture has been similarly mined and managed. Literary exports from the Arctic include the story of Sedna, the songs collected by Rasmussen, and the film *Atanarjuat (The Fast Runner)*.[12] Nonetheless, Inuit continue to suffer from underrepresentation in southern university classrooms. Even in Native literature classes, Inuit writers and storytellers have a marginal presence, if they are present at all. In the 1980s, Robin McGrath wrote a dissertation and a series of articles on Inuit literature, and in 1988, Penny Petrone published the collection *Northern Voices: Inuit Writing in English*.[13] Yet these trailblazing texts failed to ignite a great deal of interest amongst literary scholars, and in a 2004 *Windspeaker* article, the Inuk writer and politician Zebedee Nungak spoke out about the difficulties that Inuit writers face in distributing their work: "With nobody actively seeking such material," he grieved, "any number of journals, diaries, and manuscripts gather dust in many an obscure shelf."[14]

In 1977, the unification of Inuit into "one indivisible people with a common language, culture, environment and concerns" happened largely for strategic reasons: to gain recognition and respect from southern governments.[15] Could a similar strategy be employed in order to increase recognition of Inuit literature in classrooms and printing houses? What would happen if literary critics were to follow the example of the ICC and unite texts from across Inuit Nunaat into a common literature, or literary tradition? This article will ask whether the strategic concept of an Inuit circumpolar literature is justifiable, even as a temporary measure. Is an Inuit literary history possible?

An Inuit "Nation"?

This type of question has been under discussion in indigenous literary studies for a number of years now, in particular since the 1999 publication of Craig Womack's (Oklahoma Creek/Cherokee) *Red on Red: Native American Literary Separatism*.[16] Building on Robert Warrior's (Osage) principles of intellectual sovereignty, Womack constructed a tribal-specific study of Creek literature and argued that indigenous oral traditions were deeply political texts, inseparable from the concerns of their communities.[17] Since the appearance of *Red on Red*, a number of other indigenous critics have published studies that draw upon the specific intellectual traditions of different Indian nations, and together they have formed a critical school now known as indigenous "literary nationalism." In 2006, the Cherokee scholar Daniel Heath Justice published *Our Fire Survives the Storm: A Cherokee Literary History*, and, in 2008, the collectively edited anthology *Reasoning Together: The Native Critics Collective* included a number of tribal-specific studies by indigenous scholars, including Phillip Carroll Morgan (Choctaw), Christopher B. Teuton (Cherokee), Janice Acoose (Saulteaux/Métis), Lisa Brooks (Abenaki), and Tol Foster (Creek).[18] In the meantime, renewed attention has been given to earlier scholars, such as Simon Ortiz (Acoma Pueblo), who have based their critical methodologies on the specificities of their home communities.[19] Further afield, the Canadian poet Robert Bringhurst's somewhat controversial work has drawn attention to the genius of traditional Haida literature, while Richard Dauenhauer and Nora Marks Dauenhauer (Tlingit) have worked tirelessly to document Tlingit oral traditions.[20] These scholars have made it apparent that generalized approaches to indigenous literatures are insufficient, as they fail to account for the distinct artistic and intellectual traditions of individual nations.

Indigenous literary nationalism, however, places a great deal of importance on national specificity. With its interest in the foundations of individual literary traditions and in the social and political relevance of texts, literary nationalism resonates in many ways with the discipline of literary history.[21] As a critical practice, literary history has origins in the nationalist movements of nineteenth-century Europe; it often focuses on the ways in which the literary productions of particular groups embody national character or identity.[22] Literary historians are witnesses to the ways in which nations narrate themselves. David Perkins, author of *Is Literary History Possible?*, points out that although literary history has swung in and out of favor, it has become newly relevant in the context of late-twentieth-century social justice movements, which "produce literary histories for the same motives, essentially, that inspired the national and regional literary histories of the nineteenth century. These groups turn to the past in search of identity, tradition, and self-understanding."[23] The literary nationalists might describe this project slightly differently, as, for example, Warrior did, when he wrote *Tribal Secrets: Recovering American Indian Intellectual Traditions*, or as Kimberley M. Blaeser did in "Native Literature: Seeking a Critical Center."[24] After centuries of state-sponsored attempts at suppressing indigenous cultures, Native critics are working to *reclaim* precolonial literary traditions; in this way, they resist being confined to the experience of colonization.[25]

Justice writes, "Indigenous nationhood is a necessary ethical response to the assimilationist directive of imperialist nation-states."[26] Similarly, literary nationalism—which promotes indigenous nationhood through its study of tribal literatures—is strategic; it works to bolster the threatened sovereignty of Native peoples. Yet tribal nationalism, Justice argues, is distinct from the nationalism of nation-states, in part because of "the ability of Indigenous nationalism to extend recognition to other sovereignties without that recognition implying a necessary need to consume, displace, or become absorbed by those nations."[27] Likewise, the indigenous literary nationalists have always been careful to point out that theirs is not the only acceptable way of reading indigenous texts. As Womack put it in *Red on Red,* "I believe that *one approach* to Native literatures should be a study of the primary culture that produces them."[28] Despite this commitment to critical tolerance, indigenous literary nationalism proceeds always with the cautionary tales of twentieth-century state nationalism in mind. At the same time that they describe the literary traditions of particular indigenous nations, the literary nationalists must grapple with the risks of their approach—in particular, with the possibility that it may mimic the homogenizing activities of nation-states.

The danger is that in articulating national literatures strategically—in order to resist the assimilationist tactics of the colonial nation-states—critics may inadvertently downplay the diversity that exists *within* tribal traditions. Justice returns to this issue in his contribution to *Reasoning Together.* Reflecting on his work in Cherokee literary history, he observes that "no community is monolithic and without dissent or even conflicting ideas about what exactly constitutes the group.... My initial supposition that there was a single, unitary idea of 'Cherokeeness' was both naive and, ultimately, impossible, especially given the long and tangled realities of Cherokee social history."[29] The dangers of emphasizing coherence and unity exist whether the critic is imagining nations or literatures; the possibility of creating totalizing narratives is one that literary history as a discipline has struggled with.[30] As Perkins explains, "The writing of literary history involves selection, generalization, organization, and a point of view. It selects for representation only some of the texts and relevant events in the tract of past time it supposedly describes; it collects these into general entities (e.g., romanticism); it adopts a point of view toward them; and it makes them constituents of a discursive form with a beginning, a middle, and an end, if it is Aristotelian narration, or with a statement, development, and conclusion, if it is an argument."[31] In Hayden White's terms, the literary history is "emplotted" and, therefore, subject to the desires of the literary historian.[32] As a narrative, it attempts to give shape to an entire tradition and bestow a logical coherence onto that tradition's components.[33] It is inevitable that certain elements will be omitted, and that the specificities of individual texts will be subordinated to the character of the literature as a whole. Literary history, like literary nationalism, is therefore complicated by the diversity of the nation.

This problem is especially pertinent in the Inuit context, in which the very existence of a "nation" is in question. As the anthropologist Robert G. Williamson writes, "Traditionally, though the Eskimo conceived of themselves generally and generically as *Iniut* [*sic*]—'The People', they never had any strong sense of total ethnic-group loyalty, still less of a sense of identification on a pan-Eskimo or national scale."[34] However, if someone had asked the delegates gathered at Barrow whether an Inuit nation could be said to exist, they might have said yes—although they might not have used the term *nation.* The Latin root of the word *nation* (*natio*) refers to birth and evokes a group of people connected by kinship ties.[35] When the ICC declared the existence of an Inuit "people," they were suggesting a very similar concept. I argue that as long as we do not confuse the term *nation* with the idea of the nation-state, we can think of nationhood and peoplehood as being very closely related phenomena.[36] In an 1882 lecture given at the Sorbonne, Ernest Renan asked the question "Qu'est-ce qu'une nation?" or "What is a nation?"[37] He discussed the factors of shared race, language, religion, and "interests," but one by one eliminated them as the defining feature of nationhood. Geography, he conceded, is an important factor; however, the true core of the nation lies in a kind of shared consciousness amongst its members—in "the possession in common of a rich legacy of memories . . . [and in] the desire to live together, the will to perpetuate the value of the heritage that one has received in an undivided form."[38] This idea that nationhood is determined not by a set of shared characteristics but rather by a kind of imaginary covenant between members was later expanded upon by Benedict Anderson. The nation, Anderson said famously, "is an imagined political community."[39] It is based on a narrative of a shared common history, identity, and, often, enemy.

Reading Stories of "Others" for Nationalist Themes

When the ICC declared its constituents to be "one indivisible people with a common language, culture, environment and concerns," they formed the quintessential imagined community, or nation.[40] Although the words spoken at Barrow certainly gave the concept of an Inuit nation a new kind of reality, I would argue that it was not an idea conjured out of thin air. Rather, the resolutions voiced in 1977 were the product of a long history of precolonial Inuit national sentiment. Evidence of this is to be found in the traditions of stories across Inuit Nunaat—stories that take as a central theme the idea of what it means to be Inuit, often by describing what it means to *not* be Inuit.

The classic Inuit stories cover a wide range of topics, yet a consistent theme is the presence, and sometimes the threat, of other (non-Inuit) beings. As the editors of *Uqalurait: An Oral History of Nunavut* point out, "Inuit folklore is full of stories about the murderous nature of strangers."[41] Even when they are not murderous, these Others tend to be characterized by a wonderfully disconcerting weirdness. In the brother and sister stories, for instance, a pair of traveling siblings visit the land of the *kukilingiattiaraaluit*, the "ones with the long nails," and the *itiqanngittut*, the "ones without anuses."[42] Other stories tell of visits to villages of bears and of a whole range of *uumajuit* (animal spirits) and *inurajait* (human-like beings).[43] This latter category includes *ijirait* (shape-shifting land spirits, or "hidden ones"), *inukpasugjuit* (giants), and *inugarulligaarjuit* (little people), to name only a few.[44] These Others often live in ways that parallel Inuit life, but they inevitably reveal some (frequently horrific) difference, which marks them as distinctly non-Inuit, or nonhuman.

In the chapter "Reading the Oral Tradition for Nationalist Themes: Beyond Ethnography," Womack argues that classic indigenous stories have a deeply political aspect; they serve—and have always served—to articulate a national identity.[45] As Womack puts it, "oral traditions—legends and myths, if you will—performed in their cultural contexts have always been nationalistic and are told for the purpose of cultivating a political consciousness."[46] Stories provide listeners with a sense of communal identity; they describe "what it means to be from a clan, a town, a nation."[47] J. Edward Chamberlin points out that "we all have stories that hold us in thrall and others at bay."[48] Stories of Others are an effective way of defining who we are, by reminding us of who we are not.

This sense of Otherness might also come into play in Inuit stories about their relations from different regions; however, this is not the same difference that separates Inuit from non-Inuit. Simon Anaviapik, a Tununirmiut elder, tells a story about traveling as a child to the Nattilik region.[49] At first, his family was struck by the strangeness of the other Inuit: "They seemed almost like animals to us in their own dialect." However, similarities quickly became apparent, and the strangeness fell away. "It did not take very long for the language difficulty to clear up," Anaviapik says, "That's how it is when you're all Inuit; problems are easily solved."[50]

When different Inuit regional groups encountered each other, it was likely that they would know many of the same stories. As Rasmussen recorded myths and legends in each of the communities he visited, he noted their resemblance to the versions he knew back in Greenland: "Out of fifty-two stories which I wrote down among the Padlermiut at Hikoligjuaq, no fewer than thirty were identical with ones I had already heard in Greenland, and this despite the fact that for thousands of years past, no intercourse had taken place between the two groups of people."[51] Rasmussen may have been over-estimating the lack of contact between different groups of Inuit, and it may be an exaggeration to describe Inuit stories from different regions as "identical." Homogeneity, however, is not the point; the more important detail is the existence of a common tradition of stories that work to define Inuitness by raising the specter of Otherness. As Justice argues in *Reasoning Together*, "no community is monolithic and without dissent or even conflicting ideas about what exactly constitutes the group. . . . Though members of a group might differ in their understandings of that community's composition, they nonetheless work to articulate the shifty, unstable, but ultimately embodied notion of purposeful collectivity."[52]

The epic tale of Kiviuq is perhaps the prototypical articulation of the distinction between Inuit and Others. In a story told across the Arctic, the hero Kiviuq (also spelled Kivioq, Kiv(v)iok, or Keeveeok, and known in Alaska as Qayaq) is swept out to sea during a storm and spends many years—some would say thousands—exploring the lands far beyond his home and encountering a whole host of strange and terrifying beings. In one version, Kiviuq encounters a woman called Igutsaqjuaq (Big Bee [Woman]), who angrily cuts off her own eyelids when she believes them to be blocking her light.[53] Later, Kiviuq meets a man chopping driftwood who has a wide opening from his mouth through to his anus; Kiviuq has to reassure the man craftily that he did not approach him from behind and so did not look through the hole in his body. The wonderful strangeness of these characters might again be read as part of a treatise on Otherness, which further serves to remind the listeners of their own shared humanity, or normalcy. As Kiviuq wanders far from home, he explores the boundaries of the Inuit nation.

Aside from fantastic beings, the classic stories are also populated with non-Inuit people, like the Iqqiliit (Dene), the Allait or Unaliit (Cree), the

Qallunaat (white people), and the Tuniit (or Dorset, the people who inhabited the central and eastern Arctic prior to the arrival of the Thule Inuit).[54] The stories of this latter group are a mainstay of the Canadian Inuit storytelling traditions and have recently made an appearance in contemporary Inuit fiction. In the 2004 collection *Our Story: Aboriginal Voices on Canada's Past*, the Iglulingmiut writer Rachel A. Qitsualik published the story "Skraeling," which tells of an Inuk who encounters a group of Tuniit (and later, Vikings) during the Thule eastward migration of 1000 BC.[55] In the village of the Tuniit, the main character Kannujaq finds an Inuk boy who has lived there for his entire life. At the end of the story, the boy, Siku, leaves with Kannujaq to return to his people. As they prepare for the journey, Siku asks Kannujaq: "What . . . am I to say my mother is, if not a Tunik? *What are we?* "[56] "'I don't know,' Kannujaq replied. But he thought about a word his grandfather had used. 'Perhaps we are *Inuit.*'"[57] In this moment, it is clear that although the year is 1000 BC, it is also 1977 AD, when the ICC delegates spoke the Inuit nation into being. One might imagine that Qitsualik is writing an antecedent to the meeting at Barrow and testifying to the precolonial origins of Inuit national consciousness.

As Rasmussen points out, stories from the various regions of Inuit Nunaat do have remarkable similarities; this alone might indicate the possibility of a unified vision of the literature. However, attempts to make stories from Greenland match stories from Alaska will always require some selective listening and will by necessity downplay the unique cultural and political contexts of the different regions. A more acceptable strategy for a literary history, therefore, might be to consider the way in which the form and function of the literature—rather than its content—remains consistent. Justice, in his contribution to *Reasoning Together*, comes to the conclusion that "though there are many different ways of understanding what it is to be Cherokee—some more suited to the preservation of Cherokee nationhood, communitism, and decolonization than others—each way is still an attempt to give shape to an idea of what it is to be, think, and live Cherokee."[58] Here, the idea of the nation—and by extension the literary tradition—is not so much a clearly definable *thing* but rather a *process*. As works of Inuit literature from different regions and historical periods endeavor to describe what it means to be Inuit, they are involved in the process of nation building, or imagining communities. This is the thread that might pull them together—or if not together, at least in the same direction.

Inuit on the International Stage

The idea of an Inuit nation may not be the primary political framework of Arctic communities; it might only flicker to life in moments of encounter, as people recognize their differences from others or their similarities to each other. The rest of the time, it might be the more tangible, local realities that take precedence: the questions of Nunavut identity, Labrador dialect, or Alaskan oil drilling. But those occasional moments of unification—that theoretical sense of peoplehood, or nation—might be justification enough for an

Inuit literary nationalism. Let's not forget that this tying together—this search for connective sinews, or threads—is strategic, ultimately, as nationalisms always are.[59] Like the ICC's declaration of unity, the idea of a coherent Inuit literary tradition has the potential to confer a sense of sovereignty onto Inuit literature and to "re-affirm [its] right to self-determination."[60] An Inuit literary history might encourage students and scholars to recognize Inuit literature as a distinct and self-sufficient artistic tradition, deserving of serious study.

In the course of these discussions, readers might take a moment to ask why cohesion—whether of a people or literature—is so politically compelling. Why does a monolithic tradition get more attention than a fragmented or miniscule one? Is it part of a literary sensibility—a desire for narrative unity? Or is it pure military strategy? A nation that spans four countries is formidable, and the same goes for its literature; that kind of breadth, we think, must equal value, or at least a respectable design—as demonstrated by its ability to expand and endure. If nations and literatures are large and organized enough, then it is clearly unwise or impossible to ignore them. The current need for cohesion in studies of Inuit literature might simply be a side effect of the material's obscurity in the mainstream. The possibility of learning about Inuit literary traditions might be appealing to many students, especially with the ground-work laid by indigenous studies and Isuma Igloolik Productions.[61] However, the availability of Yupiit, Iñupiat, Inuvialuit, Nattilingmiut, Aivilingmiut, Iglulingmiut, Nunavimmiut, Nunatsiavummiut, and Kalaallit literatures for study might be a bit overwhelming for most southern students; it might send them back to the comforting embrace of John Milton or N. Scott Momaday.[62]

Although an Inuit literary history may never be able to achieve an accurate representation of the complexities of the literature as a whole, it would at least provide an entry point for students and scholars. Literary histories can never be truly thorough; this is not their purpose. As Perkins observes, "The only complete literary history would be the past itself, but this would not be a history, because it would not be interpretive and explanatory."[63] A literary history is intentionally fictional, and it entails all of the benefits that storytelling has to offer. To call history a fiction, White says, "in no way detracts from the status of historical narrative as providing a kind of knowledge. . . . [T]he encodation of events in terms of such plots structures is one of the ways that a culture has of making sense of both personal and public pasts."[64] The trouble lies only in the possibility that emplotment may occur undetected, all the while giving the impression of objectivity, factuality, and finality.

In discussing the possibility of a unified Inuit literary history, however, I am attempting to emplot quite openly and with freely available motives. In late 2009, heads of government and environmental organizations met at a United Nations conference in Copenhagen to negotiate a multinational plan for climate change mitigation.[65] During the two weeks that the meeting was in progress, however, the Obama administration granted Shell the rights to exploratory oil drilling in the Chukchi Sea off the coast of Alaska.[66] Such threats to Arctic ecology are a rallying point for the environmental move-ment; melting glaciers and shrinking sea ice have become powerful symbols of a global crisis. In the Canadian context, the Arctic has also become an important political touchstone in the policies of Prime Minister Stephen Harper's government, as vamped-up concerns about sovereignty threats and the control of northern shipping routes regularly appear in the prime minister's speeches. Rival Canadian political leaders visit Nunavut frequently, and each has promises for northern development and prosperity. The Arctic is no longer located on the periphery of American and Canadian national consciousness; rather, it is increasingly becoming a key player on the international political stage. For many North Americans, however, the landscape north of the tree line still has a kind of frontier status—simultaneously wild, threatened, and rich in resources. The problem is that images of frozen, treeless terrain and polar bears stranded on ice floes are telling an incomplete story about the north, and the majority of southerners are unaccustomed to thinking about the Arctic as a peopled landscape with an extensive cultural and political history. But as the changing geological and political climates continue to create challenges for northerners, this is now more than ever an essential shift in perspective.

Once Inuit sovereignty and literature have a more viable position in the southern imagination, we can look forward to specific, regional studies that take the full complexity of local history and geography into account. At the moment, however, it might be most prudent to explore the strategic potential of the ICC's narrative of Inuit cultural unity for literary studies: a unified literary history, like a unified political history, has the capacity to make space for Inuit voices to be heard in the south. So is an Inuit literary history possible? In view of the Arctic's current role as an international political chesspiece, the answer is yes; and not only that—it is necessary.

NOTES

1. Rasmussen's mother was Inuk (the singular of Inuit), and Kalaallisut (Greenlandic Inuktitut) was his first language. Knud Rasmussen, *Across Arctic America: Narrative of the Fifth Thule Expedition* (Fairbanks: University of Alaska Press, 1999), xxxvi.

2. As Philip Lauritzen mentions (*Oil and Amulets: Inuit: A People United at the Top of the World* [St. John's, NL: Breakwater Books, 1983], 23), Inuit representatives from the Chukotka region in Siberia did not attend the first Inuit Circumpolar Council (hereinafter referred to as ICC) meeting. However, they are now full members of the ICC; Mary Simon, *Inuit: One Future—One Arctic* (Peterborough, ON: The Cider Press, 1996), 14.

3. See Peter Kulchyski and Frank James Tester, *Tammarniit (Mistakes): Inuit Relocation in the Eastern Arctic, 1939–63* (Vancouver: University of British Columbia Press, 1994) and *Kiumajut (Talking Back): Game Management and Inuit Rights 1900–70* (Vancouver: University of British Columbia Press, 2007); or Marybelle Mitchell, *From Talking Chiefs to a Native Corporate Elite: The Birth of Class and Nationalism among the Canadian Inuit* (Montreal, QC, and Kingston, ON: McGill-Queen's University Press, 1996).

4. The Canadian national Inuit organization's name translates to "Inuit are united in Canada." Mary Simon, "Inuit and the Canadian Arctic: Sovereignty Begins at Home" (address, Canadian Club of Victoria, Victoria, BC, 25 September 2008),

http://itk.ca/President-Speaking-Tour (accessed 1 October 2008); Simon, *Inuit: One Future—One Arctic*, 15.

5. ICC, "Final Report—First Inuit Circumpolar Conference, 1977," Eben Hopson Memorial Archives, http://www.ebenhopson.com/icc/ICCBooklet.html (accessed 13 March 2008); emphasis added.

6. Michèle Therrien, *Le Corps Inuit (Québec Arctique)* (Paris: Société d'Études Linguistiques et Anthropologiques de France, 1987), 144.

7. André Légaré, "The Spatial and Symbolic Construction of Nunavut: Towards the Emergence of a Regional Collective Identity," *Études/Inuit/Studies* 25, no. 1–2 (2001): 159.

8. Both Iñupiat and Inuvialuit can be translated as "the real people." Therrien, *Le Corps Inuit*, 144.

9. The extension *-miut* means *people of*. Although traditional ethnonyms like Nattilingmiut or Aivilingmiut are still in use, they have now been supplemented by -miut terms for particular communities (i.e., Iqalungmiut, or the people of Iqaluit) or for new regional designations (i.e., Nunavummiut, or the people of Nunavut). Note that these are now geographic rather than ethnic markers; the term Nunavummiut can include all residents of Nunavut, including the 15% who are non-Inuit.

10. Therrien, *Le Corps Inuit*, 144; my translation.

11. Innuit Tapirisat of Canada was the previous name of the Inuit Tapiriit Kanatami; quoted in Lauritzen, *Oil and Amulets*, 26.

12. The story of Sedna, or the origin of the sea mammals, is one of the better-known Inuit stories. For an example of a Sedna story, see "Uinigumasuittuq: She Who Never Wants to Get Married," in Alexina Kublu, "Stories," in *Interviewing Inuit Elders Volume 1: Introduction*, ed. Jarich Oosten and Frederic Laugrand (Iqaluit: Nunavut Arctic College, 1999), 153–61.

See Knud Rasmussen, ed., *Eskimo Poems from Canada and Greenland* (Pittsburgh: University of Pittsburgh Press, 1973), or Edward Field, trans., *Eskimo Songs and Stories: Collected by Knud Rasmussen on the Fifth Thule Expedition* (New York: Delacorte Press, 1973).

Atanarjuat (The Fast Runner), DVD, directed by Zacharias Kunuk (Igloolik, NU: Igloolik Isuma Productions, 2001).

13. Robin McGrath, *Canadian Inuit Literature: The Development of a Tradition* (Ottawa, ON: National Museums of Canada, 1984); Penny Petrone, ed., *Northern Voices: Inuit Writing in English* (Toronto: University of Toronto Press, 1988).

14. Zebedee Nungak, "Contemplating an Inuit Presence in Literature," *Windspeaker* 22, no. 1 (April 2004), http://find.galegroup.com.myaccess.library.utoronto .ca/itx/start.do?prodId =CPI (accessed 14 September 2008).

15. ICC, "Final Report."

16. Craig Womack, *Red on Red: Native American Literary Separatism* (Minneapolis: University of Minnesota Press, 1999).

17. As articulated in Robert Warrior, *Tribal Secrets: Recovering American Indian Intellectual Traditions* (Minneapolis: University of Minnesota Press, 1994).

18. Daniel Heath Justice, *Our Fire Survives the Storm: A Cherokee Literary History* (Minneapolis: University of Minnesota Press, 2006); Daniel Heath Justice, Christopher B. Teuton, and Craig Womack, eds., *Reasoning Together: The Native Critics Collective* (Norman: University of Oklahoma Press, 2008).

19. Ortiz's 1981 essay "Towards a National Indian Literature: Cultural Authenticity in Nationalism" (originally published in *MELUS* 8, no. 2: 7–12) was republished in the 2006 collection *American Indian Literary Nationalism* by Robert Warrior, Jace Weaver, and Craig Womack (Albuquerque: University of New Mexico Press, 2006), 253–60.

20. Robert Bringhurst, trans., *A Story as Sharp as a Knife: The Classical Haida Mythtellers and Their World* (Vancouver, BC: Douglas and McIntyre, 1999); Richard Dauenhauer and Nora Marks Dauenhauer, eds., *Haa Kusteeyí, Our Culture: Tlingit Life Stories* (Seattle, London, and Juneau, AK: University of Washington Press and Sealaska Heritage Foundation, 1994). Though not technically part of the indigenous literary nationalist movement, the works of Bringhurst and the Dauenhauers have related goals and concerns.

21. Womack's more recent work stresses the need for critics to place historical context at the fore. See "A Single Decade: Book-Length Native Literary Criticism between 1986 and 1997," in Justice, Teuton, and Womack, ed., *Reasoning Together*, 3–104.

22. As David Perkins explains, "the advantages of nineteenth-century literary histories were manifold and enormous. The premise that the history of literature exhibits the development of 'the national conscience,' as [Benedetto] Croce put it, provided a sense of purpose and wide social significance of the work." David Perkins, *Is Literary History Possible?* (Baltimore, MD: Johns Hopkins University Press, 1992), 4.

23. Ibid., 10. See also p. 181.

24. Warrior, *Tribal Secrets*; Kimberley M. Blaeser, "Native Literature: Seeking a Critical Center," in *Looking at the Words of Our People: First Nations Analysis of Literature*, ed. Jeannette Armstrong (Penticton, BC: Theytus Books, 1993), 51–62.

25. The Cherokee writer Thomas King explains this issue: "While post-colonialism purports to be a method by which we can begin to look at those literatures which are formed out of the struggle of the oppressed against the oppressor, the colonized and the colonizer, the term itself assumes that the starting point for that discussion is the advent of Europeans in North America. . . . [T]he idea of post-colonial writing effectively cuts us off from our traditions, traditions that were in place before colonialism ever became a question, traditions which have come down to us through our cultures in spite of colonization, and it supposes that contemporary Native writing is largely a construct of oppression." Thomas King, "Godzilla vs. Post-Colonial," *World Literature Written in English* 30, no. 2 (1990): 11–12.

26. Justice, *Our Fire Survives the Storm*, 8.

27. Ibid., 24.

28. Womack, *Red on Red*, 25; emphasis added.

29. Daniel Heath Justice, "'Go Away, Water!': Kinship Criticism and the Decolonization Imperative," in Justice, Teuton, and Womack, ed., *Reasoning Together*, 153.

30. Linda Hutcheon, "Adventures in Literary Historyland" (keynote address, Cambridge History of Postcolonial Literature Conference, Toronto, 19 September 2008).

31. Perkins, *Is Literary History Possible?* 19.

32. Hayden White, "The Historical Text as Literary Artifact," in *The Norton Anthology of Theory and Criticism*, ed. Vincent B. Leitch (New York and London: W. W. Norton and Company, 2001), 1712–29.

33. As Perkins says, "Unless one perceives such syntheses, one cannot write literary history. The assumptions that the various genres, periods, schools, traditions, movements, communicative systems, discourses, and epistemes are not baseless and arbitrary groupings, that such classifications can have objective and valid grounds in the literature of the past, is still the fundamental assumption of the discipline, the premise that empowers it." *Is Literary History Possible?* 4.

34. Robert G. Williamson, *Eskimo Underground: Socio-Cultural Change in the Canadian Central Arctic*, Occasional Papers II (Uppsala, Sweden: Institutionen för Allmän och Jämförande Etnografi vid Uppsala Universitet, 1974), 31.

35. "Nation," in *The Oxford English Dictionary Online*, http://www.oed.com (accessed 13 February 2007).

36. The concept of "peoplehood," as developed by Tom Holm, J. Diane Pearson, and Ben Chavis in "Peoplehood: A Model for the Extension of Sovereignty in American Indian Studies," is dependent on four intertwined attributes: a shared language, sacred history, ceremonial cycle, and place, or territory. In *Wicazo Sa Review* (Spring 2003): 7–24. An invention of the "modern," industrialized era, nation-states are political bodies defined by a "fusion of their component populations." Ernest Renan, "What Is a Nation?" trans., Martin Thom, in *Nation and Narration*, ed. Homi K. Bhabha (New York: Routledge, 1990), 10. The nation-state is a political entity that can encompass multiple "ethnic" nations and is usually endowed with various institutions for managing its citizens. As Max Weber argues in his essay "Politics as a Vocation," "a state is a human community that (successfully) claims the *monopoly of the legitimate use of physical force* within a given territory." In *From Max Weber: Essays in Sociology*, trans. Hans Heinrich Gerth and Charles Wright Mills (London: Routledge, 1998), 78.

37. Renan, "What Is a Nation?" 8–22.

38. Ibid., 19.

39. Benedict Anderson, *Imagined Communities: Reflections on the Origin and Spread of Nationalism* (London: Verso, 2006), 6.

40. ICC, "Final Report."

41. John Bennett and Susan Rowley, eds., *Uqalurait: An Oral History of Nunavut* (Montreal, QC, and Kingston, ON: McGill-Queen's University Press, 2004), 130.

42. The brother and sister stories are a series of tales that culminate in the creation of the sun and moon. See "Aningagiik: Brother and Sister Legends," in Alexina Kublu, "Stories," in Oosten and Laugrand, ed., *Interviewing Inuit Elders Volume 1*, 162–81.

43. Thomas Kusugaq, *Eight Inuit Myths/Inuit Unipkaaqtuat Pingasuniarvinilit*, trans. Alex Spalding (Ottawa, ON: National Museums of Canada, 1979), 1–14; Mariano Aupilaarjuk et al., *Interviewing Inuit Elders Volume 4: Cosmology and Shamanism*, ed. Bernard Saladin d'Anglure (Iqaluit: Nunavut Arctic College, 2001), 51.

44. Ijirait are also called *tarriaksuit* or *tarriassuit* (shadow people) in South/East Baffin. Aupilaarjuk, *Cosmology*, 51–54; Bennett and Rowley, *Uqalurait*, 150–59.

45. Womack, *Red on Red*, 51–74.

46. Ibid., 61.

47. Ibid., 62.

48. J. Edward Chamberlin, *If This Is Your Land, Where Are Your Stories?: Finding Common Ground* (Toronto: Alfred A. Knopf Canada, 2003), 2.

49. The Tununirmuit are a North Baffin Inuit group in the Pond Inlet (Mittimatalik) area. The Nattilingmiut, or Netsilingmiut (people of the place where there are seals), are from the area around Taloyoak in the Kitikmeot region of Nunavut. Bennett and Rowley, *Uqalurait*, 340.

50. Ibid., 126.

51. Rasmussen, *Across Arctic America*, 87–88.

52. Justice, "'Go Away, Water!'" 153.

53. Recently, the tale was made into a film by John Houston, which features tellings of the Kiviuq story by elders Henry Evaluardjuk, Annie Peterloosie, and Samson Quinangnaq. *Kiviuq*, DVD, directed by John Houston (Halifax, NS: Triad Film Productions, 2007).

54. Iggiliit is a rather disparaging term meaning *louse eggs*. Alex Spalding, "iqqilik," in *Inuktitut: A Multi-Dialectal Outline Dictionary* (Iqaluit: Nunavut Arctic College, 1998), 30. Allait is from *allaq*, or *stranger*. Lucien Schneider, in *Ulirnaisigutiit: An Inuktitut-English Dictionary of Northern Quebec, Labrador and Eastern Arctic Dialects* (Laval, QC: Les Presses de l'Université Laval, 1985), 19. Like Iqqiliit, the term can also denote "Indians" more generally. Qallunaat appear in the Sedna/Nuliajuk story: they are said to be descendants of the puppies that Nuliajuk had with her dog-husband, who were set afloat in a *kamik* (boot). In some versions, the rest of the puppies were sent overland to become the Indians. Aupilaarjuk et al., *Interviewing Inuit Elders Volume 2: Perspectives on Traditional Law*, eds. Frédéric Laugrand, Jarich Oosten, and Wim Rasing (Iqaluit: Nunavut Arctic College, 2000), 189.

55. Iglulingmuit means "the people of Igloolik" in the North Baffin region; Rachel A. Qitsualik, "Skraeling," in *Our Story: Aboriginal Voices on Canada's Past* (Toronto: Doubleday Canada, 2004), 36–66.

56. Qitsualik, "Skraeling," 65; emphasis added.

57. Ibid., 66; emphasis in original.

58. Justice, "'Go Away, Water!'" 153.

59. In Inuktitut, the word *ivaluk* can mean both *sinew* and *thread*.

60. ICC, "Final Report."

61. The makers of the film *Atanarjuat (The Fast Runner)*.

62. This list represents but a sampling of possible identifications under the generic "Inuit" umbrella.

63. Perkins, *Is Literary History Possible?* 13.

64. White, "The Historical Text as Literary Artifact," 1716.

65. "United Nations Climate Change Conference Copenhagen 2009," http://en.cop15.dk (accessed 28 December 2009).

66. Yereth Rosen, "Natives, Greens Seek to Block Shell Drilling Plan," *Reuters*, 15 December 2009, http://www.reuters.com/article/idUSN152607920091215? (accessed 28 December 2009).

AMERICAN INDIAN CULTURE AND RESEARCH JOURNAL 34:2 (2010) 81–101

Dę'ni:s nisa'sgao'dę?: Haudenosaunee Clans and the Reconstruction of Traditional Haudenosaunee Identity, Citizenship, and Nationhood

THERESA MCCARTHY

Among the Haudenosaunee the clan system is an ancient tradition of matrilineal descent that has maintained the social, political, economic, and spiritual cohesion of the people for centuries. Following the American Revolution and the relocation of large numbers of Haudenosaunee people from our traditional homelands in what is now New York State, this system became disrupted. Much of the damage was enacted through nineteenth-century federal policies supporting the dispossession of our territories, which imposed definitions of *citizenship* and *leadership* on the nations or tribes. As a result, many Haudenosaunee gradually lost a sense of who they are as a distinct people with relationships and responsibilities to each other that transcend the Canadian/American border, as well as their currently bounded reserve/reservation communities. Although it is important to enumerate these consequences, it is also critical to recognize that disruptive colonial frameworks continue to reside in a context in which the Haudenosaunee paradigms that anchor cultural, political, and land-based relationships have never been successfully effaced. Illuminating this continuity through the lens of a community-based clan research and education initiative at Six Nations of Grand River in Ontario, this article presents a fuller expression of the meaning of clans evidenced by attention to Haudenosaunee languages and translation and the cultural narratives comprising historic Haudenosaunee traditionalism. The following examination of grassroots and scholarly inter-ventions, alongside contexts of displacement and relevance, corresponds with

Theresa McCarthy (Onondaga Nation, Beaver Clan) is an assistant professor in the Department of American Studies at the University at Buffalo. Her research focuses on the continuity of Haudenosaunee traditionalism and languages within contemporary Six Nations/Haudenosaunee communities, especially Six Nations of Grand River in Ontario, Canada.

the concomitant pedagogical processes of reflection, action, and transformation encouraged by the clan research educational initiative. Emphasizing the viability of clan-based knowledge in transforming and transcending conceptual boundaries and more tangible borders that continue to affect the Haudenosaunee today, this article explores the ongoing practical relevance of this ancient system to current challenges involving assertions of citizenship, leadership, territorial mobility, and land rights.

HAUDENOSAUNEE CLAN RESEARCH AT SIX NATIONS: GRASSROOTS AND SCHOLARLY INTERVENTIONS

There are a number of different ways to look at how Haudenosaunee clan knowledge has been sustained at Grand River. Maintenance of this knowledge is most commonly associated with Haudenosaunee traditionalist institutions, such as Longhouses and the Confederacy Council, and the generations of extended families that have upheld their responsibilities to Haudenosaunee traditionalism spiritually and ceremonially in relation to these contexts as a regular part of their daily lives. There have also been other ongoing community-based educational and research initiatives situated somewhat beyond these spaces that are also aimed to support access to this knowledge. These grassroots efforts are especially important for those who may not have been exposed to this knowledge as a normative part of socialization by taking more direct, explicit approaches to teaching and learning about Haudenosaunee traditionalism. Although not officially associated with traditionalist institutions, such initiatives are often guided by lifelong Longhouse and Confederacy adherents and require extensive commitments of time and energy on the part of these educators and initiative proponents. Intended to compliment and reinforce the broader collective and institutional maintenance of Haudenosaunee knowledge, such efforts also encourage more personal processes of decolonization. As examples of what Taiaiake Alfred calls "self conscious traditionalism," they help to promote "shifts in thinking and action that emanate from recommitments and reorientations [to original teachings and values] at the level of the self that, over time and through proper organization, manifest as broad social and political movements to challenge state agendas and authorities."[1]

At Six Nations of Grand River, ongoing Haudenosaunee clan research initiatives are among numerous other grassroots educational efforts that advance the contemporary practical relevance of Haudenosaunee traditionalism. The research and educational initiative undertaken by my clan, the Onondaga Beaver clan, initially got underway in the early 1990s. At that time, although a few individual clan members were already engaged in genealogical research into the extended family's matrilineal relations, concerns had been mounting among other members of the Beaver clan about the increasing lack of representation of clan members in the Confederacy Council, especially when important issues like education reform at Six Nations were under deliberation. As Sago:ye:satah, leading proponent of the initiative recalls, "some of us knew that a big part of the problem came from the conflict between our traditional identity as Haudenosaunee people and that other identity that's been forced upon us, but we decided we needed to do more than just talk about it, it was time to take action. It was time to make an investment in bringing our people back."[2]

My involvement in the clan research initiative began in 1998 when I received an invitation by phone to a meeting from an Onondaga Beaver clan relative who was largely unknown to me. The earliest Beaver clan meetings I attended seemed like extended family reunions, but these were based more on us "getting to know each other" rather than celebrating lifelong, familiar family connections. Efforts involved drawing clan members together to determine "who's who," "who's related to who," and "who's associated with which family" because there are two Onondaga Beaver clan titles at Six Nations. Identifying clan members prompted further outreach to relatives residing within as well as outside the reserve community. As interest and participation in this initiative grew, these meetings began to take on a more concentrated research-based and educational focus. We became involved in taking a more systematic approach to "getting our house in order" through complementary efforts that include:

- Identifying clan members and developing a clan registry.
- Assembling inventories of clan names, sorting out Confederacy-related titles, and working toward filling vacancies.
- Devising a mediation framework for conflict resolution.
- Ensuring the voice of clan members in decision making about lands, reparations, and future development, a main objective being our eventual (re)representation as fully functioning clans in the Confederacy Council.
- Assembling resources to enhance competence in our official Onondaga language.
- Becoming more aware of and active in protecting the Grand River watershed ecosystem.
- Promoting environmental and economic sustainability through attention to traditional foods and resource-based technologies.
- Illuminating roles and responsibilities through attention to relevant teachings about traditional governance, social and economic systems, and ceremonial and spiritual worldviews with their associated values and principles.

All of these efforts recognize how the need to reclaim this knowledge corresponds with the need to help foster further accessibility to it, so that associated Haudenosaunee clan-based systems and practices can be again understood and exercised more extensively.

A related component of clan research-based education evolved more or less naturally in the learning process. Inevitably, the more people learn about clan-based knowledge, the more we usually move further into understanding why and how this knowledge has been disrupted. This sentiment echoes Patricia Monture-Angus's recommendations for enhancing indigenous governance structures, "knowledge of the imposed systems of power and control are also important, as it is through this knowledge that the people can make informed choices about how to continue to move away from these impositions in the future."[3] Promoting awareness of the fact that disruptive colonial frameworks continue to reside in a context in which the Haudenosaunee paradigms anchoring cultural, political, and land-based relationships have never been successfully eliminated is an equally critical dimension of this educational process.

As my involvement in the clan research initiative continued, fellow clan-relative participants began to assign me tasks that made use of the time and resources accessible to me as a graduate student. Under their direction I assembled a fellowship application focused on promoting Haudenosaunee cross-border relationships. This afforded me the opportunity to go to the University at Buffalo to work with John Mohawk from 2000 to 2001.[4] From this point on, my contributions to the clan research project consisted of using the time of my fellowship to gather information by looking at relevant scholarship, doing archival research, conducting personal interviews, and working with John and other Six Nations peoples and scholars in the United States. Basically I was to do anything on the "academic" side of things that might support the project's overall objectives to help advance reassertions of Haudenosaunee citizenship and leadership, or, as Sago:ye:satah more succinctly put it, "repatriating our people to their traditions."[5]

Guided by my work with Mohawk, and with the invaluable help of many members of the Onondaga Beaver clan and several Six Nations elders and community members every step of the way, my research continues to focus on how indices of continuity and viability reinforce the ongoing, practical relevance of ancient Haudenosaunee clan knowledge and the clan system. Specifically, it addresses how the clan system reaffirms and advances a capacity to transform and transcend conceptual boundaries and more tangible borders that continue to affect the Haudenosaunee today—especially the nation-state borders that bisect our territories and the infinite boundaries on either side that crosscut it. These lines, limits, parameters, and perimeters, reified experientially through colonial laws and policies, tend to get stuck in our heads. Over time, many of us have come to accept these lines designed to promote our physical and conceptual separation from our lands, each other, and ourselves as a peoples. There are still many Haudenosaunee on all sides of these borders and boundaries for whom these connections have endured despite colonial impositions. But for those of us who are relative newcomers to these understandings, a more conscious effort is needed in engaging elemental questions of meaning and purpose that inform the structure, function, and responsibilities associated with the clan system. For some, this means going back to square one by engaging the primary question, "What does it mean to belong to a clan?" And from this point, moving further into recognizing that having a clan isn't just about something you are, it's about things that you do and how these understandings and actions are situated in Haudenosaunee teachings and cosmology. Building from this basis, one can then proceed to explore how the continuity of these meanings and actions pertain to the simultaneous processes of nation being and nation building. Approaching these intersecting processes in this way helps us to reshape and recast current challenges that we as Haudenosaunee peoples continue to confront today.

BACKGROUND ON HAUDENOSAUNEE CLANS: CONSIDERING
HAUDENOSAUNEE LANGUAGES AND PARADIGMS

When you combine a fuller expression of the meaning of clans—evidenced through attention to Haudenosaunee languages and translation—with the elaboration of the structure and function of this system as related through historic Haudenosaunee traditional cultural narratives, you can see how continuity in connections enables the people to deal with separation. This brings sharper clarity to an understanding of clans as being about relationships to lands and Creation and the active expression of these relationships by and among the people as families. The telling and foretelling of cumulative Haudenosaunee narratives reiterate circumstances of some form of separation as a prevalent theme. Each time this happens, the structure and function of the clan system further develops and is refined with the emphasis on maintaining the continuity of the land-Creation-peoples familial relationships and responsibilities that clans embody.

Attention to Haudenosaunee languages and traditionalism helps to initiate an illustration of these linkages. In her dissertation "What Happened to the Iroquois Clans?: A Study of Clans in Three Nineteenth-Century Rotinonhsyonni Communities," Mohawk historian Deborah Doxtator argued that the English term *clan* is misleading and provides an elaboration of land, space, and place as the conceptual basis for Haudenosaunee clans. "The word *otara* in Mohawk," she explains, "means land, clay or earth as well as clan and in asking an individual what clan they belong to (*oh nisen'taroten*), one is literally asking 'what is the outline or contour of your clay?' referring to the land you can access and the territory to which you belong. . . . Land relationships are the basis of understanding clans and political structures."[6]

This rootedness in land is also reflected in the Creation story. According to the late Cayuga Nation, Snipe Clan Confederacy Chief Jake Thomas, "if you go back to the time of Creation, when the Creator made mankind, he made them by molding them from the earth—that's why we call it *Q:gwehǫ́:weh. Q:gweh* is what we are from . . . *Qg:weh* means the real thing from mother earth—that's what we are."[7] This extends further into "*Q:gwe:hǫ́:nęha,* meaning our way of life."[8] Like *otara* in Mohawk, *o'shya:de:nyǫ',* or clan, in Cayuga is not simply a fixed noun. It also incorporates a verb base, signifying an additional dimension of connection to the ecological landscape. Fluent speaker and longtime teacher of the Cayuga language Lottie Keye explains that by asking people to identify their clan in Cayuga, or Dę'ni:s nisa'sgao'dę, you are asking "what family of animal grouping do you belong to?"[9] Haudenosaunee clans are constituted in "patterns of activity" rooted in place, territory, and ecology.[10] Belonging to a clan is processual and actualized in everyday life through living relationships and responsibilities. These relationships and responsibilities are reciprocally connected to the land and emanate outward to incorporate the reciprocal relationships and responsibilities of the Haudenosaunee to each other.

The teaching of the origin of clans provides another way to show these processes at work in the context of Haudenosaunee paradigms. The condensed illustration of the origin of clans highlighted here is from a version of the teaching Chief Thomas shared with me shortly before he passed away in 1998. Thomas's multilingual proficiency and the extent of his experience translating Haudenosaunee traditionalism into English provide substantial assurance that Haudenosaunee language–based understandings and interpretations are attended to in his rendition of this teaching.

Drawing out some of the key themes, what follows is Thomas's rendition of Haudenosaunee clan origins:[11]

> Following the time of Creation, when the people had continued to multiply and had been given ceremonies to show their gratitude for all that the Creator had provided for them, there eventually started to be problems. The Creator had ordained that the women would be the ones to give birth and that the people would only have a certain number of days to live in this world. But eventually the people that were created and had multiplied grew so they couldn't understand when people died, what caused people to die and their bodies to grow cold. They didn't know what happened and could not comfort one and other. They didn't know how to comfort each other when death came in the family, and some times the same family would have a death and it would just overlap the births with grief and because they felt so bad about it, it also caused sicknesses and depression. By then, the Creator had also given them ceremonies, but they seemed to forget about these ceremonies, and they also could not attend them because they had such problems with grief.

As the story continues, the elders at that time assemble to try to solve these problems. A young man at this meeting seems to have the answer. He takes the people on a journey in which they all come to a river and try to cross it on a grapevine. The vine breaks but only after some of the people do manage to get across the river to its other bank; an equal number are left behind on the shore. According to the teaching, this is precisely what was intended to happen. The young man tells them, to quote Thomas, "Now this is what I mean, this river is what divides us and that will be ongoing from here on, that will be ongoing for tradition. That's the way it's going to be for generations to come, we're going to be all separated. It doesn't mean that we're really going to be *separate*, but this is the only way." The next morning the people are told to go out from their camps, and when they return they are to report the first things they see. This reporting establishes what the people's clans will be. They tell the man, "I saw a hawk," "I saw a beaver," an eel, a wolf, a turtle, and so on. In response the young man says,

> Now you know what all you saw, and that'll be your clan. Each one of you are to follow the generation, all the one's you saw, it will follow the mother's blood line. And that is what the reason we now have clans, so that the clan, the wolf will comfort the bear, or the bear will also comfort the wolf at any time there's anything stressful or any discomfort, it'll be up to each one wherever.

And now the death part. It's up to you if you have a problem in the bear or with the deer then the wolf will come to comfort you and you will also support one another on this side, the bears, the deer, you will all support one another. But that's where it'll divide the clan system, all your clans you will all support one and other. And that will be your identity that will be always on the women, it will always follow the women. And this is the way it will be that you can comfort one and other because you can't comfort yourself if you have a problem and that's why somebody else has got to come and comfort you and bring your spirit back up and so that's where it started with the clan system.

The teaching about the origins of the Haudenosaunee clan system reminds us of what clans are, how this system came to be, and its purpose. Clans provide a means of how extended families work in providing consolation, comfort, support, and mediation to each other and are derived from what the women initially see (or what is revealed to them)—the hawk, the deer, the bear—as they look to the ecosystem. Clan responsibilities establish a connectedness among the people that can repair their personal and interpersonal detachment by the anguish of loss and grief as well as transcend their experiences of physical separation by the river. Rooted in Creation and (re)affirmed in ceremonies, these principles are extended in subsequent Haudenosaunee teachings, including the Great Law of Peace. As Thomas states, "as the people continued to multiply and branch out into various settlements across the land, they once again began to forget about their ceremonies, their instructions, how they were related to one another, and gradually they began to start fighting and warring with one and other." The theme of clans abridging separation, while maintaining continuity in principles, is brought forward in time and reflected in the teaching of the Great Law of Peace. Again the people begin to forget their ceremonies and how they are related to one another and gradually start fighting and warring with one another. According to the Great Law, clans become the basic building blocks of the system of Confederacy government, reestablishing relatives, responsibilities, political voice, economic activities, and linkages between families in the past as well as among future generations. As the clan system is extended to structure unity and governance within the Great Law by breaking down hostility and discouraging war, it also reaffirms clan-based understandings in order to provide consolation, support, and mediation, as in the teaching of clan origins. Through the Great Law, clan responsibilities are also considerably magnified in their capacity to establish a connectedness among the people that can transcend their separation across the vast geographical space of the homeland territories.

HAUDENOSAUNEE CLANS: REINTERPRETING CONTEXTS OF DISPLACEMENT AND RELEVANCE

Released just before his sudden passing in 2006, Mohawk's *The Iroquois Creation Story* became a final contribution to his incredible legacy. Mohawk's reworking of ethnologist J. N. B. Hewitt's translation of the "Creation Story," told to him by Onondaga Chief John Arthur Gibson of Grand River in 1890, also includes Gibson's version of the Haudenosaunee clan origins teaching.[12] Noteworthy interpretive and translational intersections arise when considering Mohawk's and the late Chief Thomas's respective representations of historic Haudenosaunee traditionalism. Thomas was always thinking first in one of the five Haudenosaunee languages in which he was fluent and endeavoring to translate these *back to us* in English in his efforts to share these teachings with broader audiences. Although Mohawk did not have to contend with a language barrier as directly as Thomas, he did have to reconcile and navigate through Hewitt's interpretive filter. Mohawk sought to reinscribe Hewitt's translation of Gibson's renditions with Haudenosaunee sensibilities in order to project these *out to us* in English more effectively. Both Mohawk and Thomas invested a lifetime emphasizing the generative capacity of Haudenosaunee knowledge. Understanding the complexities of contemporary circumstances, and how easy it is to become disheartened by them, comprised a significant part of Mohawk's and Thomas's efforts. These efforts involved reminding us that in forgetting there has always been remembering.

Speaking characteristically of historic Haudenosaunee narratives, as Mohawk explained in the foreword to *The Iroquois Creation Story*, "Such stories urge upon us the expectation that things have been known to happen in a certain way, and are likely to happen that way again."[13] This is certainly true when we look at the recurring themes in historic traditionalism and their relevance to how prolonged interactions with settler nation-states have long been our main sources of separation—disrupting the social, political, economic, and spiritual cohesion of Haudenosaunee people as maintained through the clan system. But there is also recurrence in an overarching theme that renders the continuity of connections despite separation as something that is always possible and always happens. For this, Mohawk reminds us, we are extremely fortunate. Continuity is maintained, as core values and principles are brought forward as the basis of dealing with and reconciling new challenges. The stories that are told don't just describe this capacity for continuity; they also come to constitute it. Or as Mohawk eloquently puts it, "for as long as the Haudenosaunee exist . . . [we] will continue to tell this story."[14]

The experiential, historic, and ongoing stories of our separation, as advanced within Six Nations communities and, more recently, by indigenous and allied scholars, increasingly undermine the very legitimacy of colonial frameworks that have attempted to justify the disaggregation of peoples and lands. Such analyses often effectively reinforce the contemporary and practical relevance of Haudenosaunee traditionalism and, in doing so, incite movement away from what Rick Ponting and Cora Voyageur identify as a "deficit paradigm" approach to the interpretative representation of First Nations knowledge and experience.[15] Most significantly, Haudenosaunee citizens' ongoing assertions of the continuity and validity of their distinct nationhood have been increasingly successful in reconfiguring nation-state interactions with Haudenosaunee peoples. What becomes increasingly clear as consideration of disruption and displacement unfolds is how is the traditional theme of separation conveyed in historic narratives takes on a new and different relevance. Even so, with reinvigorated attention to clan knowledge and structures there resides an enormous potential through which the separation wrought by these complex contexts may be challenged, subverted, and overcome.

Although the Canadian-US "border" is a construct that is foreign and without meaning in Haudenosaunee cosmology, it has had very real, substantive implications for the social and political cohesion of Haudenosaunee people over time. Following the American Revolution and the movement of a large portion of the Six Nations population to the Grand River in Ontario in 1784, the Haudenosaunee were divided geographically but not necessarily culturally or socially. In the early decades of the 1800s the Confederacy Council rekindled its fires at Grand River and remained the form of governance committed to all Six Nations people, including those who came to Grand River and those who remained in the homeland territories within the emergent borders of New York State and the province of Quebec. Derivations of this larger council, in the form of either smaller clan councils or national clan councils, administered the specific needs of the specific settlements in their various locations throughout the Grand River tract.[16] Despite the relocation of a large portion of the population, with the reestablishment of Confederacy government to preside over the Haudenosaunee in both territories, clan relationships and the intrinsic connections among the people were initially preserved and maintained.[17]

Disruption to this unity and the severing of these relationships intensified, however, through the consolidation of Canada, alongside the United States, as a separate colonial nation-state. The imposition of a distinct political structure and colonial regime contributed to a legacy of increasing fragmentation within traditional Haudenosaunee sociopolitical culture. Although there is not space in this article for an extensive analysis of the multidimensional effects of colonial processes on Six Nations peoples, numerous Haudenosaunee scholars continue to enrich multiple facets of this discourse through their contributions.[18]

A particularly predatory cluster of Canadian federal policies have had the greatest impact on clan-based relationships among the Six Nations people at Grand River, as well as other Haudenosaunee communities on the Canadian side of the border. These have further entrenched disconnection from Haudenosaunee who remained on the other side of either the Niagara or St. Lawrence rivers in the United States.

After the British North America Act of 1867 transferred jurisdiction of Canadian affairs from the British Crown to the new Canadian government, attempts to transform recognition of the Six Nations legally from sovereign allies into mere wards intensified. On the heels of precursory legislation including the Enfranchisement Act of 1869, with its direct provisions to alter traditional social and political structures, it was through the unilateral decision of the new Canadian government that the Indian Act of 1876 was implemented. Influenced by European notions of descent, pedigree, property rights, and the access of lands and resources through their privatization, this act continues to prescribe a system of patrilineal registration in order to delineate all "Indians" who were of federal concern. In Canada, it becomes the most prominent legal basis for recognition of the federal government's trust relationship and fiduciary ties to First Nations. Métis scholar Bonita Lawrence argues that although the Indian Act set out a framework for defining *Indians*, band affiliation, and access to contingent rights, it was "in fact Canada's way to preempt the rights of Indigenous nations to govern themselves, signify[ing] that colonial [powers], not Native people, controlled Native destinies."[19] Though the Indian Act is often assumed to be a means for dispensing compensation for historic treaty agreements and other Crown negotiations, Lawrence rightly contends that "there can be no greater violation of the nation-to-nation relationship specified in the treaties, when Indigenous citizenship in every sense of the word is defined by a body of colonial administration."[20]

For the Haudenosaunee at Grand River, the Indian Act requirements for "Indian" recognition are obviously antithetical to how clans and nations are matrilineally reconciled. The act's potential to jeopardize the future of the Confederacy Council's decision-making capacity and its ability to preside over the people as a form of governance were immediately apparent. Six Nations historian Susan Hill has written extensively about how the nineteenth-century reestablishment of Confederacy governance met with increasing federal government pressure to administer the Grand River settlement in ways that went against clan lines and broader Haudenosaunee spiritual and sociopolitical philosophies and structures. Although the Indian Act further compelled the alienation of lands and resources on the Grand River tract, Hill's research carefully delineates the various ways in which the Confederacy Council of this era diligently attempted to protect and guide this new settlement according to traditional principles and to reconcile these in the development of land policies involving allotment, inheritance, territorial boundaries, natural resources, and communal lands.[21]

Under the duress of government interference and the rapid diminishment of the Grand River tract land base, the fluidity of movement and migrations of clan relatives between the homeland territories and Grand River are increasingly cut off, and the focus of Confederacy chiefs becomes more localized.[22] Some ethnohistorians and anthropologists have oversimplified interpretations of the inward or more internal focus of the Confederacy's attention to Grand River concerns, rather than broader Haudenosaunee concerns, during the era of resettlement.[23] It is important to counter assumptions that a localized orientation simply characterized the Confederacy's outlook from the point of its reestablishment at Grand River. Analyses of this time period must attend to realities involving the reduction of the Grand River tract to one-sixteenth or 4.8 percent of its original size in sixty-three years (1784–1847), as well as to how this history of land reduction served to consume rather than fortify Six Nations' financial resources.[24] Although the urgency of these circumstances clearly legitimated attention to more localized priorities, these generalizations also miss how Haudenosaunee knowledge was actually sustained through the councils' apparently inward ceremonial focus under the extreme pressures of this era.

Notably, the nineteenth-century era also coincides with the acceleration of the federally mandated residential school system. The system was in full swing in Canada and the United States by the late 1800s. What it did, among other things, was to target, through children, the elimination of traditional spirituality and Native languages, two aspects of Haudenosaunee culture that animated, supported, and reinforced the continuity of clan relationships.

By the turn of the twentieth century the Indian Act had been amended so that it included stringent provisions for the implementation of federally regulated elective band council governments on reserves. In 1924, this system was forcibly installed at Six Nations when armed Royal Canadian Mounted Police officers deposed the Confederacy Council and remained in the community to ensure the transition to the elective system. This contributes to intensifying displacement from understanding clan relationships, both within and outside the boundaries of Six Nations, as the clan-based Confederacy system is decentralized, forced to operate "underground," and is, therefore, no longer overtly accessible as an immediate aspect of political life in the community.

ADDRESSING THESE CONSEQUENCES THROUGH THE HAUDENOSAUNEE CLAN SYSTEM

Important academic work that elaborated on the intellectual and political integrity of North American indigenous nations increasingly accelerated by the 1980s.[25] Numerous indigenous and allied scholars continue to advance distinct understandings of Haudenosaunee sovereignty and nationhood within the realm of academic literature.[26] Coinciding with philosophical and practical articulations of nation-based autonomy that have been maintained in Six Nations communities, these scholarly efforts reiterate the imperative of relational responsibilities, spiritual reciprocity, and connectedness among human beings, the land, and other elements of Creation as consistent with Haudenosaunee principles.[27] A number of these efforts further clarify sharp distinctions or contrasts between Haudenosaunee- and Western European–derived concepts of sovereignty, emphasizing tendencies for the latter to be framed by notions of individualism, hierarchy, unidirectional power, absolute authority, materialism, coercion, and domination.[28] These valuable analyses of indigenous nationalism may be complemented and enhanced by consideration of how knowledge of Haudenosaunee clans might encourage a constructive force among future generations, and thus how active and knowledgeable clans remain integral to contemporary assertions of Haudenosaunee nationhood and citizenship.

Within Six Nations community contexts, whether expressed routinely in the course of everyday life or defiantly in direct clashes with the state, the inherent sovereignty of the Haudenosaunee has been continually articulated as the right to determine citizenship, leadership, and freedom of movement within territorial homelands, and the guaranteed respect for distinct spirituality, traditions, and values; none of these were to be viewed as constrained by the imposition of Canada and the United States as nation-states.[29] This sovereign status, the Haudenosaunee have historically claimed, was never relinquished. It was acknowledged in the earliest treaties, such as the Guswentah, or Two Row Wampum, which established the parameters of coexistence with Dutch, French, and English colonists in the 1600s. In the case of the Six Nations people who came to Grand River, Ontario, specifically, this sovereignty was affirmed, once again, through their alliance with the British and through Grand River tract land negotiations with the Crown following the American Revolution.[30]

By no means is the intent of this article to diminish or downplay the overall consequences of colonial intrusion on the recognition and expression of Haudenosaunee nationhood, nor is it to suggest that in light of continuity such understandings have been seamlessly and uncontentiously preserved. Contemporary community-based education initiatives promoting Haudenosaunee traditionalism among a broader base of the Six Nations population at Grand River and beyond continue to encounter crucial questions regarding the meanings, functioning, and protocol associated with clan-based paradigms of citizenship and leadership. For example, there continues to be disparity in views related to the practical roles of women and clan mothers in leadership, the assignment of clan names to individuals, the adoption of "clanless" citizens, the valid expression of consensus, the status of adopted nations, and the reattribution of "borrowed" Confederacy titles to their appropriate extended-family lineages.[31] Although matters such as these have incurred varying levels of debate and discord, their eventual reconciliation will come from none other than Haudenosaunee citizens.[32] When understood in these terms, our vantage point shifts from a focus on these concerns solely as by-products of colonial processes that compromise Haudenosaunee sociopolitical integrity, to an acknowledgment of these matters, and citizens' ongoing engagement with them, as internal "domestic issues," constituted in inherent, emergent, and practical expressions of Haudenosaunee nationhood.[33]

The vantage point that specifically situates our consideration of yet-to-be resolved questions and concerns also enhances our appreciation of the ongoing efforts of citizens to promote continuity in Haudenosaunee cultural and political distinctiveness. Despite some rather pessimistic portraits of colonial frameworks as ingrained almost to the point of "naturalization" in indigenous consciousness, there is mounting indication of outright rejection and increasing subversion of the influence and power of nation-state regimes.[34] The maintenance of the Haudenosaunee clan-based system of Confederacy governance throughout almost four centuries of colonial oppression is one of the most decisive examples; however, there are other, potentially less obvious ways in which to consider indices of cultural continuity and colonial subversion.

Haudenosaunee clan-based knowledge has withstood efforts to reduce our nationhood to the racial constructs perpetuated by settler nation-states. Undoubtedly it will be the further undoing of these ideas despite varying levels of their internalization by many people. Considerable progress has been made in the area of reconciling identity and citizenship according to clan-based paradigms. For example, during the four years (1996–2000) I spent researching grassroots educational initiatives that promoted Haudenosaunee languages and traditionalism at Grand River, I witnessed the broadening of community awareness of the illegitimacy of the Indian Act as a direct result of educators' efforts in disseminating information about Haudenosaunee clans. This is not to imply that it was possible to convey understandings of the full scope of knowledge involving clans to initiative participants within the limitations of a workshop or a succession of educational sessions; traditionalist educators were often quick to impress upon participants that learning is an ongoing process, continually elaborated throughout the course of one's lifetime. Even so, once participants gained further access and exposure to the continuity of a culturally distinct constitution of identity and belonging, it was remarkable how quickly the ideological authority of the 130-year-old Indian Act was stripped away. As this ideological shift continues to spread among a broader base of the Six Nations population, a marked increase in its practical expression, and its application to the resolution of outstanding concerns and grievances (both internally and with the state), can only be expected.

In the area of the continuity of clan-based leadership, despite its deposition at Six Nations in 1924, the Confederacy Council has continued to maintain its responsibility to, and recognition by, Haudenosaunee people in Canada and the United States. At Grand River specifically, it has played a crucial, though largely unpublicized, role in the ongoing protection of Six Nations' distinct rights, which the Indian Act–mandated elective band council system was specifically designed to eliminate. The Confederacy Council remains connected to, rather than separate from, Haudenosaunee cosmology.[35] Thus, the Great Law continues to be asserted through the Confederacy Council's maintenance, despite settler governments' refusal to recognize Haudenosaunee sovereignty. In reality this council continues to practice nation-to-nation diplomacy with the new governments that have arisen in Haudenosaunee territories.[36] Upholding a central commitment to the people, it continues to exert its power in the present, notwithstanding historic attempts at interference and disruption.

Grappling with the ongoing history of colonial coercion and interference has meant confronting the legacy encouraged by these processes. Part of this legacy is reflected by vacancies in chief titles and associated Confederacy offices; it is also reflected in a few remaining instances of duplicated titles on the Canadian and American sides of the border. Efforts to address these circumstances reaffirm the fundamental significance of clan mothers charged with these responsibilities. These efforts relatedly promote cohesion by reaffirming the significance of clan relatives working together across Haudenosaunee communities in order to enhance the coherence of the Confederacy system.

By extension, emphasis must also be placed on the way clans reflect and validate a continuity that is also strategic, particularly in association with much politicized processes of contesting and resisting colonial constructs. They provide a means for reconciling Haudenosaunee citizenship that has remained consistent in comparison to the enormous inconsistencies of our treatment by nation-state citizenship regimes. In Canada, these approaches have moved through eras of total exclusion, provisional enfranchisement, and unilateral imposition, which incrementally established contingencies based upon what Six Nations peoples, as well indigenous peoples more broadly, were required to give up. These terms of "Canadian citizenship" resided not in the reinforcement or reconciliation of ongoing relationships but rather as a regulatory regime conditional upon the relinquishing of lands, socio-economic and political structures, rights, languages, traditions, children, dignity, and so forth.

Along with his renowned proficiency in illuminating the cultural history of Haudenosaunee traditionalism, Chief Thomas was also adept at promoting its relevance to contemporary circumstances. According to Thomas, Canadian Prime Minister Pierre Trudeau publicly stated to Aboriginal attendees of a First Ministers conference in 1983, "that if you no longer speak your language and no longer practice your culture, then you have no right to demand aboriginal rights or claim land from the Canadian government, because you are assimilated with the ruling power."[37] Recognition of such strategies continually reinforced Thomas's convictions about the crucial significance of maintaining Haudenosaunee languages and traditionalism. Sago:ye:satah similarly felt that these sentiments were another reason to spur people into action, "We must be aware that this is one of the main ways the government has justified stealing our land and denying us our rights is by trying to change us. It's just like destroying evidence, so that they can continue to maintain that we have no claim to sovereignty."[38] Notably, arguments almost identical to Trudeau's enabled a US federal court ruling that denied cultural damage reparations to Alaskan Native communities directly affected by the enormous oil spill caused by the *Exxon Valdez*.[39] Such conjecture also presented a formidable obstacle in Gitxan and Wet'suwet'en's battle with the Supreme Court of Canada to confirm legal recognition of their title to their unceded territory in *Delgamuukw v. the Queen*.[40]

In an interview on a local radio-show broadcast publicizing the Onondaga Beaver clan research initiative at Six Nations in 1998, Sago:ye:satah related the significance of Haudenosaunee clan-based continuity to community residents:

> Because we believe that your identity is where your rights flow from. Myself as my traditional identity I have rights from that. As my Canadian identity, my name Kenny Hill as they call me, I don't have many rights in that sense because we're all under the Indian Act and in the words of the government with that English name, so we really don't have the rights that flow from our treaties; the only way we can access those rights is through that traditional identity and the respect for the things that flow from those treaties and all those concepts that inform them, that's where really our rights flow from.[41]

Referring to the significance of his "Indian name," indicative of his clan affiliation, Hill establishes the crucial connection of clan identity and citizenship to Haudenosaunee autonomy affirmed through treaties and the exercising of treaty rights. Such assertions are a vital means to question and counter the Indian Act's legitimacy in maintaining the power to limit, through its imposed terms and criteria, the Canadian government's fiduciary responsibility by legislatively delineating all "Indians" who are of federal concern. Evidenced by arguments outlined previously in this article, alongside the observations of Chief Thomas presented in the preceding text, it is well-known that the rigidity and assimilative orientation of this legislation has always been intended to extinguish these very fiduciary obligations by promoting domestication and extinguishment of indigenous nationhood. On a broader scale, recognition of these strategies has become prominent in indigenous assessments of federal "healing" and "justice" initiatives. Responses to these initiatives have continued to advance arguments that as long as classifications of indigenous nationhood and identities are defined and legally/politically recognized in terms set by colonial regimes, opportunities for reconciliation will continue to be "compromised if not fully limited."[42] Regarding Six Nations specifically, Hill and Thomas agree that what the government is trying to say when it comes to rights or land claims is that the Six Nations people of today are not the same as those who migrated from their homelands. Thus Haudenosaunee clan knowledge promoted through education and research becomes an important means of verifying this continuity.

Haudenosaunee clans continue to verify the continuity of peoples' citizenship in nations that have long predated the consolidation of Canada and the United States as nation-states and the formation of legal, political, and economic institutions in either country. It is imperative that not only Six Nations peoples but also Canadian and American citizens recognize this reality more widely. Within broader legal and political arenas, such acknowledgment helps to clarify why it is so important that negotiations involving lands and land rights occur with delegates of the Confederacy governance structure with whom treaties were made historically. In these matters, state-sanctioned band councils, whether installed forcibly or welcomed favorably in Six Nations reserve/reservation communities, simply did not exist during this era and reasonably have no jurisdiction. In legitimating claims based on nation-states' unfulfilled responsibilities and inconsistencies, the significance of appeals to the continuity of Haudenosaunee traditionalism is substantive and cannot be dismissed as recent exercise in "cultural invention, nationalist fabrication or symbolic abstraction."[43] Presently at Six Nations there can be no better example of this than the ongoing negotiations between the Haudenosaunee Confederacy and the Canadian government over Grand River tract land rights. After refusing to recognize the Confederacy's jurisdiction for eighty-four years, government representatives now contend that their willingness to enter into negotiations was a direct result of the Confederacy's support of recent Six Nations community efforts to press for the clarification of title to disputed Grand River tract lands. This moment potentially represents an important turning point in Haudenosaunee history; it is an opportunity to continue to interrupt and dislodge the unidirectional flow of power that has historically characterized interactions with nation-states that is a direct result of Haudenosaunee continuity.

The point is that the meanings, connections, structures, functions, and practices associated with Haudenosaunee clan knowledge and the clan system are still living—and solidly remain in and of the present—even while work is being done to enable this system to be understood further and exercised more extensively. In our Onondaga Beaver clan research initiative, and in other such initiatives that are ongoing within and across Haudenosaunee communities, efforts to reclaim and reassert those land-based connections and that connectedness among peoples as relatives and families hinge upon how clans comprise the value of relationships and the responsibilities to console, comfort, support, and mediate as conveyed in the teaching about their origins and according to the Great Law. We can engage these principles and frameworks in promoting broader education and awareness only because they continue to be asserted in the ceremonials of thanksgiving and condolence that have been carefully protected and maintained for centuries by our people.

Although understandings of Haudenosaunee identity and leadership through clan relationships have been diminished by the complex and ongoing colonial processes in Canada and the United States, they have not been destroyed. In constituting our political and cultural distinctiveness, clans anchor the historical rootedness of our nationhood on this land base; validating a continuity will be integral to our future. This in turn can help demonstrate that Six Nations people are not yet assimilated and have maintained a viable means to contest and resist colonial constructs. There have always been Haudenosaunee citizens on both sides of the border—clan mothers, chiefs, faith keepers, traditional orators and historians, educators, language speakers, elders, adults, youth, and children—who have maintained the continuity of this cultural knowledge and are among the Haudenosaunee's most invaluable resources. Actively promoting Haudenosaunee clan research and education in Canada and the United States will assist in accessing information, facilitating dialogue, and sharing histories with the ultimate objective to learn about and link clan relatives to each other in order to advance the cohesion of Haudenosaunee people. This will enhance our ability to reach across whatever legislation, border, or boundary that would try to divide us.

Acknowledgments

This article, and the larger project of which it is part, would not exist without the cooperation I've received from those who work so tirelessly to preserve and promote Haudenosaunee traditionalism at Six Nations. Nyá:węh to all the members of the Onondaga Beaver clan, especially Sago:ye:satah and his family and Tatgahdohs, who taught me much about belonging and its requisite responsibilities. I will always cherish the memories and the mentorship I received from John Mohawk and Chief Thomas. I am indebted to my good friends, who also happen to be my fellow colleagues from Six Nations, Sue Hill, Rick Monture, and Dawn Martin-Hill, for their constant support. Thank you very much to Rob Innes for the invitation to be included in this volume and for the ensuing patience this required. Thank you also to the editors of *AICRJ*, whose editorial suggestions helped to improve the quality of this article.

NOTES

1. Taiaiake Alfred, *Peace, Power and Righteousness: An Indigenous Manifesto* (Toronto: Oxford University Press, 1999), quoted in Taiaiake Alfred and Jeff Corntassel, "Being Indigenous: Resurgences Against Contemporary Colonialism," *Government and Opposition* 40 (2005): 611, http://web.uvic.ca/~gta/pdfs/goop_166.pdf (accessed 25 August 2006).

2. Sago:ye:satah, telephone conversation with author, 5 December 2009.

3. Patricia Monture-Angus, "Community Governance and Nation Re-Building: Centering Indigenous Learning and Research," 2004, 7, http://www.fngovernance .org/pdf/MontureNationReBuilding.pdf (accessed 10 October 2007).

4. Despite my prior involvement in the Onondaga Beaver clan research initiative upon arriving at the University at Buffalo, I was still far from grasping the broader significance of these efforts. This was one area where John Mohawk really helped me. One of the skills he was notorious for among his students was that you could give him your most rudimentary, unformulated ideas, and he would listen to them, take them, and craft them into the most eloquent research questions or arguments. Then he'd subtly spin them back to you, in such a way that would leave you impressed with yourself for having come up with them in the first place. It was hard not to get excited over John's passion for ideas, and, for those of us who were his students, these ideas remain imprinted on so much of our work. He affected so many people's abilities to "see" the important connection between local and global indigenous action, something that remains very difficult for many to conceive and convey.

He maintained an unshakable faith in our ability to reason; the pragmatism of Haudenosaunee teachings and spiritualism; the transformative capacity of consciousness; and the power of words, oration, and persuasion, not only to reiterate experiences but also as our most important tools to mould new realities and propel action in order to enhance our continuity. Much of the knowledge John promoted wasn't his alone; and he was always clear about this. This is reflected in just how much apparently "authorless" or unattributed John Mohawk writing is currently in circulation. John always emphasized that Haudenosaunee knowledge has been collectively and dynamically produced across infinite generations of peoples, while remaining consistently rooted in this land base. He has nevertheless made crucial contributions to this knowledge. I continue to be inspired by his ability to get it across.

5. Sago:ye:satah, conversation with author, Six Nations of Grand River Territory, 1 August 2008.

6. Deborah Doxtator, "What Happened to the Iroquois Clans?: A Study of Clans in Three Nineteenth-Century Rotinonhsyonni Communities" (PhD diss., University of Western Ontario, 1996), 6. In her dissertation, Doxtator further articulates the historical significance of land to the Haudenosaunee clan system, as well as to Haudenosaunee nationhood:

> Before the nineteenth century the Rotinonhsyonni [Haudenosaunee] people had great ethnic diversity among their clans. The biological lineage of individuals in the centuries prior to the 1800s was not as important as the physical presence of the person sharing the common land of the community. . . . In Rotinonhsyonni thought, an individual without a community and a land base to which to belong was "socially dead." For a nation not to have people organized

into communities with which to maintain control over territories was to be "no longer a people" . . . . Without people in clans to use and connect with the land, the nation would cease to exist. In many ways the land, its nature and the kinds of relationships that the people had with it, influenced the social organization of the Rotinonhsyonni people (54–55).

7. Confederacy Chief Jake Thomas was a highly respected historian and orator of Haudenosaunee traditionalism, in his own community and in other Six Nations and Aboriginal communities across North America. He was fluent in five of the Six Nations languages. Thomas dedicated a large part of his life to promoting Haudenosaunee traditionalism and languages though education and educational resource development. Part of his commitment to facilitating Native and non-Native access to Haudenosaunee knowledge involved translating and reciting a number of central Haudenosaunee teachings into English. In the 1990s Thomas gave three public recitations of the Great Law of Peace in English at Six Nations. These recitations, from nine to twelve days in duration, provided opportunities for those not fluent in a Haudenosaunee language to access this foundational teaching about the historic foundation of the Haudenosaunee confederacy. I am very grateful for the chance I had to work with Thomas when conducting my dissertation research. He passed away in 1998 at the age of 76.

8. Chief Thomas, interview by author, Six Nations of Grand River, 13 August 1997.

9. Lottie Keye, conversation with author, Hamilton Regional Indian Centre, Hamilton, ON, 16 January 2001.

10. Doxtator, "What Happened to the Iroquois Clans?" 58.

11. The following 4 quotations are from the Thomas interview; the emphasis is his.

12. See John C. Mohawk, *Iroquois Creation Story: John Arthur Gibson and J. N. B. Hewitt's Myth of the Earth Grasper* (Buffalo, NY: Mohawk Publications, 2005), 85–96. In the Gibson version, the young man who initiates the system takes his leave of the people with this parting message of reassurance:

"That which we have arranged," the young man said, "is so durable that it will last as long as our families will continue to exist. It will last as long as the grasses grow and the trees grow. It will last as long as the rivers flow. Now I have finished arranging your affairs."

Similar to the Thomas rendition, as the people begin to disperse they are reminded that "it shall continue to be in the future, that there will always be clans on both sides of the river" (96).

13. Ibid., xi.

14. Ibid., viii, v.

15. See Rick J. Ponting and Cora J. Voyageur, "Multiple Points of Light: Grounds for Optimism among First Nations in Canada," in *Hidden in Plain Sight: Contributions of Aboriginal Peoples to Canadian Identity and Culture*, ed. David R. Newhouse, Cora J. Voyageur, and Dan Brown (Toronto: University of Toronto Press, 2005), 425–54. Here Ponting and Voyageur note the prominence of a "deficit paradigm" in social science treatment of First Nations, emphasizing suffering, conflict, problems, and First Nations' overall status as victims. They argue that such tendencies often preclude consideration of evidence of success, positive developments, and grounds for optimism in First Nations' struggles to "loosen the grip of colonialism."

16. Doxtator, "What Happened to the Iroquois Clans?" 217–75.

17. Ibid., 232.

18. See Alfred, *Peace, Power and Righteousness*; Taiaiake Alfred, "Sovereignty," in *Sovereignty Matters: Locations of Contestation and Possibility in Indigenous Struggles for Self-Determination*, ed. Joanne Barker (Lincoln: University of Nebraska Press, 2005), 33–50; and Taiaiake Alfred, *Wasase: Indigenous Pathways of Action and Freedom* (Peterborough, ON: Broadview Press, 2005); Susan Hill, "SKANATA YOYONNIH—One Village Has Been Made: The Nineteenth Century Consolidation of the Six Nations Grand River Territory." Paper presented at the Canadian Historical Association—85th Annual Meeting, York University, Toronto, 26 May 2006; Kahente Horn-Miller, "Otiyaner: The 'Women's Path' through Colonialism," *Atlantis* 29, no. 2 (2005): 57–68; Kathleen Jamieson, *Indian Women and the Law in Canada: Citizens Minus* (Ottawa, ON: Advisory Council on the Status of Women, 1978); Dawn Martin-Hill, "She No Speaks and Other Colonial Constructs of 'The Traditional Woman,'" in *Strong Women Stories: Native Vision and Community Survival*, ed. Kim Anderson and Bonita Lawrence (Toronto: Sumach Press, 2003), 106–20; Rick Monture, "'In the Free and Independent Manner Natural to Indians': Joseph Brant and the Translation(s) of Iroquois Sovereignty." Paper presented at American Studies Association Meetings, Washington, DC, November 2005; Rick Monture, "'Sovereigns of the Soil': Joseph Brant, Deskaheh and the Haldimand Deed of 1784." Paper presented at the Annual Conference on Iroquois Research, Rensselaerville, NY, October 2006; Patricia Monture-Angus, "Women and Risk: Aboriginal Women, Colonialism and Correctional Practice," *Canadian Women's Studies* 19, no. 1–2 (1999): 24–29; Audra Simpson, "Paths Toward a Mohawk Nation: Narratives of Citizenship and Nationhood in Kahnawake," in *Political Theory and The Rights of Indigenous Peoples*, ed. Duncan Ivison, Paul Patton, and Will Sanders (Cambridge: Cambridge University Press, 2000), 113–36; Audra Simpson, *To the Reserve and Back Again: Kahnawake Mohawk Narratives of Self, Home and Nation* (Duke University Press, forthcoming).

19. Bonita Lawrence, "Indian Status and Entitlement," in *Mixed Blood Urban Native Peoples and Indigenous Nationhood*, ed. Bonita Lawrence (Vancouver: University of British Columbia Press, 2004), 209–26.

20. Ibid., 223.

21. Hill, "SKANATA YOYONNIH"; Susan Hill, *The Clay We Are Made Of: An Examination of Haudenosaunee Land Tenure on the Grand River Territory* (Winnipeg: University of Manitoba Press, 2010).

22. Doxtator, "What Happened to the Iroquois Clans?" 217–75; Sally M. Weaver, "The Iroquois: The Consolidation of Grand River Reserve in the Mid-Nineteenth Aboriginal Ontario in the Mid-Nineteenth Century, 1847–1875," in *Aboriginal Ontario: Historical Perspectives on the First Nation*, ed. Edward S. Rogers and Donald M. Smith (Toronto: Dundurn Press, 1994), 189–96; Sally M. Weaver, "The Iroquois: The Grand River Reserve in the Late Nineteenth and Early Twentieth Centuries, 1875–1945," in Rogers and Smith, eds., *Aboriginal Ontario*, 233–41.

23. Thomas S. Abler, "Seneca Moieties and Hereditary Chieftainships: The Early Nineteenth-Century Political Organization of an Iroquois Nation," *Ethnohistory* 51, no. 3 (2004): 459–88; William N. Fenton, *Locality as a Basic Factor in the Development of Iroquois Social Structure*, Bureau of American Ethnology Bulletin 149, no. 3 (Symposium on Local Diversity in Iroquois Culture), ed. William N. Fenton (Washington, DC:

Government Printing Office, 1951): 39–54; Annemarie Anrod Shimony, *Conservatism among the Iroquois at the Six Nations Reserve* (Syracuse, NY: Syracuse University Press, 1994).

24. Theresa McCarthy, "'It Isn't Easy': The Politics of Representation, 'Factionalism' and Anthropology in Promoting Haudenosaunee Traditionalism at Six Nations" (PhD diss., McMaster University, 2006), 134.

25. Howard Adams, *A Prison of Grass: Canada from a Native Point of View* (Toronto: New Press, 1975); Akwesasne Notes, ed., *Basic Call to Consciousness* (Summertown, TN: Native Voices, 1978); Russel L. Barsh and James Y. Youngblood, *The Road: Indian Tribes and Political Liberty* (Berkeley: University of California Press, 1980); Harold Cardinal, *The Unjust Society: The Tragedy of Canada's Indians* (Edmonton, AB: Mel Hurtig Publishers, 1969); Harold Cardinal, *The Rebirth of Canada's Indians* (Edmonton, AB: Mel Hurtig Publishers, 1977); Vine Deloria Jr. and Clifford M. Lytle, *The Nations Within: The Past and Future of American Indian Sovereignty* (Austin: University of Texas Press, 1984); George Manuel and Michael Posluns, *The Fourth World: An Indian Reality* (New York: Collier Macmillan Canada, 1974).

26. Alfred, *Peace, Power and Righteousness*; "Sovereignty"; and *Wasase*; Hill, *The Clay We Are Made Of*; Horn-Miller, "Otiyaner: The 'Women's Path' through Colonialism"; Simpson, *To the Reserve and Back Again*; James Tully, *Strange Multiplicity: Constitutionalism in an Age of Diversity* (Cambridge: Cambridge University Press, 1995).

27. Alfred, "Sovereignty."

28. Alfred, "Sovereignty"; and *Wasase*; Monture, "In the Free and Independent Manner Natural to Indians"; "Sovereigns of the Soil"; and "'Much Might Be Written': A Literary and Intellectual History of Six Nations of the Grand River, 1784–2005" (draft of PhD diss., McMaster University, 2007); Simpson, "Paths Toward a Mohawk Nation"; Andrea Smith, *Conquest: Sexual Violence and American Indian Genocide* (Cambridge, MA: South End Press, 2005); Tully, *Strange Multiplicity*.

29. Monture, "In the Free and Independent Manner Natural to Indians."

30. Monture, "Sovereigns of the Soil."

31. McCarthy, "It Isn't Easy," 279–348.

32. For an excellent discussion of adoption practices according to Haudenosaunee principles see Aaron L. VanEvery, "Let Us Put Our Minds Together as One: To Be a Citizen of the Haudenosaunee" (master's thesis, University at Buffalo, 2009).

33. Kahnawake Mohawk anthropologist Audra Simpson has contributed significantly to scholarly recognition of distinctly cultural, experiential, and practical expressions of indigenous nationhood evidenced by Kahnawake residents' efforts to revise their membership code, based on a quantified delineation of blood quantum, to a system that is more aligned with Haudenosaunee values and philosophies. Problematizing colonialism and Euro-Western notions of nationhood as "analytic norms" that have dominated inquiry into these circumstances, Simpson argues that the internal conversations, dialogue, and even the discord constituting this revision process continues to shape Kahnawake's collective sense of self. These interactions, and the meanings and experiences they engage and produce, establish the basis of how indigenous, and specifically Mohawk, nationhood is advanced and effectively reframed in Simpson's work. See Simpson, "Paths Toward a Mohawk Nation"; and *To the Reserve and Back Again*.

34. Bonita Lawrence, "Gender, Race and Regulation of Native Identity in Canada and the United States: An Overview," *Hypatia* 18, no. 2 (2003): 3–4; Joe Sawchuk, "Negotiating an Identity: Métis Political Organizations, the Canadian Government and Competing Concepts of Aboriginality," *American Indian Quarterly* 25, no. 1 (2001): 73–92.

35. Mohawk, *Iroquois Creation Story*, v.

36. Richard Hill Sr., conversation with author, 12 January 2006.

37. Chief Jacob Thomas with Terry Boyle, *Teachings from the Longhouse* (Toronto: Stoddart Publishing Company, 1994), 141–42; Thomas interview.

38. Sago:ye:satah, conversation with author, Six Nations of Grand River Territory, 1 August 2008.

39. Joseph Jorgenson, "Ethnicity, Not Culture? Obfuscating Social Science in the *Exxon Valdez* Oil Spill Case," *American Indian Culture and Research Journal* 19, no. 4 (1995): 5–13.

40. Terry Glavin, "The Fall of Dimlahamid: The Gitxsan Wet'su'weten and the Fallout of the Delgamuukw Decision," in *Nation to Nation: Aboriginal Sovereignty and the Future of Canada*, ed. John Bird, Lorraine Land, and Murry Macadam (Toronto: Irwin Publishing, 2002), 175–85.

41. Sago:ye:satah, *The Monday Night Phone-In Radio Show*, CKRZ 100.3 FM Radio: Voice of the Grand, 21 January 1998.

42. Monture-Angus, "Women and Risk," 25; See Alfred, *Peace, Power and Righteousness*; and *Wasase*.

43. Simpson, "Paths Toward a Mohawk Nation," 115.

AMERICAN INDIAN CULTURE AND RESEARCH JOURNAL 34:2 (2010) 103–124

In the Eyes of the Beholder: Understanding and Resolving Incompatible Ideologies and Languages in US Environmental and Cultural Laws in Relationship to Navajo Sacred Lands

SHARON MILHOLLAND

Meeting the legal requirement and moral imperative to protect both the physical and spiritual integrity of sacred lands depends on applying traditional indigenous philosophies and bodies of knowledge. Although important progress is evident in US environmental and cultural laws written to acknowledge the needs, rights, and interests of Native peoples in the management of sacred lands, a significant amount of work remains. Native peoples still face working within a body of federal law that imposes values, concepts, and languages of the dominant Western society and barely recognizes the traditional Native knowledge systems and values necessary for meaningful protection and access to sacred lands. Consequently, the legal tools intended to protect sacred lands often conflict with traditional indigenous values relative to land and religious practices, privilege the values of the dominant society, erode tribal identity and sovereignty, and leave sacred lands vulnerable to desecration or destruction.

In the United States, federal and state environmental, cultural, and religious freedoms protection laws mandate cooperation and consultation with Native peoples to protect effectively, and permit access to, sacred places on federally held lands. The federal government is charged with a legal trust duty to tribal governments to exercise the highest standards of good faith and integrity in order to protect Indian lands, resources, and cultural heritage. Regardless of this substantial legal framework, Native nations across

Sharon Milholland is a private consultant in Tucson, Arizona. She earned a PhD in American Indian studies from the University of Arizona and has fifteen years of experience managing cultural resources on federal lands in the southwestern United States.

the United States have repeatedly expressed concerns that consultation and collaboration efforts with state and federal land-management agencies are inconsistent and inadequate.[1] They believe that land management prescriptions and practices are unilaterally determined, geographically limited in scope, and not culturally compatible.[2] Native nations complain that various forms of industrial, commercial, and recreational development continue to threaten essential sacred places.[3]

For example, in the state of Georgia, the Muscogee people are battling proposed interstate highway expansion that threatens to restrict access to, and damage, mound temples and historic villages in the Ocmulgee Old Fields.[4] In Nevada, the Western Shoshone Nation is fighting to protect its sacred Yucca Mountain from transformation into this country's central repository for nuclear waste.[5] Southeastern California is the stage for the Quechan tribe's struggle to halt the permit for an open-pit gold mine that threatens to obliterate sacred sites and a sacred trail network in Indian Pass.[6] In the Pacific, Native Hawaiians are fighting telescope development on top of their elder ancestor, Mauna Kea. This volcano on the island of Hawaii is the highest point in Pacific Polynesia and is the "highest portal to the Hawaiian Universe."[7] In Alaska, the Gwich'in are fighting proposed oil drilling in the National Arctic Wildlife Refuge. These grounds are sacred because they are habitat for caribou, the very source of Gwich'in subsistence and nationhood.[8]

To Native peoples, compliance with existing environmental and cultural laws by itself does not result in meaningful and effective sacred lands protection and access. Intent and interpretation of the language of existing environmental and cultural laws are at issue. Effective strategies for sacred lands protection and access are those that scrutinize existing law and management practice for incompatible and hegemonic ideologies and languages. Resolving the problem of incompatible ideologies and languages in laws treating sacred lands can include tribal governments working with Congress to integrate traditional indigenous worldviews directly into the law. More importantly, resolution depends on cultivating a willingness among legislators, public land managers, project proponents, and stakeholders to commit to the practice of fulfilling sacred lands' protection needs according to traditional indigenous philosophies prior to drafting new legislation or implementing negotiations or environmental evaluations mandated in existing US law.[9]

In this article, I raise a few examples of incompatible concepts and languages in US federal environmental and cultural laws affecting the management of indigenous sacred lands. I explain these examples by describing the management of a selection of Navajo (Diné) sacred places and elsewhere. Through fundamental concepts rooted in postcolonial theory and critical race theory, I suggest an intellectual framework for understanding why traditional indigenous values and knowledge are marginalized and why incompatible Western values have been privileged and enshrined in US law and policy in relationship to the management of Native sacred lands. Finally, I want to introduce you to *hozho*, the Navajo philosophy of harmony and natural beauty, which is intimately related to the Navajo orientation to their land.[10] This is an abstract, complex, highly spiritual doctrine of Navajo philosophy and spiritual practice. The environmental and cultural laws and policy of the United States are not inclusive of the philosophy of *hozho*. By considering the Navajo traditional philosophy of *hozho*, I discuss how incorporating traditional indigenous values and knowledge in sacred lands management can resolve values conflict for Native peoples, as well as raise some complex issues regarding the introduction of traditional cultural and spiritual concepts into the language of tribal or federal law.

INCOMPATIBLE IDEOLOGIES AND LANGUAGES BETWEEN US ENVIRONMENTAL OR CULTURAL LAWS AND TRADITIONAL NAVAJO VALUES AND KNOWLEDGE

Native worldviews regarding the sacredness of the land are essential when making decisions about the land. Certain distinctive landscapes are valued as an essential and vital part of Indian being, and a moral duty to protect these places exists in order to secure the future survival of the earth, sun, stars, and all forms of life.[11] "A culture's vitality is literally dependent on individuals [living] in community with the natural world."[12] The land's features, and the sense of place and kinship they create, are central to the identity of a Native individual and a people.[13]

> The land with its water, plants, and animals is a spiritual creation put into motion by the gods in their wisdom. These elements are here to help, teach, and protect through an integrated system of beliefs that spell out man's relationship to man, nature, and the supernatural. To ignore these teachings is to ignore the purpose of life, the meaning of existence.[14]

> The importance Native Americans traditionally place on "connecting" with their place is not a romantic notion that is out of step with the times; instead, it is the quintessential ecological mandate of our time.[15]

Navajo Sacred Lands and Traditional Philosophy

Sacred places, belief systems, and spiritual practices are unique to each Native culture. To the Navajo, sacred lands generally include locations mentioned in oral tradition, places where something supernatural has happened; plants, minerals, and healing waters may be collected; or humans communicate with the supernatural world by means of prayers and offerings.[16] A special type of sacred place is the "built" Anasazi site, such as masonry pueblos, burial areas, or rock image panels.[17] Because warfare was an important part of Navajo life, ceremonial sites connected to battle are also sacred.[18] In terms of their physical form, most sacred places are distinctive features on the natural landscape.

The Navajo people describe the perimeter of their homeland, or the Diné Bikeyah, with four sacred mountains. The mountains are where the natural and spiritual universes join, and they embody the values that are most pervasive in Navajo life: "healing the sick, protecting the people and their goods, bringing rain for crops and livestock, and insuring tranquility in life."[19] These mountains are essential to Navajo being and a significant source of food, water, medicinal plants, and places of worship.[20] The four sacred mountains marking the terrestrial boundaries of their traditional territory are the most powerful of the Navajo sacred landscapes.[21]

> Our Navajo spiritual and social laws are represented by the sacred mountains, as well as the four seasons and the four parts of the day. The foundations of our rules and laws for our lives are within our sacred mountains, the four seasons and the four parts of the day. The sacred mountains were placed here to give us the understanding of our strength and courage. They shield us from evil, harm, and danger. . . . We think of them as our home, as the foundation of our hogan and our life.[22]

Traditional Indigenous Values and Knowledge Are Marginalized

The complex environmental and cultural legislative and regulatory framework governing indigenous sacred places that are in the stewardship of the United States does not always recognize the Native system of moral values, elegantly expressed as "the quintessential ecological mandate of our time," as an obvious and justifiable source of guiding principles. Rather, environmental and cultural protection laws embody the ideologies and languages of Western science and property law. Legislators defined sacred places, religious objects, and American Indian human remains as "historic property" or "cultural resources." They also defined Western scientists as the most qualified authorities to understand and care for this property through laws like the 1906 Antiquities Act, the 1966 National Historic Preservation Act (NHPA), and the Archaeological Resources Protection Act.[23]

At the time Congress enacted these statutes, legislators did not take into account the unique values and philosophies of Native peoples, such as *hozho*, in the treatment of this cultural property.[24] In the United States, property law is defined in accordance with the dominant society's values, and the ability to hold property is consistent with the ability to wield power.[25] Consequently, decision makers for federal land-management agencies largely privilege scientific, recreational, and economic values over indigenous traditional values in managing cultural property. Whether by deliberate or inadvertent decisions or actions, the federal government has culturally constructed, socially sanctioned, and legally legitimized the removal of the voices and values of Native peoples from the management of their cultural property. In the end, the legal tools designed to manage sacred lands conflict with traditional indigenous values relative to land and religious practice, privilege the values of the dominant society, erode tribal identity and sovereignty, and leave sacred lands vulnerable to desecration or destruction.

Postcolonial Theory, Critical Race Theory, and Indigenous Sacred Lands

To understand why traditional indigenous values and knowledge are marginalized, and why incompatible Western values have been privileged and enshrined in US law and policy in relationship to the management of Native sacred lands, I examine this legal architecture under the lens of critical theory. Postcolonial theory and critical race theory can be linked together to form an intellectual framework for analysis of American Indian affairs because the subjects of race and political standing for indigenous peoples are unavoidably intertwined.[26] American Indians are a distinct racial group that entered into formal treaties with the US government on a nation-to-nation basis. Understanding how social, political, and legal institutions in the United States create and maintain hierarchical power structures with Native governments, and then fail to resolve power and values conflicts, can be explained through central tenets emerging in these two bodies of theory.

Postcolonial theory is a rapidly evolving field of scholarship generally sharing skepticism about value neutrality in Western institutions. The term *postcolonial* is inclusive of a wide spectrum of definitions of power-holding Western institutions and ideologies in societies having colonial histories. Although "post" colonialism suggests that colonial practices and ideologies are erased, colonized lands and peoples actually have residual colonial institutions, including government, courts, education, mass media, and the church, that continue to shape national identity even in a postcolonial political era.[27] Exploring the nature and degree of how the institutions in power sustain and legitimize their political positions is one focus of postcolonial theory.[28] The concept of incommensurability is the condition in which dominant Western institutions construct concepts and languages are so incompatible with non-Western values and goals that these are leveraged into the margins, and the dominant society maintains power in order to privilege its own values and goals.[29]

Critical race theory is another rapidly evolving intellectual tradition expanding across multiple disciplines that essentially questions the existence of neutral principles of constitutional law. *Black's Law Dictionary* defines it as "a reform movement within the legal profession . . . whose adherents believe that the legal system has disempowered minorities. Critical race theorists observe that even if the law is couched in neutral language, it cannot be neutral because those who fashion it have their own subjective perspective that, once enshrined in law, has disadvantaged minorities and even perpetuated racism."[30] Critical race theory emerged in the mid-1970s among legal scholars who built on the insights of critical legal studies and feminism in response to a need for a new theory to address racism occurring after the civil rights era of the 1960s. Critical race scholars argue that the practice of relying on precedent in civil rights litigation lacks effectiveness in securing rights for people of color in any sustained way. Critical race scholars also claim that arguments for rights for minorities have procedural solutions focused on the appearance of equality rather than substantive solutions focused on actual equality. Further miring equal rights advancement for minorities, those rights are usually limited when they conflict with the interests of the powerful.[31]

The first assumption of critical race scholarship is that for people of color racism is commonplace and can be encountered in aversive or deliberate form.[32] Second, critical race theory holds that the concept of race is a social invention and that these social concepts of race are enshrined in the law.[33] Third, critical race theory recognizes the "voice of color" as a unique collection of personal stories of individuals who have been ignored or alienated by the dominant institutions.[34] Critical race theorists posit that progress to eradicate racism occurs only when it is to the advantage of the dominant society to do so, a concept known as *interest convergence*.[35] The concept of interest convergence emerged from the work of Derrick Bell, one of the intellectual founders of critical race theory.[36] In his analysis of the 1954 US Supreme Court ruling in *Brown v. Board of Education*, he asserts that civil rights advances always coincide with the self-interest of the dominant society.[37] Conversely, impediments to civil rights advancement can also be rationalized by the self-interest of the dominant society.

Incommensurability, Interest Convergence, and Indigenous Sacred Lands

The concepts of incommensurability and interest convergence are evident in US environmental and cultural protection laws relative to the preservation of indigenous sacred places. A very broad example of incommensurability in this body of law is the distinction between the cultural environment and the natural environment, rather than considering them as integrated. This body of law also transforms spiritual responsibilities and "the quintessential ecological mandate of our time" to a set of bureaucratic procedures often just giving the appearance of adequate treatment. One of the most important specific demonstrations of incommensurability and interest convergence in the legal language of sacred lands management is the codification of the fundamental term *sacred land*.

Indigenous sacred lands have generally been described as natural features such as rivers, waterfalls, springs, mountains, buttes and spires, or built features such as burial areas, rock image panels (pictographs or petroglyphs), medicine wheels, vision quest monuments, dance arbors, sweat bath enclosures, and gathering areas where sacred trees, plants, stones, water, or other natural materials are collected.[38] Lawmakers have seized on the physical place and the built environment in order to create a single legal definition that is narrow in scope and not necessarily consistent with how Native peoples regard sacred or holy places. The Sacred Sites Executive Order 13007 (24 May 1996) directs agencies administering federal lands to accommodate access to, and ceremonial use of, Indian religious sites to the "extent practicable" as determined at the discretion of a land manager. This order defines *sacred site* in the following manner: "'Sacred site' means any specific, discrete, narrowly delineated location on Federal land that is identified by an Indian tribe or Indian individual determined to be an appropriately authoritative representative of an Indian religion, as sacred by virtue of its established religious significance to, or ceremonial use by, an Indian religion, provided that the tribe or appropriately authoritative representative of an Indian religion has informed the agency of the existence of such a site."[39]

Another effort to codify the term *sacred* occurs in the Native American Sacred Lands Act (H.R. 2419).[40] This bill strives to enact Executive Order 13007 into law and provide authority to place federal land into trust for the benefit of the Indian tribe or tribes for which the land is considered sacred.[41] The latest draft of this bill was motivated in direct response to the Quechan tribe's fight against the development of an open-pit gold mine in Indian Pass, California. In general, the bill intends to protect indigenous sacred sites from aggressive energy development. Additionally, this bill provides authority for federal land managers to enter into cooperative agreements with tribes in order to manage a sacred landscape on federal land and any lands adjacent to sacred places.[42] The bill also underscores the importance of Native science and oral history as valid lines of evidence supporting the definition and significance of sacred sites. It also provides a more accurate definition of *sacred land*. "The term 'sacred land' means any geophysical or geographical area or feature which is sacred by virtue of its traditional cultural or religious significance or ceremonial use, or by virtue of a ceremonial or cultural requirement, including a religious requirement that a natural substance or product for use in Indian tribal or Native Hawaiian organization ceremonies be gathered from that particular location."[43]

Important criticism remains, however, regarding the sufficiency of this definition and the appropriateness of attempting to codify definitions of the sacred.[44] Arguably, a single statutory definition cannot capture the grand multiplicity of perspectives on what is "sacred." The concept of "sacred" is broad, abstract, and imbued with such deep personal spiritual meaning transcending the physical and the metaphysical, that the notion of creating a single definition of *sacred* extends beyond incommensurable and approaches impossible. Native peoples are qualitatively different from each other in cultural and spiritual heritages. Definitions of what constitutes "sacred" are accordingly particular. The meaning of the sacred, or sacred lands, is relative to individual geographical areas; individual cultures or tribes, bands, clans, or societies within the tribe; or men and women within the tribe.

The "sacred" also embodies a tribe's unique experience and language. Different groups of people may see the same phenomenon as either sacred or secular. Sacredness of a place can derive from human actions of great significance, nonhuman actions of great significance, or from higher powers having revealed themselves to human beings.[45] Stories about places without any obvious physical definitions may still encompass sacredness.[46] Tribal philosophers and scholars who have compared Native faiths and the concept of sacred have concluded that tribes have some general spiritual ideas and practices in common, and that these generalities are more appropriate for secular discussion.[47] For example, a generally accepted broad description of *sacred*, rather than a legal definition, is "something special, something out of the ordinary, and often it concerns a very personal part of each one of us because it describes our dreams, our changing, and our personal way of seeing the world. The sacred is also something that is shared, and this sharing or collective experience is necessary in order to keep the oral traditions and sacred ways vital. . . . Having a guiding vision in common as a people and maintaining it with renewals, ceremonials, rituals, and prayers."[48]

The National Environmental Policy Act of 1969 (NEPA) is one of the most significant pieces of environmental legislation enacted in the United States.[49] It requires rigorous assessment of the ecological and cultural impacts of federal undertakings and preservation of important historical, cultural, and natural aspects of our national heritage. This law contains concepts and language that are incommensurable with Native worldviews on sacred lands management. For example, indigenous cultures and spirituality are intertwined with the land, and the effects of an action on the land also impacts Native culture, spirituality, and sovereignty. Yet the NEPA does not adequately consider the effects of proposed projects on indigenous societies and cultures in a way that is meaningful to Native peoples. Specific examples of concepts and language central to the NEPA in which Indian people must participate and integrate their values, understandings, and bodies of knowledge are *social impact assessment* and *mitigation.*

Social impact assessment is a part of the environmental impact analysis required by the NEPA. Social impact includes "the consequences to human populations of any public or private action—that alter the ways in which people live, work, play, relate to one another, organize to meet their needs and generally cope as members of society. The term also includes cultural impacts involving changes to the norms, values, and beliefs that guide and rationalize their cognition of themselves and their society."[50]

Socioeconomic variables and values primarily define and measure social impact. These variables include per capita income, housing availability, and employment opportunity. Social impact also considers, to a lesser extent, the potential effect to cultural resources. Defining and measuring potential impact to all cultural resources that are important to Native peoples are inadequate. Traditional indigenous values defining environmental and cultural sustainability fall in between the socioeconomic environment described under the NEPA and the cultural environment defined under the NHPA.[51] The effects of a proposed action over sacred places, like highway construction or surface mining, are usually limited to a discussion about material, or archaeological, remains and their intrinsic scientific or educational values. Social impact analysis of effect resulting from an action on sacred natural places does not routinely include discussions of ceremonies, stories, songs, dance, language, technology, or art forms linking land and cultural identity.

The process outlined in NEPA guidelines for defining impact to cultural properties generally includes defining concrete boundaries for places of cultural or spiritual interest. Assigning rigid physical boundaries to places of spirituality and power is an incommensurable practice to Native peoples. For example, the sacred mountains defining the Diné Bikeyah are imbued with such deep personal spiritual meaning transcending the physical and the metaphysical, that the notion of demarking a physical boundary around discrete locations of "sacredness" is an incommensurable concept. "There are no boundaries. Boundaries don't make sense. All ceremonies go to the four sacred mountains. Ceremonies and mountains are inside us. The land is within us and we take it with us. You can't put a boundary around that."[52]

Legal and administrative boundaries ultimately supplant cultural boundaries for sacred lands definition and protection. To illustrate, the Dinétah is a Navajo sacred landscape spanning several hundred square miles in northwestern New Mexico. According to origin stories, the modern Navajo people, Nihookáá Diné, emerged into the modern world within the Dinétah. This region is also the birthplace of some of the most important spiritual beings in Navajo creation. Gobernador Knob, or Ch'ool'íí, a prominent dome-shaped rock outcrop, is the birthplace of Changing Woman. She created the four pairs of Diné who became the originators of the four original clans.[53] The fundamental values for Navajo identity, culture, and "charter of life" are based on Changing Woman's life.[54] Dził Ná oodiłii, commonly known as Huerfano Mesa, is the first terrestrial hogan marking the center of the Navajo world around which the people were to travel.[55] Gobernador Knob and Huerfano Mesa are situated within the Dinétah and are two of the six most sacred and revered mountains in the Navajo physical and metaphysical universe.

Today, the Dinétah is not managed as a whole or culturally defined sacred or heritage landscape. Most of this region is divided among multiple federal, state, and private landowners, as well as the Navajo Nation. The physical and spiritual integrity of the Dinétah as a holy land is deteriorating from large-scale energy, commercial, and recreational development. The Dinétah is located in the San Juan Basin, one of the largest natural gas fields in the United States. Oil and gas production in this region has been ongoing for more than fifty years.[56] In 2003, the US Bureau of Land Management (BLM) approved additional large-scale oil and gas resources development.[57] The proposed wells, pipeline, and road network expand over one hundred thousand acres of northwest New Mexico, including the sacred lands of the Dinétah. The Navajo Nation rejected BLM approval of this proposal, expressing concerns over the adverse effects to Ch'ool'íí and Dził Ná oodiłii and inadequate compliance with federal environmental and cultural protection statutes.[58]

Ch'ool'íí and Dził Ná oodiłii, along with several other important cultural properties within the Dinétah, are individually managed as a discretely defined Area of Critical Environmental Concern (ACEC).[59] An ACEC is a special management designation applied to protect and prevent irreparable damage to important historical, cultural, and scenic values; fish or wildlife resources; or other natural systems or processes, or to protect human life and safety from natural hazards.[60] What is problematic about the ACEC concept relative to sacred landscapes is that an ACEC is a narrowly defined management unit encompassing a natural or human-built physical feature. Consequently, the larger cultural or spiritual landscape is arbitrarily fragmented into noncontiguous "islands of preservation." Additionally, the cultural landscape of the Dinétah is fragmented into multiple federal, tribal, and state management jurisdictions, missions, and management priorities, none of which are organized around the traditional cultural concept of the Dinétah or the traditional philosophy of *hozho*.

Finally, preservation of resources in the ACEC is limited to visible surface features and does not normally include the air space or the substrate.

Although surface gas wells, pumping stations, roads, and pipelines are not permitted inside the ACEC, the sacred properties inside this protective unit are still vulnerable to desecration or destruction as consequences of directional drilling from locations outside of the ACEC boundary or from hydraulic fracturing. Directional drilling is the process of drilling a curved or angled well in order to reach a target that is not directly beneath the drill site, and where a vertical hole may not be optimal, such as when trying to reach a gas reservoir located beneath a body of water.[61] Hydraulic fracturing, or fracking, involves high-pressure injection of fluids into the bedrock to break up formations surrounding the oil and gas, allowing it to flow more freely. According to the Environmental Protection Agency, fracturing fluids can include a long list of hazardous materials and carcinogens, such as diesel fuel and formaldehyde. Fracking can result in physical damage to surface features, and any injected fluids that remain trapped underground are sufficiently toxic to contaminate groundwater.[62]

Another incommensurable NEPA and NHPA concept relative to the treat-ment of sacred places is the idea of "mitigating" adverse effects to sacred lands. Common mitigation measures implemented by project proponents include avoiding the impact altogether, minimizing impacts by limiting the degree or magnitude of the action, rectifying the impact by repairing or restoring the affected environment, reducing or eliminating the impact over time by preservation and maintenance operations, or compensating for the impact by replacing or providing substitute resources or environments.[63] Indigenous sacred lands can be places of spiritual power and can have physical and metaphysical elements or metaphysical or intangible characteristics. Places of power can be esoteric and even dangerous; therefore, the standard alterna-tives provided under NEPA regulations, or standard archaeological practice, cannot apply to sacred lands or traditional cultural properties (TCPs). Tribes argue that mitigating adverse effects to the metaphysical or spiritual compo-nents of sacred lands is not always possible.[64] The only option for mitigating impact to sacred lands is no action at all.[65]

Navajo elders echoed these opinions in reaction to the treatment of Dook'o'oosłííd (San Francisco Peaks), the westernmost of the four Diné sacred mountains, located in northeastern Arizona.[66] Dook'o'oosłííd is a living being created and brought from the underworld by the Holy People. It is the residence of the Holy People who guide and support the Diné. This mountain range is a significant source of food, water, and medicine, and it is an essential place of worship.[67] Navajo elders living near Dook'o'oosłííd first argue that desecration of sacred lands cannot be mitigated. Second, they suggest that if mitigation or "repair" of sacred lands is a possibility, mitigation is not limited to measures applied by non-Navajos like a federal agency or project proponents. Navajo people, specifically medicine people, need to aid the mountain.

> Stop talking about the mountain. Only climb the mountain with song and prayer . . . and the snow will come back. We need to teach this to everyone and our future generations.[68]

Effect to the physical properties or significance of traditional cultural properties cannot be mitigated by any measure other than avoidance. If TCPs are adversely affected their power can be diminished or lost. This loss can be measured by success in healing.[69]

Today, the US Forest Service manages Dook'o'oosłííd. Although there are numerous commercial and recreational uses of forest resources on the mountain, the citizens of the Navajo Nation consider a facilities improvement project at the seven-hundred-acre Snowbowl Ski Area as one of the most egregious threats of desecration to this sacred landscape. More specifically, variable levels of natural snowfall affect ski area operations, and in drought years, snow levels are not sufficient for the Snowbowl to remain open long enough each year to make the business profitable. To augment natural snow levels, Snowbowl management has proposed using reclaimed wastewater from the city of Flagstaff to make artificial snow and then spread it throughout the ski area. Navajo Nation President, Joe Shirley Jr., stated, "To Navajos, the use of effluent on one of its four sacred mountains surrounding the Navajo Nation is an outrageous desecration of a holy site. The proposed development of the sacred *Dook'o'oosłííd* would be like having a child witness the brutal violation of its mother, leaving it emotionally and psychologically scarred forever."[70]

The Navajo Nation along with twelve other tribes sued the Forest Service for its 2005 decision permitting the Snowbowl Ski Area to upgrade its existing facilities and utilize treated sewage effluent for snowmaking.[71] *Navajo Nation et al. v. U.S. Forest Service et al.* (January 2006) is the most recent case testing the Religious Freedom and Restoration Act (RFRA).[72] The 1993 RFRA affirms the language and intent of the American Indian Religious Freedom Act to recognize the inherent right of Native peoples as a group to believe, express, and exercise their religious beliefs and declares it the policy of the United States to protect that right.[73] The RFRA further mandates that the federal government shall not "substantially burden" a person's exercise of religion unless that burden is in the "compelling interest" of the government.

For tribal governments, the legal fight to save Dook'o'oosłííd from desecration evolved into an argument over the definition of *substantial burden.* Tribal attorneys argued that the purity of the water and the soil on the peaks would be compromised by the use of recycled sewage and would, therefore, put a substantial burden on the ability of tribal members to practice their traditional faith.[74] The US District Court judge rejected arguments from the tribes that upgrading existing facilities and dispersing snow made with reclaimed water within the Snowbowl Ski Area present a substantial burden to thirteen Native nations considering the mountains sacred. After a three-member panel of the Ninth Circuit Court of Appeals reversed the lower court's decision and sided with the tribes, the court later reheard the case and, in an eight to three vote, finally rejected the tribal RFRA claim.[75] The court concluded that the Forest Service decision to permit the use of treated effluent does not require Native peoples to act contrary to their religious beliefs.[76]

The Navajo Nation petitioned the US Supreme Court to review the Ninth Circuit ruling. In June 2009, the Supreme Court officially declined to hear the case.[77] This decision leaves the Ninth Circuit's interpretation of substantial burden in place and marks the end of the intertribal, four-year struggle to protect the mountain with a religious freedom argument. This standing judicial interpretation of substantial burden also serves as another example of incommensurability and interest convergence in US law. A dominant Western institution interpreted the concept of substantial burden in a manner that privileges economic and property values. Consequently, this decision impedes the fundamental human right of Native peoples to worship at a reverent natural place that is free of desecration. Snowbowl management remains focused on implementing planned improvements at the resort.[78] Additionally, in October 2009, the Navajo Nation Council voted to consider legislation that would allow the tribe to try to buy the Snowbowl.[79]

Preservation and protection of this nation's most important historic and cultural resources is at the core of the NHPA.[80] The NHPA "represents the cornerstone of federal historic and cultural preservation policy, and it is the most widely litigated federal statute in the area of cultural property law."[81] The National Register of Historic Places (NRHP), authorized by the NHPA, gives recognition to places meeting "historical significance" criteria in American history, architecture, archaeology, engineering, and culture. Places significant to indigenous peoples were not adequately recognized until 1992 when amendments to the act provided explicit recognition of traditional religious and cultural values and places important to American Indians, Alaska Natives, or Native Hawaiian organizations and stated that these may be eligible for National Register listing. For the first time, an indigenous TCP could be defined and evaluated for National Register eligibility against criteria that are inclusive of traditional cultural perspectives and priorities.[82] An important advantage of listing sacred sites on the National Register is that it honors the property and its significance as an indigenous spiritual place and signals the property's worthiness of protection for traditional cultural reasons.

Managers and scholars have raised questions about the effectiveness of listing an indigenous sacred place on the NRHP, designating it as a National Historic Landmark, or naming it to the Endangered Historic Places List, or other similar historic or heritage designation.[83] To illustrate, Mount Graham, or Dzil Nchaa Si An, is a sacred mountain to the Western Apache and is "eligible" for listing on the National Register. This mountain, home to sacred beings, is central to Apache religion and life.[84] Designating this TCP as eligible to the National Register is a positive administrative step toward recognizing the nature, extent, and importance of the mountain as a sacred place, but designation of a property does not guarantee its protection according to the expectations of Native people.

Although Mount Graham is eligible for listing on the National Register, the current land steward, the Forest Service, is considering permit renewal for continued operations of three existing telescopes within the University of Arizona's Mount Graham International Observatory (MGIO). As many as seven telescopes have been approved for construction within the MGIO.[85] According to the Western Apache, construction of the MGIO, and associated infrastructure, has profoundly desecrated Dzil Nchaa Si An and has elicited significant controversy among Apache traditional practitioners, the Forest Service, project proponents, and the local communities over Apache demands for telescope removal.[86] In the end, a National Register listing, or a positive eligibility determination for a sacred mountain like Dzil Nchaa Si An, does not, by itself, define a special protocol for sacred lands management, nor does it necessarily achieve the desired protection of the physical or spiritual integrity of the property. Site protection is a public-interest decision that is made at the discretion of the property manager. Finally, determining the significance of indigenous sacred lands within a Western process is incommensurate with Native values. Listing properties on the National Register follows a rigid bureaucratic process in which disclosure of sensitive traditional cultural information occurs to convince the US government, and the general public, of its significance and that a sacred place is sacred and worthy of preservation.

RESOLVING INCOMPATIBLE IDEOLOGIES AND LANGUAGES

Traditional Navajo Values and Knowledge

Meeting the legal requirement and moral imperative to protect the physical and spiritual integrity of sacred lands depends on traditional indigenous philosophies and bodies of knowledge. For the Navajo Nation, a sacred lands management policy, applied on and off the reservation, should be based on a combination of the principles of *hozho*, natural law, tribal law, and federal environmental and cultural resources protection law. *Hozho* is an abstract, complex, highly spiritual doctrine of Navajo philosophy and spiritual practice described as "perfection so far as it is attainable by man, the end toward which not only man but also supernaturals and time and motion, institutions, and behavior strive. Perhaps it is the utmost achievement of order."[87] This Navajo philosophy of harmony and natural beauty is intrinsic to how Navajo people treasure their land and is, therefore, intrinsic to sacred lands preservation. It is also the incentive and direction for all Navajos to work together. "Religious leaders need to be involved in creating a Navajo Nation sacred lands management policy. Sacred lands need to be foremost managed as sacred. They constitute a part of Navajo identity which is defined by language, land base and culture. This is the guiding philosophy for sacred lands treatment."[88]

A sacred lands management policy based on the doctrine of *hozho* may have important spiritual and practical benefits. Such a plan could be applied to all Navajo traditional territory, the Diné Bikeyah, which is inclusive of all sacred places located on reservation and nonreservation lands. A sacred lands policy based on the doctrine of *hozho* may resolve some of the incommensurable ideologies and languages embedded throughout federal environmental and cultural protection laws. With a central plan guiding local decision making across the Diné Bikeyah, sacred lands will be treated competently and consistently according to a vision based on tradition and to what constitutes compliance with all Navajo Nation and federal environmental and cultural protection laws. A sacred lands policy grounded in *hozho* may be an important means to assure that all Navajo people representing a wide spectrum of interests have the opportunity to express concerns and take part in decisions.

> A uniform policy would eliminate the influence of single individuals. The person with authority for decision-making at the time has tremendous influence over policy and individual site protection. This applies to tribal positions as well as federal positions. Individual people, philosophy, and policy all work together to influence sacred lands management.
>
> A uniform policy would also address the need to decide what is the role of economic development on sacred lands both on reservation and off. An internal disagreement among Navajo Nation citizens exists regarding alteration of a sacred place from a proposed action related to economic development. Some feel that sacred lands should never be altered for economic development regardless of who benefits (including Navajo communities).[89]

Some Navajo citizens expressed concerns over the absence of a commitment to the traditional philosophy of *hozho* in the treatment of sacred lands. Navajo people collectively need to decide what their commitment to sacred lands protection and tradition is going to be in relationship to decisions about proposing or permitting projects like communications towers, energy production, or tourism development. One Navajo citizen stated, "Sacred lands should be treated as sacred lands," because the consequences of not protecting sacred lands and conducting ceremonies extend far beyond noncompliance with tribal or federal environmental and cultural laws.[90]

The wisdom shared by Navajo elders is that complying with the law is not what the Navajo or anyone else should be worried about. Our collective concern should be about the health and survival of local communities practicing traditional subsistence off the land. Without proper understanding of, and respect for, the profound effects of landscape loss to traditional cultures and ways of life, federal management practices remain agents of adverse change in indigenous cultures. One Native scholar describes the most severe of these consequences as "environmental genocide."[91] The elders clarified that beyond the well-being of the Navajo people, the larger issues are caring for the environment in order to ensure the survival of all humanity.

A sacred lands policy based on the doctrine of *hozho* may raise as many complex issues as it resolves because this would be an attempt to blend traditional sacred doctrine with secular US law. For example, because the doctrine of *hozho* can be characterized as an abstract, complex, highly spiritual, unconscious operation, then it is largely unavailable for precise explanation or codification.[92] It may be a challenge for Navajo Nation lawmakers to introduce concepts of true *hozho* into a secular policy that also incorporates Western concepts of property law and science. Additionally, lawmakers may be challenged to blend *hozho* with the doctrines and sacred beliefs of other cultures, including other Native cultures. For example, the Hopi tribe would vigorously seek to have their doctrines and beliefs considered in the management of their traditional cultural places that are under Navajo or federal jurisdiction. Finally, the doctrine of *hozho* is a spiritual paradigm in which to manage cultural property that, for some communities, may be a source of economic development and heritage tourism. Native communities and individuals may have to debate the compatibility of spiritual and economic paradigms for sacred lands management.

INNOVATIVE STRATEGIES FOR SACRED LANDS MANAGEMENT

Traditional indigenous philosophies and bodies of knowledge are essential to meet the legal requirement and moral imperative to protect the physical and spiritual integrity of sacred lands. A culture's vitality is dependent on individuals living in community with the natural world. The land's features, and the sense of place and kinship they create, are central to the identity of a Native individual and a people. Sacred lands loss, desecration, or neglect can result in spiritual, practical, cultural, and political risk to Native peoples.[93] Eroded sacred lands diminish the spiritual practices that are central to religious belief systems, personal and cultural identity, and human survival. One Navajo elder pointed to contamination of ground water and plant communities on Dook'o'oosłííd as a practical example of potential adverse effect to the health and survival of local communities living directly off the land. Environmental and human rights are at risk for all Native nations because the Forest Service and the Ninth Circuit Court of Appeals have forced the Navajo Nation into a compelling, but very risky, decision to argue their position on the Snowbowl Ski Area expansion proposal to an, historically, unsympathetic Supreme Court. Now the Navajo Nation is forced to contemplate using limited economic resources to attempt to purchase the ski area in order to protect not only the mountain but also their faith, culture, and sovereignty.

In the United States, a complex environmental and cultural legislative and regulatory framework governs indigenous sacred places that are in federal stewardship. Unfortunately, this legal architecture, intended to protect sacred lands, ultimately conflicts with traditional indigenous values relative to land and religious practice, privileges the values of the dominant society, erodes tribal identity and sovereignty, and leaves sacred lands vulnerable to desecration or destruction. An examination of the ideologies and languages in US environmental and cultural protection laws demonstrates sacred lands management is another arena of tribal rights and environmental justice in which the critical theory concepts of incommensurability and interest convergence are operative. Effective strategies for sacred lands protection and access are those that identify and reflect on incompatible and hegemonic ideologies and languages in the law and in practice and then take action to transform them. The examples of terms and concepts I discuss in this article, codifying a definition of *sacred land*, defining and measuring *social impact* and *mitigation*, delineating discrete boundaries for sacred landscapes, determining historical significance, and defining *substantial burden* on the free exercise of religion, do not form an exhaustive list. They comprise a small sample of unambiguous demonstrations of how the law privileges Western values of science and property rights over indigenous spiritual values in the treatment of sacred lands and fails to balance the inequity by imposing procedures largely giving the appearance of equality rather than actual equality.

For Native peoples, just complying with existing environmental and cultural laws does not alone result in meaningful and effective sacred lands protection and access. Meeting the legal requirement and moral imperative to protect the physical and spiritual integrity of sacred lands depends on a commitment to traditional indigenous philosophies and bodies of knowledge. Resolving the problem of incompatible ideologies and languages in sacred lands protection law and practice may include integrating traditional indigenous worldviews directly into federal and tribal law. For the Navajo Nation, a uniform sacred lands management policy could be based on a combination of the principles of *hozho*, natural law, tribal law, and federal environmental and cultural resources protection law.[94]

Discussions about the Navajo Nation revealed that directly integrating the sacred ideologies and languages of Native tradition into secular law may result in important spiritual and practical benefits, as well as present its own unique suite of complex issues.[95] It may be a challenge for Navajo Nation lawmakers to introduce concepts of true *hozho* into a secular policy that also incorporates Western concepts of property law and science. Additionally, lawmakers may be challenged to blend *hozho* with the doctrines and sacred beliefs of other cultures, including other Native cultures. Finally, the doctrine of *hozho* is a spiritual paradigm in which to manage cultural property that, for some communities, may be a source of economic development and heritage tourism.

Regardless of these issues, directly integrating traditional ideology into sacred lands protection laws is a significant step in developing innovative strategies for sacred lands management. Also important, effective sacred lands protection depends on cultivating a willingness among federal lawmakers, land managers, project proponents, and stakeholders to commit to honoring traditional values and working with Native governments and traditional practitioners in order to identify and change incommensurate and hegemonic ideologies and languages prior to drafting new legislation or implementing negotiations or environmental evaluations mandated in existing US law.[96] Although not impossible, this will be a formidable challenge because the larger social and political context involves convincing those with the power to share it.

NOTES

1. Derek C. Haskew, "Federal Consultation with Indian Tribes: The Foundation of Enlightened Policy Decisions, or Another Badge of Shame?" *American Indian Law Review* 24, no. 1 (1999–2000): 21–74; Jack Trope and Dean Suagee, "Consultation Protocols for Protecting Native American Sacred Places, Preliminary Draft, 10/28/03." Paper presented at the Summit on Consultation Protocols for Protecting Native American Sacred Places, 2003 November 14–16, Santa Fe, NM; Kyme McGaw and Rob Roy Smith, "Rethinking Sacred Sites Consultation: Achieving Meaningful Tribal/ Federal Relations." Paper presented at the Summit on Consultation Protocols for

Protecting Native American Sacred Places, 2003 November 14–16, Santa Fe, NM; Richmond Clowe and Imre Sutton, "Prologue," in *Trusteeship in Change: Toward Tribal Autonomy in Resource Management,* ed. Richmond L. Clowe and Imre Sutton (Boulder: University Press of Colorado, 2001), xxi; Shirley Powell and Sharon Hatch, "The Falls Creek Archaeological Area and Contemporary Native Americans: Background, Consultations, and Recommendations." Special report prepared for the US Department of Agriculture Forest Service (hereinafter referred to as USDA FS), San Juan National Forest, Durango, CO, September 1999.

2. National Congress of American Indians (hereinafter referred to as NCAI), "Essential Elements of Public Policy to Protect Native Sacred Places," Resolution #SD-02-027. Adopted at the Annual Session of the NCAI, San Diego, CA, 2002.

3. Christopher Vecsey, ed., *Handbook of American Indian Religious Freedom* (Chestnut Ridge, NY: Crossroad Publishing, 1991); Erica-Irene Daes, *Protection of the Heritage of Indigenous People* (New York: United Nations, 1997); Frank Occhipinti, "The Enola Hill Controversy: Deconstructing an American Indian Sacred Site" (PhD diss., University of Colorado, 2000); Imre Sutton, "Indian Cultural, Historical, and Sacred Resources: How Tribes, Trustees, and the Citizenry Have Invoked Conservation," in Clowe and Sutton, eds., *Trusteeship in Change,* 165; Jill Oakes et al., ed. *Sacred Lands: Aboriginal World Views, Claims, and Conflicts* (Edmonton, AB: Canadian Circumpolar Institute Press, 1998); Vine Deloria Jr., *God Is Red* (Golden, CO: Fulcrum Publishing, 1994), 271.

4. Christopher Quinn, "Mounds of Controversy: Is Sacred Tribal Land in the Path of Progress?" *Atlanta Journal-Constitution,* 14 April 2002; Heather S. Duncan, "Sites of Ancient Culture in Macon Ga., Could Be Destroyed in Firm's Expansion," *Macon Telegraph,* 5 November 2003; US Department of the Interior, National Park Service (hereinafter referred to as DOI NPS), "Ocmulgee National Monument" (US National Park Service), http://www.nps.gov/ocmu/historyculture/index.html (accessed 20 May 2009).

5. Brian Hansen, "Nuclear Waste," *CQ Researcher* 11 (June 2001): 489–504; U.S. Department of Energy, Office of Civilian Radioactive Waste Management, *Recommendation by the Secretary of Energy Regarding the Suitability of the Yucca Mountain Site for a Repository Under the Nuclear Waste Policy Act of 1982* (February 2002), 6, http://www.ocrwm.doe.gov (accessed 12 June 2009); Geoffrey Fattah and Suzanne Struglinski, "Pressure Used to Stop Nuclear Dump, Lawsuit Says," *Deseret Morning News,* 19 July 2007.

6. Courtney Ann Coyle, "Coyle: Defending Quechan Indian Pass—Again," *Indian Country Today,* 10 September 2008, http://www.indiancountry.com (accessed 27 January 2010); Larry Hogue, "Victory for Indian Pass," DesertBlog: News and Views from the Desert Protective Council, comment posted 10 June 2009, http://www.dpcinc.org/blog (accessed 27 January 2010).

7. Office of Mauna Kea Management, "Mauna Kea Comprehensive Management Plan: Fact Sheet," 2 May 2008, http://www.MaunaKeaCMP.com (accessed 14 March 2009).

8. Erica Bolstad, "Committee Votes Against Directional Drilling in ANWR," *Anchorage Daily News,* 29 June 2009; Sarah James, "We Are the Caribou People," *Earth Island Journal* 17, no. 2 (Summer 2002): 48; Zachary Coile, "The Last Refuge: Caribou Migration, Drilling Plan Symbolic of Battle between Oil and Environment," *San Francisco Chronicle,* 28 August 2005.

9. Robert A. Hershey, e-mail message to author, 27 March 2009.

10. David Suzuki and Peter Knudtson, *Wisdom of the Elders: Sacred Native Stories of Nature* (New York: Bantam Books, 1992), 156; Wilson Aronilth Jr., *Diné Bi Bee Óhoo'aah Bá Silá: An Introduction to Navajo Philosophy* (Tsaile, AZ: Navajo Community College, 1994). Aronilth applies the more comprehensive term Sa'ah Naagháí Bik'eh Hozhóón, 14.

11. Deloria, *God Is Red*, 279.

12. Gregory Cajete, *Native Science, Natural Laws of Interdependence* (Santa Fe, NM: Clear Light Publishers, 2000), 94.

13. Steven Field and Keith H. Basso, eds., *Senses of Place* (Santa Fe, NM: School of American Research Press, 1996).

14. Robert S. McPherson, *Sacred Land, Sacred View: Navajo Perceptions of the Four Corners Region* (Salt Lake City, UT: Brigham Young University, 1992), 11.

15. Cajete, *Native Science*, 211.

16. Klara Bonsack Kelley and Harris Francis, *Navajo Sacred Places* (Bloomington: Indiana University Press, 1994), 38–40.

17. Peggy V. Beck et al., *The Sacred: Ways of Knowledge, Sources of Life* (Tsaile, AZ: Dine College Press, 2001), 70.

18. Kelley and Francis, *Navajo Sacred Places*, 40.

19. McPherson, *Sacred Land, Sacred View*, 17.

20. James Riding In, "Spiritual Genocide: The Snowbowl Case." Paper presented at the Seventh Annual Conference of the American Indian Studies Consortium, Arizona State University, Phoenix, 15 February 2006; "The Snowbowl Effect, When Recreation and Culture Collide," DVD, directed by Klee Benally (Flagstaff, AZ: Indigenous Action Media, 2005).

21. Kelley and Francis, *Navajo Sacred Places*, 170.

22. Wilson Aronilth Jr., *Foundation of Navajo Culture* (Tsaile, AZ: Navajo Community College, 1991), 31.

23. *American Antiquities Act*, Public Law 59–209, June 1906 (34 Stat. 225, 16 U.S.C. 431–433); *National Historic Preservation Act*, Public Law 89-665, 15 October 1966 (16 U.S.C. 470 et seq.); *Archaeological Resources Protection Act*, Public Law 96-95, 31 October 1979 (16 U.S.C. 470aa–mm).

24. Jack F. Trope and Walter R. Echo-Hawk, "The Native American Graves Protection and Repatriation Act Background and Legislative History," in *Repatriation Reader: Who Owns American Indian Remains*, ed. Devon Mihesuah (Lincoln: University of Nebraska Press, 2000), 129.

25. Angela Riley, "Indian Remains, Human Rights: Reconsidering Entitlement under the Native American Graves Protection and Repatriation Act," *Columbia Human Rights Law Review* 34 (2002): 49–94; John W. Ragsdale Jr., "Some Philosophical, Political and Legal Implications of American Archaeological and Anthropological Theory," *University of Missouri at Kansas City Law Review* 70 (2001): 1.

26. Bill Ashcroft et al., *Key Concepts in Post Colonial Studies* (London: Routledge, 1998); Colin Perrin, "Approaching Anxiety: The Insistence of the Postcolonial in the Declaration on the Rights of Indigenous Peoples," in *Laws of the Postcolonial*, ed. Eve Darian-Smith and Peter Fitzpatrick (Ann Arbor: University of Michigan Press, 1999), 19–37; Edward Said, *Orientalism* (New York: Vintage, 1978); Franz Fanon, *The Wretched of the Earth* (New York: Grove, 1968); John McLeod, *Beginning Post-Colonialism* (Manchester, UK: Manchester University Press, 2000); Patrick Williams and Laura

Chrisman, *Colonial Discourse and Post-Colonial Theory: A Reader* (New York: Columbia University Press, 1994).

Derrick A. Bell Jr., *Faces at the Bottom of the Well: The Permanence of Racism* (New York: Basic Books, 1992); Kimberle Crenshaw et al., *Critical Race Theory: The Key Writings That Formed the Movement* (New York: The New Press, 1995); Richard Delgado and Jean Stefancic, *Critical Race Theory: The Cutting Edge* (Philadelphia: Temple University Press, 2000); Richard Delgado and Jean Stefancic, *Critical Race Theory: An Introduction* (New York: New York University Press, 2001); Robert A. Williams Jr., "Vampires Anonymous and Critical Race Practice," *Michigan Law Review* 95 (1997): 741.

27. Said, *Orientalism*; Fanon, *The Wretched of the Earth.*

28. Ania Loomba, *Colonialism/Postcolonialism: The New Critical Idiom* (New York: Routledge, 1998).

29. Peter Fitzpatrick, "Passions Out of Place: Law, Incommensurability and Resistance," in Darian-Smith and Fitzpatrick, eds., *Laws of the Post-Colonial,* 39–55.

30. Bryan A. Garner and Henry Campbell Black, *Black's Law Dictionary* (St. Paul, MN: West Group, 1999).

31. Crenshaw et al., *Critical Race Theory,* 103–22; Delgado and Stefancic, *Critical Race Theory,* 21–23.

32. John F. Dovidio and Samuel L. Gaertner, "Aversive Racism and Selection Decisions: 1989 and 1999," *Psychological Science* 11, no. 4 (July 2000): 315–19.

33. Ian F. Haney Lopez, "The Social Construction of Race," in Delgado and Stefancic, eds., *Critical Race Theory,* 168.

34. Delgado and Stefancic, *Critical Race Theory,* 9.

35. Ibid., 7.

36. Derrick A. Bell Jr., "*Brown v. Board of Education* and the Interest-Convergence Dilemma," *Harvard Law Review* 93 (1980): 518.

37. *Brown v. Board of Education,* 347 U.S. 483 (1954).

38. Andrew Gulliford, *Sacred Objects and Sacred Places* (Boulder: University of Colorado Press, 2000); Joseph Bruchac and Thomas Locker, *Between Earth and Sky: Legends of Native American Sacred Places* (San Diego, CA: Harcourt Brace Jovanovich, 1996); Keith H. Basso, *Wisdom Sits in Places* (Albuquerque: University of New Mexico Press, 1996).

39. Executive Order no. 13007: Indian Sacred Sites, sec. 1 (b) (iii), "Accommodation of Sacred Sites" (24 May 1996).

40. *Native American Sacred Lands Act of 2003,* HR 2419, 108th Cong., 1st sess. (11 June 2003).

41. Ibid., sec. 6, "Transfer of Land."

42. Ibid., sec. 7, "Cooperative Agreements."

43. Ibid., sec. 1, "Short Title; Definitions."

44. Suzan Shown Harjo, "American Indian Religious Freedom Act at 25," *Indian Country Today,* 1 August 2003, http://www.indiancountry.com (accessed 28 March 2008).

45. Deloria, *God Is Red,* 275–85.

46. Basso, *Wisdom Sits in Places*; Kelley and Francis, *Navajo Sacred Places.*

47. Cajete, *Native Science*; Beck et al., *The Sacred*; Deloria, *God Is Red*; Vine Deloria Jr., *The World We Used to Live In: Remembering the Powers of the Medicine Men* (Golden, CO: Fulcrum Publishing, 2006).

48. Beck et al., *The Sacred,* 6.

49. *National Environmental Policy Act of 1969*, Public Law 91-190, 42 *U.S. Code* 4321 and 4331-4335.

50. Interorganizational Committee on Guidelines and Principles for Social Impact Assessment, "Guidelines and Principles for Social Impact Assessment," *Environmental Impact Assessment Review* 15, no. 1 (1993): 11.

51. *National Historic Preservation Act*, Public Law 89-665, 15 October 1966 (16 *U.S. Code* 470 et seq.).

52. Interview by author with anonymous Navajo elder, 6 November 2007.

53. Raymond D. Austin, personal communication, 29 March 2008. Dr. Austin is adjunct assistant professor at James E. Rogers College of Law. He served on the Navajo Nation Supreme Court from 1985 to 2001.

54. Maureen Trudelle Schwartz, *Navajo Lifeways: Contemporary Issues, Ancient Knowledge* (Norman: University of Oklahoma Press, 2001); Beck et al., *The Sacred*, 76.

55. Aronilth Jr., *Diné Bi Bee Óhoo'aah Bá Silá.*

56. US Department of the Interior, Bureau of Land Management (hereinafter referred to as DOI BLM), *Record of Decision: Farmington Proposed Resource Management Plan and Final Environmental Impact Statement* (Farmington, NM: Farmington Field Office, 2003), 1.

57. Ibid., 9.

58. Meeting with anonymous Navajo Nation government staff, 11 October 2006.

59. DOI BLM, *Record of Decision.*

60. Ibid., 133.

61. "Directional Drilling," http://www.NaturalGas.org (accessed 27 January 2010).

62. US Environmental Protection Agency, *DRAFT Evaluation of Impacts to Underground Sources of Drinking Water by Hydraulic Fracturing of Coalbed Methane Reservoirs*, EPA 816-D-02-006 (August 2002).

63. US Council on Environmental Quality, *Code of Federal Regulations*, Title 40 sec. 1508.20, "Mitigation" (1 July 1998).

64. Suzan Shown-Harjo, "Gathering to Protect Native Sacred Places: Consensus Position on Essential Elements of Public Policy to Protect Native Sacred Places (Essential Elements and Objectionable Elements)," San Diego, CA, 8–9 November 2002. Report presented to the NCAI Subcommittee on Human, Religious, and Cultural Concerns, 12 November 2002, and to the NCAI Convention Session on Sacred Lands: Protecting Our Most Precious Resources, 13 November 2002; Tom King, *Places That Count: Traditional Cultural Properties in Cultural Resources Management* (Walnut Creek, CA: AltaMira Press, 2003), 193.

65. Interview with anonymous Navajo Nation government staff, 24 August 2007.

66. Sharon Milholland, "Native Voices and Native Values in Sacred Landscapes Management: Bridging the Indigenous Values Gap on Public Lands through Co-Management Policy" (PhD diss., University of Arizona, 2008), 178.

67. James Riding In, "Spiritual Genocide"; Benally, "The Snowbowl Effect."

68. Interview by author with anonymous Navajo elder, 6 November 2007.

69. Interview with anonymous Navajo Nation government staff, 24 August 2007.

70. Navajo Nation, Office of the President and Vice President, "Navajo Nation President Joe Shirley, Jr., Calls Proposed Arizona Snowbowl Development Violation of Navajos' Mother," news release, 3 November 2005.

71. USDA FS, *Record of Decision: Arizona Snowbowl Facilities Improvements Final EIS and Forest Plan Amendment #21* (Coconino County, AZ: Peaks Ranger District, Coconino National Forest, February 2005).

72. *Navajo Nation et al. v. U.S. Forest Service et al.*, WL 62565 (D. Ariz. 2006); *Religious Freedom Restoration Act*, Public Law 103-141, 42 *U.S. Code* 21 (1993).

73. *American Indian Religious Freedom Act*, Public Law 95-341, 95th Cong., 2d sess. (11 August 1978) and amendments, HR 4230, 103rd Cong., 2d sess. (8 August 1994).

74. Howard Fischer, "Snowmaking Wins Legal OK," Capitol Media Services, 9 June 2009, http://www.savethepeaks.org (accessed 27 October 2009).

75. *Navajo Nation et al. v. U.S. Forest Service et al.*, No. 06-15371, No. 01-15436, No. 06-15455 (9th Cir., 12 March 2007).

76. Fischer, "Snowmaking Wins Legal OK."

77. US Supreme Court Docket, Case No. 08-846 (8 June 2009).

78. Cindy Yurth, "High Court Refuses to Hear Dook'o'oosłííd Case," *Navajo Times*, 11 June 2009, http://www.navajotimes.com (accessed 27 October 2009).

79. Jason Begay and Noel Lyn Smith, "Navajo Nation Considers Purchasing Arizona Snowbowl," *Navajo Times*, 23 October 2009, http://www.navajotimes.com (accessed 27 October 2009).

80. *National Historic Preservation Act*, Public Law 89-665, 15 October 1966 (16 *U.S. Code* 470 et seq.).

81. Sherry Hutt et al., *Cultural Property Law: A Practitioner's Guide to the Management, Protection, and Preservation of Heritage Resources* (New York: John Wiley and Sons, 1999), 5.

82. DOI NPS, National Register, *Guidelines for Evaluating and Documenting Traditional Cultural Properties*, Bulletin 38 (Washington, DC: National Park Service, 1990).

83. Frank Occhipinti, "The Enola Hill Controversy: Deconstructing an American Indian Sacred Site" (PhD diss., University of Colorado, 2000); King, *Places That Count*, 213.

84. Resolution of the White Mountain Apache Tribe of the Fort Apache Indian Reservation, Resolution No. 07-99-153, adopted 15 July 1999.

85. *Arizona-Idaho Conservation Act*, Public Law No. 100-696, 102 Stat. 4571, 4597 (1988); USDA FS, *Term Special Use Permit (Draft)* granted to the Board of Regents, University of Arizona (Steward Observatory), Tucson (1988).

86. Resolution of the White Mountain Apache Tribe of the Fort Apache Indian Reservation, Resolution No. 12-2003-296, adopted 17 December 2003. Elizabeth A. Brandt, "The Fight for Dzil Nchaa Si An, Mt. Graham: Apaches and Astrophysical Development in Arizona," *Cultural Survival Quarterly* 19, no. 4 (1996): 50–57; John Welch, "White Eyes Lies and the Battle for Dzil Nchaa Si An," *American Indian Quarterly* 21, no. 1 (1997): 75–109; Robert A. Williams Jr., "Large Binocular Telescopes, Red Squirrel Piñatas, and Apache Sacred Mountains: Decolonizing Environmental Law in a Multicultural World," *West Virginia Law Review* 96 (1994): 1133.

87. Gladys Reichard, *Navajo Religion: A Study of Symbolism* (1950; repr., Princeton, NJ: Princeton University Press, 1977), 45.

88. Interview with Navajo Nation government staff, 24 August 2007.

89. Ibid.

90. Ibid.

91. Manny Pino, "Assaulting Mother Earth: Natural Resource Development and Sacred Site Protection." Paper presented at the Seventh Annual Conference of the American Indian Studies Consortium, Arizona State University, Phoenix, 15 February 2006.

92. Raymond D. Austin, "Navajo Courts and Navajo Common Law" (PhD diss., University of Arizona, 2007), 81–84.

93. Deloria, *God Is Red*, 284.

94. Milholland, "Native Voices and Native Values in Sacred Landscapes Management," 192.

95. Austin, "Navajo Courts and Navajo Common Law," 81–84.

96. Hershey e-mail.

AMERICAN INDIAN CULTURE AND RESEARCH JOURNAL 34:2 (2010) 125–144

Language, Epistemology, and Cultural Identity: "*Hopiqatsit Aw Unangvakiwyungwa*" ("They Have Their Heart in the Hopi Way of Life")

SHEILAH E. NICHOLAS

Daniel Nettle and Suzanne Romaine in *Vanishing Voices: The Extinction of the World's Languages* state that indigenous peoples represent about 4 percent of the world's population but speak at least 60 percent of the world's languages.[1] They point out the reality of an ominous linguistic crisis of global proportions—languages die and continue to die, but the "trickle of extinction of the last few centuries is now turning into a flood."[2] Within the US context, they state, "Of an estimated 300 [aboriginal] languages spoken in the area of the present-day US when Columbus arrived in 1492, only 175 are spoken today, most [are] . . . possibly only one generation away from extinction."[3] Recognizing that the statistics can tell neither the "whole" story nor "all" of the stories of the world's languages, this article offers the linguistic story of the "smaller language" population of Hopi, a historically oral communal society that resides on the high plateau lands of the southwestern United States. Hopi society has not escaped the consequences of modernity increasingly evident in the declining use and functions of the Hopi language in all domains of contemporary Hopi life. The Hopi case contributes the perspective of a society whose cultural values, encoded in myriad cultural traditions that remain largely intact and continue to be practiced, mark a distinct identity. More importantly, what is revealed is that the Hopi youth have developed a strong allegiance to the Hopi way of life; they "have their heart in the Hopi way of life," or *Hopiqatsit aw unangvakiwyungwa*. The persistence of a strong Hopi identity directs a (re)focus on culture and language as a means for "recouping or reinvigorating the use of the native tongue."[4]

Sheilah E. Nicholas is a member of the Hopi tribe. She is an assistant professor in the Language, Reading, and Culture Program of the Department of Teaching, Language, and Sociocultural Studies at the University of Arizona, Tucson.

INTRODUCING THE RESEARCH

"When you learn about Hopi, you learn about that balance between your responsibilities to yourself, your society, your whole world. That's how Hopis think about it. This is passed through the language," stated a community member at a 1996 public forum on the status of the Hopi language.[5] Users of Hopi, particularly older users, perceive a direct relationship between Hopi linguistic competency and the development of a Hopi moral fiber manifest in communal attitudes and behaviors of industry, self-discipline, reciprocity, respect (*naakyaptsi*, self-respect, and *tuukyaptsi*, respect for others), responsibility, and obligation cultivated through active participation in the Hopi way of life. However, the Hopi are confronted with a breach in the Hopi cultural plan visibly evident in the attitudes and behaviors of many—youth and adult alike—who are described as *qa Hopi*, or not Hopi.

A growing awareness of this breach in the fabric of the Hopi life was openly voiced at a series of public forums held from December 1996 through February 1997. The use of the Hopi language in daily conversation and communication, particularly between the older and younger generations, had diminished. Parents and grandparents openly acknowledged that they did not speak Hopi to their children or grandchildren anymore. Younger Hopi were growing up not understanding or speaking Hopi. An immediate anxiety expressed was that many Hopi youth were engaging in substance abuse, gang membership, and domestic violence—activities that violated the principles of the Hopi way of life. In addition, community members, grandparents, and parents who actively participated in traditional activities and ceremonies pointed out the lack of cultural and linguistic preparedness among Hopi youth needed to attain a deeper, spiritual level of understanding of these activities and ceremonies. From their observations, Hopi adults and elders described Hopi youth as no longer behaving humbly or having "respect for anything." Instead, Hopi youth are perceived as *tsàatsayom*, or children who have not yet attained maturity—had not learned the precepts that guide one to think maturely and, therefore, had not learned to behave in a distinctively Hopi manner; they had not yet "become Hopi."[6]

Hopi parents and elders associated such displays of immature, inappropriate behaviors with the inability of younger Hopi to understand and speak the Hopi language. More disturbing for the older Hopi was that the Hopi language as the means of passing on Hopi history and cultural and religious knowledge from young to old was severely threatened. The gravity of their concerns was poignantly captured in the words of one community member who stated, "When we begin to lose our language, we begin to lose who we are [our cultural identity]."[7]

These concerns prompted the Hopi tribe to assess the status of Hopi language fluency in the reservation communities, which subsequently confirmed a significant language shift from Hopi to English among the Hopi people. English was spoken as the primary language in at least half of the 347 households (representing 1,293 individuals) surveyed, particularly among the younger Hopi in the households.[8] The survey results also identified Western education as a significant factor in the progression of the language shift among the Hopi people.

Myriad questions surface from this linguistic situation: How is a Hopi cultural identity formed or acquired? What is the role of the Hopi language in the identity-formation process of Hopi youth? In the trend toward English monolingualism, how do contemporary youth define what constitutes a Hopi identity? What is the impact of language shift on the identity-formation process of contemporary Hopi youth? When Hopi youth are no longer socialized through their heritage language, are they still learning the culturally appropriate social knowledge of Hopi citizenship and the esoteric knowledge that will carry the Hopi people into the future? What is the pattern or process of Hopi language shift? What and where are the sites of cultural and linguistic strength and continuity?

This contemporary Hopi linguistic situation positioned Hopi youth as shouldering both the burden of language shift and loss and the responsibility for cultural and linguistic continuity. This article draws from my research, which investigated language shift among the Hopi people and, more specifically, the role of the heritage language in the contemporary lives of Hopi youth. Three Hopi youth—Dorian, Jared, and Justin, aged nineteen at the time of the study—are at the heart of the larger study that includes their parents and members of the grandparent generation. Although the participants' collective life histories confirmed that a breach has occurred in the Hopi cultural plan, Dorian's, Jared's, and Justin's cultural and linguistic experiences also affirm the strength and influence of Hopi culture—its traditions, practices, social institutions, and religion. Moreover, the accumulated experiences of three generations of Hopi not only inform the Hopi people about the shifting process pinpointing the sites of rupture and instability and subsequent impact of language shift but also bring to light two strongholds of Hopi culture and language: Hopi oral tradition and the Hopi identity-formation process expressed in Hopi as "*Hopiqatsit ang nùutum hintsakme, Hopisinoniwtingwu,*" or "Participating along with others in the Hopi way of life, one becomes a Hopi."

This article provides an in-depth "on the ground" look at the Hopi language shift—"becoming accustomed to speaking English"—through the lenses of the study participants who represent the youth, parent, and grand-parent generations.[9] The article also gives attention to Hopi oral tradition and the Hopi identity-formation process in order to articulate the link among language, epistemology, and identity, spotlighting *what* of the traditions, practices, and religion remain salient and *why* they remain salient.

I maintain that Hopi oral tradition is the "total communicative frame-work"—manifest in ritual practices, religious ceremonies, and cultural institutions; symbolism; song words and phrases; prayer; and teachings.[10] Hopi oral tradition is the "transmission mechanism" through which the Hopi people continue to be enculturated with the cultural knowledge, history, ethics, and values of their communal society.[11] The Hopi language is maintained through these traditional conventions. Thus, practiced—*language as cultural practice*—it serves to remind, reinforce, and keep the concepts of the Hopi way of life and messages from the past indelible in the minds of the Hopi people. Moreover, it is through active participation and involvement in the Hopi way of life that an emotional commitment and allegiance to the ideals of the Hopi way of life is formed: a process I call *affective enculturation*. The affective aspect of the Hopi identity-formation process is one that transcends and supports (re)acquisition of the Hopi language. Thus I claim that this relationship and the ongoing salience of cultural practices embodied in oral tradition encourage and tangibly support youth in relearning their heritage language as a fundamental part of their contemporary everyday lives and identities.

CONTEMPORARY HOPI SOCIETY

Hopitutskwa—Hopi Lands

The Hopi are the westernmost of the Puebloan groups. They reside on a portion of their aboriginal lands designated by the 1882 Executive Order as the Hopi Reservation in the northeast part of the state of Arizona on and around the three southernmost fingers of the Black Mesa region. The current reservation boundaries encompass 1.6 million acres of their aboriginal lands (see fig. 1).[12] A geographical, linguistic, and cultural enclave within an enclave, the Hopi Reservation also lies within the larger Navajo Reservation that, in turn, lies within the boundaries of three southwestern states (Arizona, New Mexico, and Colorado) and the larger US society.

Hopisinom—The Hopi People

The Hopi people number about twelve thousand, of whom more than seven thousand reside in and around twelve villages situated across three mesas.[13] The remaining five thousand live off the reservation in various rural and urban areas across the United States as well as in foreign countries. Hopi, a matrilineal society, traces and carries clan descent through the mother's totemically named clan. Traditionally, the residential unit included the extended family, but today Hopi households are largely comprised of nuclear family units.

The Hopi people continue to live much as their ancestors did, tending to fields of corn, squash, beans, and melon as well as participating in the ceremonies that remain integral to the Hopi way of life. Each village community functions as a socially and ceremonially autonomous unit and continues to carry out traditional cultural activities that revolve around a rich ceremonial calendar (see fig. 2). Modernity and change have come to the Hopi and are evident in the incorporation of Western education and forms of governance as well as a cash economy. The tribal government and schools are the primary employers on the reservation, but a large percentage of Hopi people are skilled carvers, potters, silversmiths, basket makers, and weavers who enjoy lucrative incomes from the sale of their crafts. Local businesses—trading posts/gas stations, restaurants, and one hotel—and a medical facility also offer employment.

Hopitsaatsayom—Hopi Youth

Many of today's Hopi youth are born on the Hopi Reservation and grow up in their village communities throughout their childhood, adolescence, and

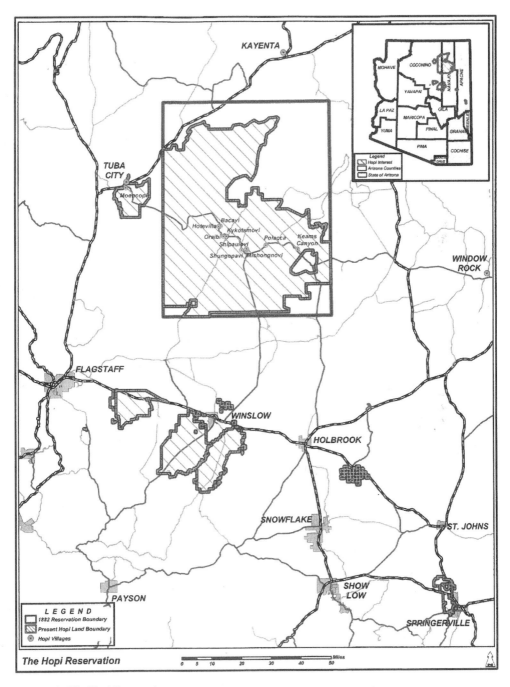

FIGURE 1. *The Hopi Reservation.*

young adult lives. Raised among their immediate and extended families, youth participate from birth in the myriad activities associated with Hopi cultural institutions—baby namings, initiations, weddings, social dances, the tradition of planting corn by hand, and religious ceremonies—that continue to be practiced in contemporary Hopi life.

Most youth attend one of seven elementary schools located in or near the village communities and transfer to the Hopi junior-senior high school for grades seven through twelve.[14] The construction of the junior-senior high school, which opened on 2 September 1986, marked the end of the mandatory boarding school era that took Hopi youth far away from home and family.

Increased mobility and access to technology have given contemporary Hopi youth greater accessibility to the mainstream world. Regular family and school excursions to neighboring towns and cities (many have also traveled to foreign countries) in addition to media and technology, especially television and the computer, have greatly broadened the exposure of Hopi youth to mainstream American and global cultures. This is in remarkable contrast to the schooling experiences of their parents and grandparents who had limited knowledge and access to the larger society prior to leaving the reservation in order to attend distant boarding schools. Consequently, contemporary Hopi youth are highly aware of and experienced with mainstream, even global, society. Most will likely venture into the wider society for varying durations of time, but others will choose to remain on the reservation.

A BREACH IN THE HOPI CULTURAL PLAN: "BECOMING ACCUSTOMED TO SPEAKING ENGLISH"

"Some of us who didn't go off to school still speak a lot of the Hopi language. Now the younger generation . . . speak English only . . . but this isn't their fault. They had to attend school for whatever reason."[15] This comment from a December 1996 forum on the status of the Hopi language established a picture of Hopi language shift as a societal-wide and intergenerational process of becoming "accustomed to speaking English" in order to benefit from Western education, participate in the wage economy, and pursue coexistence as a means of cultural survival. Thus, formal Western education was a significant factor in the shift from Hopi to English initiated in the classroom and subsequently brought into the home and the heart of family life. However, the process of Hopi language shifting and maintenance was unique to each family household. This was evident in the varying degrees of Hopi language competency and use among the three young adults—Dorian described herself as a nonspeaker of Hopi; Jared understood and spoke some Hopi; and Justin described himself as a fluent speaker of Hopi.

Such variation in proficiency has created additional tensions between the older users of Hopi and the younger, largely nonuser generations of Hopi. The comment "How are you Hopi if you can't talk [Hopi]?" made by an older Hopi speaker to one study participant points out the resultant tensions.

In the following section, the study participants, their parents, and members of the grandparent generation describe and express both a personal

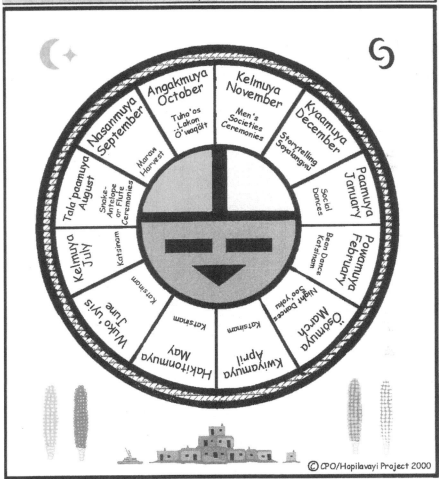

FIGURE 2. *The Hopi ceremonial calendar. Compliments of the Office of CPO/Hopilavayi Project, 2000.*

and collective Hopi perspective of language shift associated with Western schooling, which remains deeply embedded in their memories.

Hopi Youth: "In kindergarten, [we] just dropped the Hopi language"

Dorian, Jared, and Justin each recalled that Hopi was the primary language in the home; thus Hopi was the first language each heard and started to acquire in early childhood. Dorian stated, "They [significant caregivers] speak to you in Hopi and you're able to speak back, at least to some point, 'cuz you're still learning words. . . . I understood what they [family members] were saying." In addition, rather than attending preschool, Dorian was left in the care of a babysitter who spoke to her exclusively in Hopi. Jared recalled being surrounded by the Hopi language in his maternal and paternal family environments, and Justin's early childhood memory was that of learning the language associated with planting corn by hand.

However, each also remembered an abrupt linguistic shift upon entering school. Dorian said, "Before you go to school, that's how they [family members] speak to you, in Hopi . . . but when you go to school, it's like it [Hopi] just stops 'cuz you're expected to learn English." Justin recalled the same, stating, "I would mostly speak it [Hopi] until I got into school [Head Start]. . . . In kindergarten [we] just dropped . . . the Hopi language."

The impact of the Western education assimilation program was manifest in how Jared, Dorian, and Justin described their personal facility with their heritage language. Jared stated, "I can mostly understand it [Hopi], but . . . if someone asks me a question . . . I wouldn't know how to respond back in Hopi." Dorian's response to the question, "Have you ever been asked, 'Do you speak Hopi?'" was accompanied with an uncomfortable laugh. She replied, "Yes, some." When asked how this question made her feel, she answered with some difficulty stating, "I don't know. It makes [she paused and then restarted] . . . 'cuz you know, most [tribal] people say if you don't speak the language, then you're not of that tribe." Justin's reply to the same question was that his Hopi fluency level was at "about 75 percent." These statements speak volumes about how the Hopi people were coerced into accepting the agenda of schools—to teach Hopi youth to live like the white man—as a means of peaceful coexistence with the Euro-American and, subsequently, economic and cultural survival. This view of Western education can be traced back to the 1890s when generations of Hopi were subjected to compulsory Anglo-American education programs with the goal of assimilation.

The following memories of the grandparent generation conjure up a time when their Hopi world was experienced exclusively through the Hopi language. It was through the Hopi language that their memories were elicited and expressed.

Grandparent Generation: *Itam Kwiikwivit'toti*—"We became proud [arrogant]."

Marie (estimated age 65), Clara (age 82), and Vivian (estimated age 72) were the grandparent participants of the study (pseudonyms). Vivian is Dorian's paternal grandmother. Dorian's and Justin's maternal grandmothers passed away just prior to the start of the study. Marie was recruited as an alternate participant representing the grandparent generation from Justin's maternal village, and Clara represented the same from Jared's maternal home village.

Marie's description of the current status of the Hopi language pointed to a fundamental emotional and perhaps a psychological shift in attitude—shyness, bashfulness, and possibly shame—toward the Hopi language, use of the Hopi language, and predominance of English in everyday Hopi life.

"Our languages are mixed together. We are now interjecting English into our Hopi. Therefore, we are speaking a truly different language. And then we are no longer accustomed, it seems, to speaking the Hopi language. It appears as though we are shy, bashful [to speak Hopi]. . . . If we were not like that, we would be holding on to it."

For Clara, it was the younger generation of Hopi and specifically "educated"—those with advanced schooling—Hopi women who set in motion this "English only" behavior by placing the English language rather than Hopi in a position of prominence. However, Marie and Clara, as grandparents, conceded their role in the shifting process. Clara candidly admitted, "Because we don't talk to them in Hopi, that's why. It's the grandmothers', mothers' fault. And then they don't want to make up their mind [or realize, recognize] that they should talk Hopi to them. Now, these children and young women, therefore, have learned only English."

Marie concurred that when her children and grandchildren spoke to her in English, she responded with the same. Unwittingly, this linguistic practice imprinted the idea that the Hopi language "appears to be gone because they are accustomed to speaking like that [in English]." Marie and Vivian observed that English was the predominant language of use among their children and their grandchildren. Vivian's children (three of four) were raising their families away from the Hopi Reservation and therefore were not teaching their children the Hopi language, and now she supposed, "it's because they're town people and everybody [in town] speaks English." Clara recalled advising her daughter to increase her use of English in response to a humiliating incident suffered at school regarding her English speaking ability. In retrospect she stated, "But I should have said, '*Pay um uuHopilavayiy enangni*,'" or "[Along with English] use your Hopi language." Such language practices of this grandparent generation positioned English to become the *lingua franca* among their own children, the soon-to-be parent generation.

Retrospectively, this grandparent generation found the language shift to be quite perplexing. Marie stated, "*Noqw nuy noqw son put sùutokni*," or "To me, one [a first language speaker of Hopi] cannot forget [her/his language]." However, she posited that for some individuals, self-pride in acquiring English proficiency may have led to a diminishing respect for the Hopi culture and language by stating, "*Ita[m] haqawat antsa put qa kyaptsi'yyungwa pu'*," or "There are some of us who in fact seem to have lost respect for and diminished within ourselves the value and integrity of the Hopi culture and language in favor of another [language]."

Nevertheless, the language shift was a lived reality. Speaking English had become the norm among all speakers of Hopi. The impact of the language shift did not exclude the elder speakers of Hopi; the evidence was apparent in the changing linguistic structure of the language and a diminishing knowledge of the specialized lexical repositories among this generation of Hopi. Vivian stated, "We [grandmothers/elder speakers] don't speak 'good' [grammatically correct] Hopi. We don't all have a good grasp of the proper Hopi language. Even I don't know everything [vocabulary/grammar] but I [still] understand when they're [the great-grandparent generation] talking." *Wuklavayi*, a language domain used by the older generations of Hopi to express the philosophy of the Hopi way of life, had greatly declined. With the elder speakers of Hopi passing on, this language domain will be lost completely.

Parent Generation: "We're living the life of a Pahaana [white person] now."

The parent interviewees are parents of the Hopi youth in this study: Dorian's parents, Anna and Doran; Justin's parents, Lillian and Marshall (pseud-onyms); and Jared's mother, Charlene (pseudonym), a single parent. All were residing and employed on the reservation at the time of the study.

The cultural and linguistic life histories of each parent participant differed from that of their children. Doran and Lillian spent a large part of their early childhood and adolescent years away from the Hopi Reservation, although they were close enough to visit relatives and attend ceremonies frequently; English was their first and primary language. Hopi was the first and primary language for Anna, Charlene, and Marshall, prior to leaving the Hopi Reservation to attend boarding schools (Marshall's boarding school experience began at the early age of six or seven).

Unlike their parents, this parent generation made an early, preretire-ment return to the Hopi Reservation: for Anna and Charlene, prompted by the birth of their first child, and for Marshall, to carry out his religious duties. Hence these parents were raising their families in the context of Hopi life. As previously noted, each family household differed in maintaining the cultural and, particularly, the linguistic aspects of Hopi life. Moreover, each family faced a greater challenge in balancing the Hopi way of life with the Western, urban lifestyle brought to and evident on the reservation—fast paced, adhering to timelines and schedules, and incorporating wage work and professional development courses into evenings; activities that disrupt family life. Urbanization of the Hopi way of life had been occurring with each generation of Hopi leaving the reservation to experience the Pahaana way of life, bringing to Hopi new knowledge and new ways of doing things; essen-tially putting into practice a new way of life and language. Schools, which have become established institutions in the heart of Hopi communities, continue to stand for a way of life different and separate from the Hopi way of life, requiring a different and separate language. Urbanization and schooling also continue to initiate a move away from the Hopi language and culture.

In Dorian's family, school was the catalyst for language shift in home child-rearing practices. Anna stated:

> I spoke it [Hopi] pretty fluently 'til probably I started having my own kids. The older one, she started like that [hearing and speaking Hopi] 'cause she had babysitters and I was still talking in Hopi. But after she started school, that's when it [Hopi] really switched over [to English]. . . . [When they were babies], we talked to them . . . [with Hopi] baby talk . . . sing 'em all the songs. But then, eventually, it's just everything's in English now. I know I don't speak [Hopi] to my kids now. . . . I'll throw in a Hopi word now and then . . . but it's hard

to do that [speak to my children in Hopi].

Essentially, Anna had positioned her children on the periphery of the intimate aspects of family life. She stated, "When I go to my mom and sister, I'll speak Hopi with 'em. But with these two, Dorian and her younger brother, I really haven't." It is perplexing for Anna to acknowledge that she uses Hopi with her siblings and mother "without even giving it a thought," but she is unable to do the same with her children: "When I'm with the kids, it [my speaking language] just switches back to English. I wish my kids were able to talk [Hopi]." Anna now uses English to convey cultural information and instruction to her children, translations that do not adequately explain Hopi concepts. These shifting linguistic practices also affected the maintenance of her own Hopi fluency, most notably in her inability to recall or pronounce words.

Doran, a second-language learner of Hopi, stated:

> I never really learned Hopi. When I was growing up . . . it was never really encouraged for me to learn Hopi. I would hear it and I would understand a few words but when a conversation really actually started, I never understood what was going on. . . . My mom always talked English; she never talked Hopi to us. She would go home and she would talk Hopi to her brothers and her parents and to the older people but when she talked us, she would turn to us and she would talk English. . . . My uncles, both of them, talked English to us. One [uncle] more or less talked broken English, but he spoke English to us.

However, Doran's case also points out the continuing role of language in contemporary Hopi society. Several factors compelled Doran to learn Hopi when he returned to the reservation: He rekindled his participation and involvement in the kiva activities; as a family counselor, he could better serve the grandparents who were raising their own grandchildren and were most comfortable discussing intimate issues in Hopi; and in order to pursue an interest in the tribal political arena it was required that he develop a Hopi language proficiency. Doran estimated that it took him five years to develop a basic understanding of what was being said but not the ability to speak Hopi, "so I would just talk English," he stated. At the time of the study, he described himself as a speaker of Hopi after approximately sixteen years of self-learning. Despite this accomplishment, Doran acknowledged that he remained limited in expressing the deeper levels of Hopi thought to a Hopi audience or of accessing the same in the religious realm; he conveys the cultural knowledge he has relearned to his children by using English.

Charlene, whose first language was Hopi, described an unconventional start at an early age, four or five, to learning English. Accompanying her adoptive mother to work at the village day school, she was permitted to sit in the classroom of older Hopi youth while they were being schooled. Consequently, Charlene was exposed to the English language and instruction very early. The teacher's use of visuals helped her "pick up" English quickly. Ironically, her participation in class ended abruptly because her enthusiasm for learning became a distraction, and she was outperforming the older students! When she reached school age, Charlene's memories of schooling reflected the same humiliating experiences suffered by other Hopis because of her use of Hopi: "They were still . . . trying to keep us speaking English. If we did [use Hopi], they would put soap in our mouth. . . . They would cut them in half and put them on our tongue and we had to sit like that for a whole hour. . . . Either that or we get swatted on our hands or behind our knees."

Later, Charlene recalled, "When we went off [the Hopi Reservation] to high school, we all kind of lost out on that [the Hopi language]. It just seemed like it just kind of drifted off [out of use]." Distant boarding schools brought together youth from many tribes, but English quickly became the common language of intertribal friendships and marriages. English bonded Charlene to her Tewa, Shoshoni, and Nez Perce friends as well as her first husband, a member of a different tribe. Later, English remained the language of use in her home in a subsequent relationship with a city-raised, non-Hopi-speaking "full [blood] Hopi." Moreover, Charlene's attempts to establish Hopi as the language of her home were undermined by her mother, who "just started in, talking English to them, and that didn't help." Describing her current Hopi language proficiency, Charlene stated, "I speak it, but I can't really express myself in Hopi anymore and I really feel bad about that too because it reflected on my kids."

Marshall was thrust into the white man's world when he was sent to Utah with two older siblings to attend school. He stated, "I had just finished second grade. I didn't know I was going until I got on that bus with them [sisters], and at the top of the hill, I turned and [saw] my village go [disappear behind the hill]. That's when it hit me that I'm going away and so I cried all the way up to Utah." Finding himself in a bewildering situation did not end with the realization of leaving home, instead it was just the beginning of a more confusing experience called "schooling." Marshall quickly understood the subtle messages that using the Hopi language was unacceptable, and remarkably, at the age of six or seven, he quickly adapted to the situation. He recalled, "I had to make that change where I had to shut my Hopi tongue off completely and then *pay pas Pahan 'yu 'a 'a 'ta* [just be speaking English]. . . . I wasn't exactly told but then just by the actions [facial expressions, body language, I knew] I wasn't to speak any Hopi. I couldn't anyway because I didn't have anyone to talk to. So then I just got accustomed to speaking English."

Marshall made summer visits to the Hopi Reservation and eventually made a deliberate choice to make a permanent return to Hopi and position his ceremonial responsibilities at the forefront of his life: "I chose to be Hopi again. . . . I started to learn [about] my initiations." (He graduated from a high school located closer to the reservation.) The linguistic aspect of his reentry into Hopi life was anything but smooth yet was strongly influenced by the belief instilled in him by his clan uncles that he was destined to work on behalf of the Hopi people in the ceremonial realm of Hopi life; he accepted and embraced his "destiny."

As a parent, Marshall applied this strong conviction to practicing cultural traditions including making Hopi the language of use in his home. He was adamant that parents "need to be involved in the cultural doings"—learning the culture is "*practiced* [emphasis mine] in the household . . . taught down from the grandfather to the father and to the sons and nephews . . . instilling the respect for . . . the meaning of things," he explained. This is one's parental duty (conduct owed) and obligation (socially imposed responsibility) to one's children because "*I'pi—itaahimuningwu, Hopihiita, taawi; i'uuyi—itamuy tsaami'mani,*" or "All these things—our [cultural] possessions, Hopi things [like] songs; my corn—will lead us along [toward our destiny]." As such, Hopi tradition also dictates the use of the Hopi language. He supports and encourages all attempts his children and wife make in using Hopi, and he has been rewarded. In particular, he took great pride in stating that Justin uses Hopi in their kiva activities. "It goes right here [pointing to his heart] and [I realize that] I'm doing something at least," he asserted. He also maintained that learning the language "should always be in the home."

This parent generation described a linguistic shifting process from predominantly Hopi to English driven by the essentiality of English and schooling for the Hopi to participate in and benefit from the mainstream world. Embracing this ideology led to a significant breach in the cultural and linguistic structure including the family and community dynamics of Hopi society. However, these families/households demonstrated that Hopi cultural and linguistic continuity remains rooted in practicing culture, or in practicing living Hopi.

HOPI ORAL TRADITION AND THE HOPI IDENTITY-FORMATION PROCESS OF ACTIVE PARTICIPATION AND INVOLVEMENT IN THE HOPI WAY OF LIFE

Dorian's assertion, "I live Hopi, I just don't speak it," as well as the concern of the older generation of Hopi expressed in the question, "How can you be Hopi if you can't speak it," frame the discussion surrounding the Hopi ideology that by "participating along with others in the Hopi way of life, one becomes Hopi." Participation in the Hopi way of life is not contingent on a proficiency in the Hopi language. Rather, by birthright and beginning at birth, the Hopi individual embarks on a journey of becoming and being Hopi—forming a Hopi cultural identity. The Hopi clan/kinship system is the mechanism that defines the individual's place and role in terms of conduct and obligation to others within and beyond the immediate family in the secular and religious domains of Hopi life. Active participation and involvement in the Hopi way of life is the "process" by which one comes to an understanding of her or his role in the community and fulfilling the expectations of this role according to long-established cultural standards. This understanding was publicly reiterated in January 1997 at a public forum on the status of the Hopi language by a Hopi elder who stated, "If you are Hopi, you will never forget your culture because you know who you are, and you . . . know what your responsibilities are [to your family, community, people, and the world]."[16]

Participating in the sociocultural interactions, routines, and sites of Hopi traditions and practices, Dorian, Jared, and Justin gained varying degrees of competency in these socially defined contexts. Their collective experiences elucidate the principles and ethics essential to developing a distinctly Hopi identity because "words have a home in the context of culture—in the course of daily activities, in social institutions—they have meaning within these contexts."[17] Such words affect and influence the individual. Hence, in spite of the fact that, as Dorian stated, "Most of the time when you're growing up, it's English [that is used]," each of the youth participants internalized the "expected ways of thinking, feeling, and acting" rooted in corn as a way of life.

The Hopi Theory of Life: Planting Corn by Hand

According to the Hopi emergence story, the words "*Pay nu' panis sòoya'yta*," or "I have only the planting stick," were spoken by Màasaw, Guardian of the Hopi Fourth World, at the time of humankind's "emergence" into the Fourth World. The words encapsulate the Hopi life plan, Hopivötskwani, a covenant made with Màasaw to undertake the life-sustaining practices associated with the growing of *qaa'ö*, or corn, by hand in desolate but preordained lands. Inherent in the metaphor of corn as a way of life is the struggle for survival requiring a deep, abiding faith, humility, self-discipline, cohesion, and an unwavering adherence and commitment to the fulfillment of the covenant. The following teaching from Hopi oral tradition conveys this understanding: "*Itam it hìita ane tumalat qatsit namortota. Yaw son haq Hopit qatsiyat sòosok aw su'taqewni*," or "We [as a people] chose this difficult life of hard work and struggle [at emergence]. It is said that no others would willingly commit to this way of life."[18]

How the Hopi people determined to uphold this covenant constitutes their "identity, religious beliefs, ritual practices, and their daily engagements and concerns" and finds expression through the ritual practices, religious ceremonies, cultural institutions, song words and phrases, prayers, teachings, and symbolism that are practiced today.[19] Hopi oral tradition embodies the concepts of corn as a way of life, or *natwani*— the principles of reciprocity and humility, and the destiny (spiritual fulfillment and immortality) of the Hopi people.

In effect, the practice of growing corn by hand as a way of life, or practicing reciprocity and humility, teaches people how to live in harmony with others and contribute to the pursuit of life's fulfillment and spiritual immortality on behalf of the whole group. These principles are central to maintaining the cohesiveness of Hopi as a communal society, defining for them "how to be a people—in heart, thought, behavior, and conduct . . . concepts of a socioculturally structured universe."[20] Thus language as cultural practice makes a direct connection among language, epistemology, and the cultural communal ethic.

Natwanta: Practicing Making a Living, Practicing Faith

The Hopi distinguish two kinds of "practices" associated with the planting of corn by hand: *natwani* (noun), the practices of making a living, farming, and *natwanta* (verb), the practice of faith through ritual, a self-testing. Essentially, the practice of planting corn by hand is a secular and religious ritual practice, hence the expressions "planting is a religious duty" or "planting is an act of faith." The secular activity of planting emphasizes learning the skill of farming as developing self-sufficiency at the personal and collective level; planting corn by hand as work and self-discipline; and the use of the planting stick, or *sooya*, as humility.

Thus work, or *tumala*, especially that done by hand, emerges as perhaps the most important of Hopi concepts. "For the Hopi, all practices of life for Hopi well-being are work"—hoeing in the field, performing rituals, personal sacrifice, and self-discipline.[21] This concept is expressed often in daily discourse by using these Hopi words: "*Hak tumalay akw mongvastingwu, maqsontangwu*," or "One, by means of his/her work benefits from it, experiences the benefits of hardship." The reminder is that one gains spiritual growth and fulfillment through hard work and faith. In 1991 Loftin wrote, "Hard work embodies the spiritual essence of the Hopi way, chosen in the primordium by their ancestors. Through work, the Hopi people share a sense of identity with their mythic forefathers."[22] *Natwani* becomes the metaphor for the work ethic and attaining *qatsitwi*, the "know-how" for making a living. Justin stated that he was born and raised to be a Hopi farmer. His father and male relatives modeled this staunch commitment to the planting tradition explicitly. It is the way of life for a Hopi farmer, a difficult life that requires one to work hard and thereby acquire a strong work ethic. Justin perceived himself as having acquired this work ethic: "I'm a hard working person, 'cuz that's the way I was brought up. . . . I'm still doing that [working hard]."

The *sooya* symbolizes a life of humility and becomes the instrument by which the Hopi farmer tests his faith to the utmost in order to ensure life by one's own hands supported by faith. Further, as a personal endeavor, to use the *sooya* allows one to participate in the ways of the Hopi ancestors, or *hisat.sinom*; to work the earth with a reverence emanating from a perception of earth as *itangu*, or our mother, commanding proper thoughts and feelings toward a "relative"; and essentially to experience a return to and "reactualization" of the time at emergence—a reminder to the Hopi people of their petition and subsequent acceptance of the life plan set out for them by Màasaw.[23] This is reiterated by Justin: "[Hopi farming is about] how to plant with a [planting] stick, on your own instead of having somebody else doing it for you. . . . Way back then, that's how we survived—[by] planting the corn. We ate from what we planted and that's what kept us alive [physically and spiritually]."

The ritual practice of planting is also applied to the developing sense of commitment to and preparation for the economic responsibility—self-sufficiency at an individual level—to one's family as a husband and father. Justin stated, "You can talk to the plants; they're just like your children. So, [you tell them] 'Just be strong as you're growing up. Don't let anything bother you.' And they'll hear you." Although Jared is not active in the planting tradition, planting corn as a symbol of a Hopi man's economic responsibility was instilled early in his mind: "That's the man's role you know," he stated and assured that he will resume this responsibility "especially if I get married." Loftin described *natwani* as embodying the notion of self-practice, "a worldly reflection on one's self-practice and conduct" in reference to the successful growth of "crops, children, or other fruits of personal effort; if they turn out well they accrue to the individual's virtue" in ethical terms.[24] Mary Black in *Maidens and Mothers: An Analysis of Hopi Corn Metaphors* articulated a concise description of the relationship a Hopi farmer has to his corn children and extended to human children:[25]

> A symbiotic and complementary relationship is seen to pertain to corn and humans. Young plants are cared for as children by people; if they are properly cared for, encouraged and prayed for, they are able to mature. . . . Their lines of life are carried on in the ears of corn, some which become poshumi [seeds] for the next germination cycle. The rest become "mother" to the humans who cared for them—in the literal sense of actual nourishment. . . . The nourishment and energy received from corn in turn allow the humans to continue to care for the young plants . . . thus the life cycle of corn and humans complement one another and repeat through the ages.

Neither can survive without the other. Using "nurturing" words that offer counsel, advice, support, and encouragement, for example, "*Uma hapi ö'qalyani. Uma qa tsaakwiwyungni. Uma kyaktaytotini; su'qawyani,*" or "You [my corn children] desire to be strong. You are not to wither. You have a speedy growth; be confident," makes evident the integral role of language in the "proper care" of one's children. Justin stated that he uses these words of encouragement in tending to the corn in his family's field. Song lyrics also convey these messages. An elder Hopi woman recalled this practice vivid in memories of her childhood:

> *Hisat taataqt pasve taatawtinumyangwu, ispi uuyiy songawnen tiitavtotangwu. Haalaykyaakyang amumi unangtavi'yungngwu.*

> At that time, the men at their fields, would go along singing, because, in effect, they were taking care of their plants [as if they were children]. With much happiness, they were tending to them [the corn children].

In turn, one's female kin give reciprocal attention and commitment to the corn, harvesting and storing the corn brought from the fields: "They'll [grandmother, mother, aunts] clean [it], and then they'll take it off the cob, [and then] we'll save it or we'll boil it," stated Justin. This attention is extended to the woman's role in the preparation of traditional food made from corn—*nöqkwivi,* or hominy; *piiki,* or blue corn wafer bread; *somiviki,* or sweet, blue corn tamale; *kutuki,* or parched corn; and other corn dishes served during ritual performances and ceremonies. An elder Hopi woman explained,

> *Nöösiwqa pas hiikya'ta. Taaqa hiita aniwnaq, put ak itam itaaqatsiy ö'qalyangwu. Hak sinot qa iingyalngwu, pante, hak songawnen naa'ingyalngwu. Itam sunan sinom.*

> Food is of great value. When a man grows his foodstuff, by means of that, we strengthen our lives. Therefore, one should not exclude or reject the company of [guests at mealtime], if one does so, one essentially rejects oneself. We are all one people.

Inherent in this statement is a reference to the emergence of the people, or all humankind, into the Fourth World, hence, the protocol of extending an invitation to partake of the food prepared to all those who come to participate as audience members in the ritual performances and ceremonies; all are to partake of the bounty. This comprehension extends to the spirit world and resonates in Helen Sekaquaptewa's memories of sweet corn fresh from the steaming pit, ready for consumption as told to Louise Udall in *Me and Mine: The Life Story of Helen Sekaquaptewa.* She says, "The harvesting and all aspects of life had religious significance. [When the morning star reached the right position in the sky,] it was time to open the pit. While the steam poured out, [the elder] called loudly to the gods and their spirits to come and partake of this food, repeating the invitation four times—from the east, the south, the west, and the north. Being spirits, the gods eat of the vapor from the corn."[26] The preparation of food by the women is also likened to that of Mother Earth who provides substance, or *soona*, to all; we nurse from our mother, she is the provider of life, a mother to all. In turn, like Mother Earth, Hopi women are revered for their life-giving abilities.

Natwani also refers to the practice of ceremonies, practices that symbolically stand for "practicing life," or "*Itam natwantotangwu*": "We, by custom, are 'practicing,' or 'rehearsing' life." Because ceremonies also serve to remind and prompt the Hopi conscience, "participation" involves a strong conviction that there is a spiritual return to the remote past that is lived again. If one is able to project her- or himself into this realm, a solid connection to and a profound understanding of the past as significant and relevant today as well as for the future is attained. This religious task, conducted in faith and humbleness, constitutes the religious ethic. Therefore, the myriad of cultural practices, including ceremony, is referred to as *natwani* because the Hopi people continue to "practice" what has been done in actuality in Hopi history. In effect, planting corn by hand not only sustains but also continues to convey and uphold the integrity of the Hopi plan of life, or Hopivötskwani. This is reiterated in the following statement from Hopi oral tradition: "*Haqàapiy yaw qatsi qatuvostini, hak yaw pas somatsinen, sùuput namortamantani*," or "It is said, that in a time when life becomes difficult [complicated], one has to be very discerning in order to choose *the right way* [the Hopi way]."[27]

Thus, Justin, "brought up" to carry out the male duty of planting corn by hand, has been demonstrating being Hopi, and rightfully asserts, "I'm Hopi." Further, his cultural and linguistic socialization into Hopi society remain largely unaffected by the language shift from Hopi to English that surrounds him. Jared's life history, which included resisting *qa Hopi* behaviors such as gang involvement and substance abuse, demonstrates the "maturity" aspect of becoming and being Hopi—making the "right" choices in responding to such pressures expressed as "*Pam wuwni' hinti*," or "He made a smart choice." He will likely continue to make the right choices influenced by Hopi cultural values. Dorian, grounded in her experiences and knowledge of her cultural roots, asserts, "I live Hopi, I just don't speak it." The Hopi values imbued in Hopi traditions become an intrinsic part of one's cultural identity poignantly expressed in Justin's words: "Since you're Hopi you're brought up that way [in the Hopi way of life]. You can't let it go; it's just gonna be too hard [to forget this upbringing]."

CONCLUSION

Nettle and Romaine assert that only a better understanding of the historical processes leading biolinguistic diversity to the brink of extinction will allow us to change them.[28] Borrowing from Nettle and Romaine, the Hopi case study is a "bottom-up" examination of the historical process of "top-down" language shift initiated by Western assimilation programs and schooling as well as the Hopi response to the social, cultural, and economic pressures from outside and within Hopi. The shifting process, marked by changes in a "people's practices, roles, and role models," is illuminated as is the persistence, strength, and influence of culture—Hopi oral tradition and the Hopi identity-formation process, those cultural and linguistic functions identified as crucial to the continuation of intergenerational transmission and preservation of Hopi culture and habitat.[29]

The Hopi case study affirms the notion that "there are many ways that one can experience culture, language only being one of them.[30] In Hopi society, through inclusion, active participation, involvement, and interrelations with others in the myriad cultural practices—the Hopi identity-formation process conveyed through various communicative forms of the Hopi oral tradition—Hopi youth acquire the implicit messages about cultural standards of behavior and cultural knowledge embedded in these practices.

However, although "living Hopi"—practicing the customs, traditions, and religion—has anchored each in their Hopi identity, it is an identity that, in Dorian's words, is not "fully complete without the language, the tongue, the speaking." These youth, although rooted and experienced in the Hopi way of life, are linguistically ill-prepared to fulfill a duty and responsibility to pass on the cultural knowledge encoded in the Hopi language. This presents a seemingly ominous future for the vitality of the Hopi language and Hopi cultural practices and religion, but at best, these Hopi youth, secure in their Hopi identity, are confident that the sociocultural institutions and traditions through which they acquired their cultural identity and strength will endure. Each is adamant in securing the same for their own children by upholding the cultural traditions they have been taught and have learned; they have their heart in the Hopi way of life.

This commitment to the Hopi way of life has spurred a newfound motivation and urgency to "learn" the Hopi language: "[Within my lifetime] I'll still be trying to learn," asserted Dorian, "'cuz I really am set on [learning to speak] it." Nettle and Romaine state that "to choose to use a language is an act of identity or belonging to a particular community."[31] This unwavering allegiance to the Hopi way of life has maintained the Hopi people for centuries.

Maintaining, reinvigorating, and revitalizing the Hopi way of life is about keeping a uniquely Hopi personality that has survived for centuries; at the "heart" of this personality is language.[32]

The concern for and work on behalf of the Hopi language points to a reinvigoration of the collective Hopi ideological commitment to the Hopi way of life encoded in the Hopi terms *nami'nangwa* and *sumi'nangwa*—with mutual concern and care for and toward one another, and in the mood of unity—that includes the pursuit of an authentic and valid biculturalism and bilingualism in order to secure a viable future for the Hopi lifeway in the twenty-first century. Ofelia Garcia maintains that indigenous youth have been engaged in the "work" all along, through "translanguaging," or "languaging bilingually."[33] Youth, when engaging in translanguaging, are "integrating language practices from different communities with distinct ideologies"—their Hopi and their mainstream worlds—drawing from their "different semiotic systems and modes of meaning," and "in doing so, they are affirming their past and their local lives, as they project them toward a better future."[34] As such, the possibility that the younger generations of Hopi may fulfill their responsibility and obligation to pass on the Hopi way of life becomes promising.

NOTES

1. Daniel Nettle and Suzanne Romaine, *Vanishing Voices: The Extinction of the World's Languages* (New York: Oxford University Press, 2000), ix.

2. Ibid., 2.

3. Ibid., 3.

4. Kendall King, *Language Revitalization Process and Prospects: Quichua in the Ecuadorian Andes* (Clevedon, UK: Multilingual Matters, 2001), 12.

5. Comment from Minutes, Public Orientation: Hopi Language Assessment Project, Hopi Veteran's Memorial Coliseum, 23 December 1996.

6. *Hopi* as a term has multiple definitions including human being, behaving one, civilized, peaceable, polite, adhering to the Hopi way, and fluent in the language. The Hopi Dictionary Project, comp., *A Hopi-English Dictionary of the Third Mesa Dialect: Hopìikwa Laváytutuveni* (Tucson: University of Arizona Press, 1998), 99–100.

7. Comment from Minutes, Public Orientation.

8. Hopi Language Assessment Project, Presentation of Hopi Language Survey Results. Prepared for the Hopi Culture Preservation Office, the Hopi Tribe. Prepared by Diane Austin, Bureau of Applied Research and Anthropology, University of Arizona, Tucson, 13 October 1997.

9. Teresa McCarty, Mary Eunice Romero, and Ofelia Zepeda, "Native American Youth Discourses on Language Shift and Retention: Ideological Cross-Currents and Their Implications for Language Planning," *International Journal of Bilingual Education and Bilingualism* 9, no. 5 (2006): 659–77.

10. Edward T. Hall, *Beyond Culture* (New York: Doubleday, 1976).

11. Joshua A. Fishman, "What Do You Lose When You Lose Your Language?" in *Stabilizing Indigenous Languages*, ed. Gina Cantoni (Flagstaff: Northern Arizona University Center for Excellence, 1996), 80–91.

12. In 1996, the Hopi tribe was awarded a settlement by the federal government that allowed for the purchase of 420,265 acres of aboriginal lands with monies gained from the Land Settlement Act of 1882. The terms of the settlement allowed for purchase of 500,000 acres of additional aboriginal lands to be placed in trust status. "Hopi Tribe's Land Team Honored for Economic Development Plan and Land Preservation Efforts," *Hopi Tutuveni* 15, no. 23 (10 November 2005): 1–2, 11.

13. The villages of Walpi, Sitsom'ovi, and Haano are located on First Mesa, with Polacca at its base; the villages of Musangnuvi, Supawlavi, and Songoopavi are located on Second Mesa; and the villages of Orayvi, Hot'vela, Paaqavi, and Munqapi are located on Third Mesa, with Kiqötsmovi at its base.

14. Keams Canyon Boarding School (K–6), First Mesa Elementary School (K–6), Second Mesa Elementary School (K–6), Hopi Day School (K–6), Hopi Mission School (K–6), Hotevilla-Bacavi Community School (K–8), and Munqapi Day School.

15. Comment from Minutes, Public Orientation.

16. Comment from Minutes at a Public Forum, Village of Munqapi, January 1997.

17. Emory Sekaquaptewa as cited in Sheilah Nicholas, "Negotiating for the Hopi Way of Life through Literacy and Schooling," in *Language, Literacy, and Power in Schooling*, ed. Teresa L. McCarty (Mahwah, NJ: Lawrence Erlbaum, 2005), 29–46.

18. Emory Sekaquaptewa, personal communication, 25 October 2000.

19. Peter Whiteley, *Rethinking Hopi Ethnography* (Washington, DC: Smithsonian Institute, 1998), 191.

20. Elinor Ochs, *Culture and Language Development: Language Acquisition and Language Socialization in a Samoan Village* (Cambridge: Cambridge University Press, 1988), 14.

21. Emory Sekaquaptewa and Dorothy Washburn, "They Go Along Singing: Reconstructing the Hopi Past from Ritual Metaphors in Song and Image," *American Antiquity* 9, no. 3 (2004): 457–86.

22. John D. Loftin, *Religion and Hopi Life in the Twentieth Century* (Bloomington and Indianapolis: Indiana University Press, 1994), 5.

23. Ibid., 9.

24. Ibid.

25. Mary Black, "Maidens and Others: An Analysis of Hopi Corn Metaphors," *Ethnology* 234, no. 4 (1984): 279–88; quotation on p. 286.

26. Helen Sekaquaptewa as cited in Louise Udall, *Me and Mine: The Life Story of Helen Sekaquaptewa* (Tucson: University of Arizona Press, 1986), 286.

27. Emory Sekaquaptewa, personal communication, 25 October 2000.

28. Nettle and Romaine, *Vanishing Voices*, 177.

29. Ibid., 97.

30. Emory Sekaquaptewa, personal communication, 24 March 2004.

31. Ibid., 193.

32. Ibid., 192.

33. Ofelia Garcia, "En/countering Indigenous Bilingualism," *Journal of Language, Identity, and Education* (Philadelphia: Routledge Taylor and Francis, 2009).

34. Ibid., 377–79.

AMERICAN INDIAN CULTURE AND RESEARCH JOURNAL 34:2 (2010) 145–164

Respect, Responsibility, and Renewal: The Foundations of Anishinaabe Treaty Making with the United States and Canada

HEIDI KIIWETINEPINESIIK STARK

THE WOMAN WHO MARRIED A BEAVER: ANISHINAABE CONCEPTIONS OF TREATY MAKING

In 1904, Kagige pinasi, a Fort Williams Anishinaabe, recounted the story of *The Woman Who Married a Beaver* to Mesquaki anthropologist William Jones.[1] In this story, a young girl blackened her face and went to fast.[2] After a while a being approached her and asked her to come live with him. She agreed and eventually married him. The being was very rich and had many impressive things; therefore, the young woman was never in need. In time, they had four children and continued to live without want. The family was always well fed and clothed. Jones recorded:

> Now and then by a person were they visited; then they would go to where the person lived, whereupon the people would then slay the beavers, yet they really did not kill them; but back home would they come again. Now the woman never went to where the people lived; she was forbidden by her husband. That was the time when very numerous were the beavers, and the beavers were very fond of the people; in the same way as people are when visiting one another, so were (the beavers) in their mental attitude toward the people. Even though they were slain by (the people), yet they really were not dead. They were very fond of the tobacco that was given them by the people; at times they were also given clothing by the people.[3]

Heidi Kiiwetinepinesiik Stark (Turtle Mountain Ojibwe) is an assistant professor in American Indian studies at the University of Minnesota—Duluth. Her primary area of research and teaching is in the field of indigenous comparative politics, Native diplomacy and treaty, and aboriginal rights.

Her children and husband would often go to the homes of the Anishinaabe, but they always returned.[4] They brought back many gifts such as kettles, plates, knives, and tobacco, the very things used by the Anishinaabe when they ate beavers. Her husband told her that he and their children greatly loved the Anishinaabe and always enjoyed visiting them. She never left her home but heard these many things from her husband. Instead, she always remained, tidying their home. Then one day she realized that she was in a beaver lodge. She then knew she had married a beaver.

Eventually, the woman's husband passed away, and she returned to her own people. She lived many years and often told the story of what happened when she was married to a beaver.

> And she was wont to say: "Never speak you ill of a beaver! Should you speak ill of (a beaver), you will not (be able to) kill one."
>
> Therefore such was what the people always did; they never spoke ill of the beavers, especially when they intended hunting them. Such was what the people truly know. If any one regards a beaver with too much contempt, speaking ill of it, one simply (will) not (be able to) kill it. Just the same as the feelings of one who is disliked, so is the feeling of the beaver. And he who never speaks ill of a beaver is very much loved by it; in the same way as people often love one another, so one is held in the mind of the beaver; particularly lucky then is one at killing beavers.[5]

The Woman Who Married a Beaver carries with it many lessons for the listener. It serves, first of all, to prepare young children for the encounters they may have with other beings when they engage in fasting or a vision quest. This story, as Bruce White has noted, also details the intermediary role that a woman can play in her marriage.[6] Yet a striking feature of the story is its attention to the reciprocal relationship that exists between the Anishinaabe and the beavers. White says, "Further, it is a basic description of and commentary on the cooperative arrangements that many Ojibwa people believed existed between different kinds of beings in the world."[7] By living among the beavers, the woman learned the importance of Anishinaabe offerings of tobacco and gifts to the beavers' well-being. The exchange of gifts—the beaver's life in exchange for tobacco and housekeeping items—also maintains the pleasant and mutually beneficial relationship between the Anishinaabe and the beavers. The ongoing success of this relationship depends on the Anishinaabe's practice of returning the bones of the beaver to the water, as this allows the beavers to come back to life and return home. The woman learned these lessons while she lived with the beavers and passed them on to the Anishinaabe when she returned home to her own people.

What is of particular interest is how this relationship and agreement are, in many respects, comparable to treaties. I argue that this story recounts the forging and functioning of a treaty relationship between the Anishinaabe and beavers. A treaty is in place between the Anishinaabe and beavers. The beavers offer themselves up to the Anishinaabe as food, and in exchange the

Anishinaabe agree to return the bones of the beaver and make offerings so that the cycle can continue. Importantly, this treaty is predicated on mutual respect between the beavers and the Anishinaabe. The necessity of respect is illustrated by the woman's warnings that the Anishinaabe are never to speak ill of the beaver.[8] She stated that their relationship to the beaver is like their relationship to one another: just as the Anishinaabe love one another, the beaver greatly loves those Anishinaabe who speak well of them. Those who speak kindly of the beaver will find great success in trapping one. Thus, the beavers, in turn, respect the Anishinaabe by greatly loving them and giving themselves up to the Anishinaabe for food.

Another key principle in this diplomatic accord between the Anishinaabe and beavers is responsibility. Each party has a responsibility to the other: the relationship is cooperative and predicated on trust. The Anishinaabe have a responsibility to make offerings to the beavers, enabling them to live without want.[9] They also have a responsibility to return the bones of the beaver back to their homes to allow for the beaver's continuation. In turn, the beavers have a responsibility to "visit" the Anishinaabe, giving themselves as food for the Anishinaabe, which allows the Anishinaabe to live without want.

Finally, this treaty is founded on the principle of renewal. The Anishinaabe and the beaver alike must carry out the principles of respect and responsibility for the treaty to remain continually in effect. Each time the Anishinaabe offer gifts to the beavers, the beavers in turn offer themselves by allowing their physical bodies to be trapped. When their bones are returned to the water, this treaty is renewed.

These early treaties between indigenous peoples and the Animal and Star nations are perhaps the oldest recorded treaties; they are contained in stories that lay out many foundational principles of treaty making. These principles would inform Anishinaabe political thought and practice as the Anishinaabe negotiated treaties with the United States and Canada and remain pivotal to contemporary legal and political struggles that face Native nations. By thinking about this story as a treaty, we can more fully understand the values and proper behavior necessary for two or more nations to engage in creating alliances with one another, a relationship rooted in respect, responsibility, and renewal. Robert Williams states, "In American Indian treaty visions of law and peace, a treaty itself was a special kind of story: a way of imagining a world of human solidarity where we regard others as our relatives."[10] The principles of respect, responsibility, and renewal illustrated in this treaty between the Anishinaabe and beavers are foundational in Anishinaabe political thought and practice. The Anishinaabe utilized these principles in their treaty practices with the United States and Canada as a means to establish just and mutually beneficial relationships.

"OUR HEARTS AND OUR BRAINS ARE LIKE PAPER; WE NEVER FORGET": TREATY COUNCILS AND THE WRITTEN TEXT

The Anishinaabe have long had to reckon with what it means to live in a multicultural and multinational world. Beyond recognizing a collective identity, the Anishinaabe comprise distinct, separate bands that span a vast geographic region from the Great Lakes to the Plains.[11] Historically and today, the Anishinaabe are a people who share many beliefs and practices, yet individual bands are influenced by their particular histories, geographic locations, political relationships, and internal conflicts. Long before the arrival of Europeans, Anishinaabe nations were participating in social, economic, and political alliances that required engagement across national borders, kin ties, and epistemologies.[12] Nonetheless, as Vine Deloria and Raymond DeMallie state, "There has always been a question whether treaty making was a process familiar to Indian tribes or whether it was newly introduced by Europeans and inadequately understood by the Indians." But the overarching body of evidence shows that treaty making was a long-standing tradition among Native peoples. Deloria and DeMallie declare that, "As far back as we can trace the practice we find that Indians were quite familiar with diplomatic negotiations and had their own forms for making agreements."[13] Indigenous diplomatic practices are evident throughout the treaty record as Native peoples brought their own understandings of treaty making into the process.[14] The use of the pipe, exchange of wampum, and practice of gift giving are well-documented indigenous political practices that continued into their relations with European nations and later the United States and Canada.[15]

Nell Jessup Newton and colleagues argue that "the initial 'treaties' between the Americans and the Indian tribes were not written documents, but instead were formal diplomatic ceremonies lasting several days and marked by the exchange of presents, ceremonial objects, and solemn promises of friendship."[16] Even in the early formation of the United States, little attention was focused on a written agreement.[17] Legal scholar Brian Slattery similarly finds that, in Canada, "historic treaties were profoundly influenced by Indian concepts, procedures and ceremonial and differed in a number of ways from treaties typical among European states." He notes that "normally they were oral rather than written agreements. An Indian treaty typically took the form of a spoken exchange of proposals and responses, often marked by special rituals and usually taking place in several sessions extending over a number of days, leading to a firm understanding between the parties on certain matters."[18] Although initial treaty making relied heavily on US and Canadian adherence to indigenous political protocols with little aim toward a written document, these colonial nations were able to formalize this process in ways that supported their own shifting political goals and standards.[19] Thus, at the end of the eighteenth century, the shift toward a written treaty, first found with the Delaware in 1778, became standard US and British North American practice.[20]

The Anishinaabe did not conceptualize the treaty exclusively as a written document. Instead, they understood that the treaty consisted of the entire council proceedings coupled with the events preceding its development and following its implementation. DeMallie has thoroughly addressed this more holistic view of the treaty process in his research on treaty councils. Although he specifically focuses on the Dakota, his findings have broader implications and can inform our understanding of Anishinaabe treaty practices. DeMallie argues that "for the Indians the council was the traditional way of making peace or negotiating with another people."[21] Native peoples had historical diplomatic practices of negotiating and working to attain consensus when building or maintaining social and political alliances. Therefore, when First Nations entered into these practices with European nations, they fully understood their purposes. Nonetheless, DeMallie argues, "If the council as a diplomatic forum was commonly understood by both whites and Indians, the concept of the treaty was not." He finds that "for plains Indians, the council was an end in itself. What was important was the coming together in peace, smoking the pipe in common to pledge the truthfulness of all statements made, and the exchange of opinions. . . . Thus, from the Indians' point of view, the council *was* the agreement."[22]

Francis Paul Prucha also recognizes this critical distinction, asserting that "the meeting itself was the significant event, and for the Indians the exchange and acceptance of wampum strings and belts confirmed the decisions at the council."[23] The word *treaty*, while currently understood as a contract between two or more nations, historically had an alternate meaning and usage: "a 'treaty' in that sense was the 'act of negotiating,' the discussion aimed at adjustment of difference or the reading of an agreement, and by extension the meeting itself at which such negotiations took place."[24] Although the United States and Canada may have utilized the term *treaty* in its varied meanings, in time they would see the written document as the final and binding agreement.

Alternately, the Anishinaabe understood the entire council deliberations as the treaty. US and Canadian treaty commissioners primarily perceived the council, gift exchange, and dialogue as a prerequisite to acquiring the desired signatures of First Nations leaders. Although these colonial nations were frequently interested in extinguishing Indian title by having Native peoples sign their name to a treaty, or "touching the pen," the written document rarely represented the vast expressions of indigenous sovereignty, nationhood, and land tenure articulated within the council. As DeMallie states, "for individual Indian leaders, touching the pen apparently signified that they were validating all they had said at a council; in many cases the record of the treaty proceedings makes it clear that the Indian leaders did not realize their signatures committed them to *only* those statements written in the treaty."[25]

An Anishinaabe leader expressed the importance of oral negotiations to the process of treaty making. During the negotiation of Treaty Three, which concerned Anishinaabe lands in present-day Ontario with a small portion in southeastern Manitoba, this chief stressed to the Crown, "you must remember that *our hearts and our brains are like paper; we never forget.*"[26] The commissioners were aware of the Anishinaabe's remarkable ability to remember everything said during these negotiations.[27] This is reflected in the negotiation records when Canadian Treaty Commissioner S. J. Dawson cautioned the other commissioners to use great care in choosing their words. He recalled his experience with a Fort Frances Anishinaabe leader who had repeated verbatim everything Dawson had stated two years earlier.[28] Anishinaabe leader Metawaa's words at the 1833 treaty between the United States and the United Nation of Ojibwe,

Ottawa, and Potawatomi echoed the sentiments of the Treaty Three leader. He stated, "We have heard the words of our Fathers. They are good and we will hearken unto them. They shall abide in our memories."[29] Anishinaabe ability to recall the statements made in previous councils shows that they, as DeMallie suggests, understood the entire council's proceedings as constituting the treaty.

This distinction between the council as the treaty in contrast to the written document alone has led to various disputes about what was understood by the First Nations as they engaged in treaty making with the United States and Canada. The written treaties did not always faithfully reflect the terms verbally agreed to by the participating nations. This became evident to the First Nations when the government response did not mirror the promises made during the negotiations.[30] Although the Anishinaabe did not see the written document exclusively as the treaty, they gradually became aware of its importance to US and Canadian government officials. The Anishinaabe responded to the distinction of what constituted the treaty by utilizing the written format in conjunction with their long-standing practice of recording to memory everything said throughout the council.[31]

The record surrounding the 1846 treaty between the United Nation of Ojibwe, Ottawa, and Potawatomi and the United States demonstrates one way that the Anishinaabe responded to colonial preference for a written document.[32] Superintendent of Indian Affairs Major Thomas H. Harvey had met with the Anishinaabe delegations in June 1845 to discuss the prospect of a treaty that would enable the United States to remove the United Nation from its reservation in western Iowa. The United Nation was dissatisfied with this offer. Aware of the importance of the written document for the United States, they sent Major Harvey back to Washington with a written "talk" that outlined their response. This "talk" focused primarily on the United Nation's request for one million acres of land held by the Kansas Indians, as opposed to the lands proposed by the president, as well as their proposal for adjustments to the amount and duration of their annuities.

In November 1845, a delegation for the United Nation went to Washington to inquire about the president's response to their written "talk"; US treaty commissioners argued that the United Nation had not been invited to Washington and asserted that the United Nation had refused to enter into a treaty with the president. Anishinaabe leader Obto-gee-shick responded to the commissioner's recitation of their recent treaty negotiations, stating: "We have never refused him anything. When Major Harvey came to ask for our land we did not refuse, we told him it was the last piece we had to sell—take it—there is our price. We gave him a paper—it is all written down. We want our great Father's answer to that paper."[33] The United Nation recognized that the United States placed weight on the written document. Therefore, they had their requests to the president written down. When the United Nation felt that treaty commissioners had misrepresented the events surrounding a previous attempt to negotiate a treaty, they again called on this written document to assert their interests.

In order to control the tone and direction of the negotiations in Washington, the United Nation presented a formal written response to the commissioners.[34] They had this response read for them by Richard S. Elliott, their former Indian subagent at Council Bluffs, and set up measures to ensure that what was stated accurately reflected their words. Obto-gee-shick declared, "The answer he is going to give you for us comes from our hearts—the half breeds will listen to what he says."[35] Although the United Nation requested that Elliott present its written response, it ensured that he accurately represented their interests by confirming his interpretive statements through bilingual "half-breed" Anishinaabe interpreters present at the treaty.[36]

Though the United Nation left Washington without any resolution, commissioners assured the Anishinaabe that US officials would negotiate a treaty with the United Nation that summer. Recognizing the importance of written documentation for the United States, the United Nation not only formally wrote its response to US treaty commissioners, but also asked for personal copies of the written treaty. When the negotiations concluded in June 1846, Anishinaabe leader Ne-bea-me stated, "You must make us a strong paper & a good paper with the name of our great Father to it and give us one of them that we may keep it ourselves."[37] Other Native nations also requested copies of their written treaties.[38]

For instance, the Anishinaabe in Lake of the Woods requested a written copy of Treaty Three in 1873. They said that they wanted their copy to be written on parchment so that the treaty would not be "rubbed off."[39] This insistence on a copy that would withstand time was important for Lake of the Woods Anishinaabe, who saw their treaties as foundations for a long-standing relationship with Canada that carried responsibilities, rights, and privileges for both parties. These responsibilities, though not always recorded in their entirety, were thought by the Anishinaabe to be included in the written agreement. Besides insisting on a copy of the written treaty, an Anishinaabe leader at the negotiations for Treaty Three also requested the names of all the Canadian officials for accountability purposes. He stated, "I would wish to have all your names in writing handed over to us. I would not find it to my convenience to have a stranger here to transact our business between me and you. It is a white man who does not understand our language that is taking it down. I would like a man that understand our language and our ways."[40]

The United States and Canada have occasionally attempted to reconcile these distinct understandings of treaty making and resolve the issues that came out of these different perceptions by creating and relying upon special canons of treaty construction by which a document might be interpreted and construed.[41] Although the United States and Canada have sporadically adhered to these canons in court cases, they have sometimes led to favorable judicial rulings for First Nation.[42] The canons posit three distinguishing factors for interpreting Indian treaties: "(1) a cardinal rule in the interpretation of Indian treaties is that ambiguities in treaty language are to be resolved in favor of the Indians; (2) since the wording of treaties was designed to be understood by the Indians, who often could not read and were not skilled in the technical language often used in treaties, doubtful clauses are to be resolved in a nontechnical way, as the Indians would have understood the language; and (3) treaties are to be liberally construed to favor Indians."[43] In addition, the reserved rights doctrine, a closely related concept, holds that all rights not expressly ceded by a tribe in a treaty are reserved while the abrogation doctrine asserts that Congress's intent to infringe upon tribal rights must be clear and unambiguous.[44]

The canons of construction, when they are invoked, seemingly work in favor of Native interpretations of treaty making, relying on a broader examination of the historical record instead of merely the written treaty. However, Felix Cohen has pointed out that "although an interpretation of a treaty should be made in the light of conditions existing when the treaty was executed, as often indicated by its history before and after its making, the exact situation which caused the inclusion of a provision is often difficult to ascertain."[45] The canons promote and rely upon an examination of the historical record to ascertain what Native people intended when they engaged in treaties with the United States and Canada. Deloria recognizes the importance of this historical record: "We can conclude that an Indian treaty, in addition to being a formal document either ratified by Congress or unratified but nevertheless negotiated in good faith, should include the narratives of the negotiations and any prior or subsequent form of negotiation conducted according to traditional Indian procedure. By adopting this expanded understanding of the Indian treaty, one can illuminate the obscure phrases and promises contained in the written document."[46]

Journal records surrounding Anishinaabe negotiations with the United States and Canada brim with Anishinaabe conceptions of treaty making and what these agreements entail. As Deloria observed, "By looking at what the Indians said in their formal speeches during negotiations, one can determine what the Indians saw as important and what parts of the treaty should be taken seriously as a meeting of the minds."[47] Although the historical record can shed light on the important aspects of a treaty for First Nations, it can also illuminate what First Nations saw as critical principles for building and sustaining mutually beneficial relationships with other nations, namely the United States and Canada.

"OUR TREATIES WERE MEANT TO LAST FOREVER": THE TREATY AS A LIVING RELATIONSHIP

The treaty process, mirroring long-standing diplomatic practices, was seen as a way to develop international alliances with colonial and settler nations.[48] Rebecca Tsosie and Wallace Coffey state that "our ancestors recognized themselves as distinctive cultural and political groups, and that was the basis of their sovereign authority to reach agreements with each other, with the European sovereigns, and then the United States." They argue that "in each of these instances, our Ancestors exercised governmental authority to protect their lands, resources, peoples and cultures."[49] Furthermore, they point out that indigenous treaty making was primarily focused on the protection of land, resources, and peoples. Anishinaabe elder Mervin Huntinghawk echoes these sentiments: "our treaties were meant to protect our rights to the land and to provide a base for a lasting relationship with the Crown. They represent political arrangements which we gave to the Crown in order to regulate how we shared our land and resources in nation-to-nation relations." His statement illustrates how the treaty process was not a novel practice. It was a practice "given" to the Crown by the Anishinaabe. Huntinghawk, in his discussion of the treaty-making process, connects treaty elements with the longer tradition of diplomacy employed by the Anishinaabe in their relations with other Native nations.[50]

Although Huntinghawk's comments illustrate contemporary perceptions among the Anishinaabe, these views of the treaty process provide a retrospective lens for interpreting the political discourses and practices employed by the Anishinaabe in the treaty era. In many cases, the Anishinaabe called on their long-standing diplomatic practices to shape and set the tone of the treaty negotiations.[51] Additionally, Huntinghawk's comments that "our treaties were made to last forever" evidence that the Anishinaabe saw the treaty as having forged a living relationship, not merely an agreement fixed on paper.[52] This living relationship continues to be dependent on the principles of respect, responsibility, and renewal.

Throughout the treaty-making process, the Anishinaabe echoed these three principles. For example, an Anishinaabe leader from Treaty Three discussed the principle of responsibility that is rooted in notions of reciprocity: "We are the first that were planted here; we would ask you to assist us with every kind of implement to use for our benefit, to enable us to perform our work; a little of everything and money. We would borrow your cattle; we ask you this for our support, I will find whereon to feed them. The waters out of which you sometimes take food for yourselves, we will lend you in return."[53] This leader was asserting Anishinaabe sovereignty as it was connected to their placement in North America. Such an assertion established their claim to the land. The Anishinaabe leader then made specific requests of the Canadian government, offering in return the use of Anishinaabe lands and resources. His words demonstrate that the Anishinaabe saw the treaties as vehicles for building relationships vested in reciprocal responsibilities. The Canadian government would be responsible for aiding the Anishinaabe, and, in turn, the Anishinaabe would be responsible for assisting Canada.

Anishinaabe intent for treaty making was often generated by their desire to establish relationships with the United States and Canada based on peace and friendship. Anishinaabe leaders echoed this sentiment at the negotiations surrounding Treaty Three with Canada. One leader stated, "You have come before us with a smiling face, you have shown us great charity—you have promised the good things; you have given us your best compliments and wishes, not only for once but for ever."[54] Respect and kindness toward one another were critical to establishing treaty relationships. The Anishinaabe leader continued, "Let there now for ever be peace and friendship between us."[55]

The principles of respect and renewal were interdependent for the Anishinaabe of Lake of the Woods. They closed the negotiation councils by reminding the commissioner of the lasting effect of the treaty, which entailed mutual responsibilities, dependent on continuous renewal. Anishinaabe leader Mawedopenais expressed it this way, "and now, in closing this Council,

I take off my glove, and in giving you my hand, I deliver over my birth-right and lands, and in taking your hand, I hold fast all the promises you have made, and I hope they will last as long as the sun goes round and the water flows, as you have said." Mawedopenais emphasized that each nation had a responsibility to the other, with each having acquired rights from the agreement. Likewise, Lieutenant-Governor Alexander Morris seemingly recognized the responsibility that treaties carried, proclaiming, "I accept your hand and with it the lands, and will keep all my promises, in the firm belief that the treaty now signed will bind the red man and the white together as friends for ever."[56]

Yet treaty promises were not always kept by the United States and Canada.[57] These nations were frequently slow in fulfilling certain aspects of the treaties. The Anishinaabe often petitioned their treaty partners, pressing them to uphold the promises and responsibilities they had to one another. The United Nation of Ojibwe, Ottawa, and Potawatomi, while negotiating with US commissioners in Washington in 1845, expressed their understanding of the responsibilities outlined in the treaties. When the United States failed to fulfill previous treaty stipulations, the United Nation reminded the United States of its responsibility, explicitly stating, "There were two contracting parties to that treaty. The United States and ourselves. And it was not a treaty until both parties agreed to it. We were told that it could not be altered without the consent of both. We have never agreed to alter it."[58]

The United Nation continued to assert the importance of previous treaties with the United States, declaring, "This is one of the troubles that has brought us here. You now say that our Great Father cannot give us money to build our farm houses, and shops where we now are." The United States argued that they could not fulfill their treaty responsibilities to the United Nation until the tribe removed. The United Nation, having already been removed from the western shore of Lake Michigan to their current location in Iowa and Missouri, was frustrated with US attempts to remove them again with Potawatomi bands to Kansas.[59] They continued, "But the treaty calls for these things and he [the president of the United States] said when we saw him that all the stipulations of the treaty should be fulfilled."[60]

The United Nation of Ojibwe, Ottawa, and Potawatomi summarized the distinct understanding of treaty making maintained by these three separate polities when it stated, "We wished to act up to our treaties: but it seems he has changed his mind, since the last great treaty was made. Now he wants us to remove: and because we will not go to a country where we cannot live; because we will not give him our last tract of land for six cents an acre; we will not make ourselves still poorer forever than we now are, you say, he thinks we are not wise."[61] When the United States and Canada did not adhere to their treaty promises, the Anishinaabe often expressed the three principles of respect, responsibility, and renewal as a means to reorientate their relationship with the United States and Canada.

An Anishinaabe leader at the Treaty Three negotiations perhaps best expressed the importance of treaty making for the Anishinaabe when he stated, "We would not wish that anyone should smile at our affairs, as *we think our country is a large matter to us*."[62] He pushed for Lieutenant-Governor

Morris to agree to the terms set out by the Anishinaabe. Morris's response is quite telling. It shows how Canadian treaty commissioners understood treaty making in relation to the Anishinaabe. Morris responded, "I quite agree that this is no matter to smile at. I think that the decision of to-day is one that affects yourselves and your children after."[63] Although these decisions did affect the Anishinaabe and their children, these commitments also affected the Canadian government and its citizens. This agreement carried responsibilities for both sides, a point that Morris did not seem to reflect upon. The responsibilities the Canadian government had toward the Anishinaabe did not cease with a signature on paper and the payment of treaty annuities. The Anishinaabe, recognizing that treaties would affect their people for generations, understood that these relationships would need to be renewed continuously.

The Anishinaabe, in their treaties with the United States, also expressed the importance of these agreements for the future of their nations. For example, Mississippi Band of Anishinaabe leader Hole-in-the-Day (the younger), in a conference with Minnesota Governor Alexander Ramsey in October 1863, stated, "What we speak of to-day are subjects of the greatest importance to us; they are matters of life and death to us."[64] Hole-in-the-Day and his people, distraught by the paltry terms of the 1863 treaty signed in Washington, recognized that this treaty would have lasting ramifications for his people. He stated, "When we look at the treaty, we have only about a stone's [?] that is good for anything, and we see no way of bettering ourselves." Hole-in-the-Day was so troubled by what this treaty would entail for his people that he declared, "I am willing to sacrifice myself for my band, and die for them."[65] Building a relationship vested in Anishinaabe treaty principles was a way for the Anishinaabe to ensure their survival in a rapidly changing world.

Treaties were clearly not static agreements from an Anishinaabe perspective but were contingent on each nation meeting the obligations they carried. These commitments necessitated a constant renewal of friendship and peace through their fulfillment. Anishinaabe nations, when entering into a treaty with the United States and Canada, frequently built upon their previous agreements. For example, when the United States sought to negotiate an additional treaty with the United Nation of Ojibwe, Ottawa, and Potawatomi in 1846, they were reminded that their previous responsibilities would not be nullified by the success or failure of reaching a new agreement. The United Nation, in its written response, stated, "We have not come here because we wanted to sell our Country: but we have met you because our Great Father has been asking us for it for years. We have named our price, and we have no other price. If our Great Father is pleased it is well; if not, our women and children will feel glad, and, therefore, will be happy. They do not want to remove."[66]

The United Nation, though quite reluctant to remove, recognized that their survival in an ever-changing multinational terrain was dependent on their ability to establish and maintain a peaceful relationship with the United States. However, they were only willing to negotiate a new treaty that would entail their removal if certain stipulations they put forward were met. They continued their speech by declaring that "Our Great Father has been knocking at the door of our wigwams for six years. We have opened the door. If he does not come in we will close it and we do not want him to knock again."[67]

The United Nation was willing to engage in a relationship with the United States but held fast to its own demands. If a new treaty was not to be concluded, the United Nation reminded the commissioners that their previous treaties needed to be fulfilled, stating, "But if our Great Father does not want to make a treaty, on our terms, we hope he will see that all our old business is arranged."[68] The United Nation used this moment to remind the commissioners that they came to the president not to sell additional lands but to express the need for him to fulfill their previous treaty stipulations. They carefully noted that the inability of reaching a new agreement did not void previous agreements.

Anishinaabe leader Ma-ghe-ga-bo also expressed the principle of renewal at the 1837 treaty negotiations with the United States by stating, "If you offer us money and goods we will take both. You see me count upon my fingers (counting six) [.] Every finger counts ten. For so many years we wish you to secure to us the payment of an annuity. At the end of that time our grandchildren, who will have grown up, can speak to you for themselves."[69] Ma-ghe-ga-bo's words demonstrate that this agreement, within Anishinaabe understandings of treaty making, did not exclusively depend on the stipulations the Anishinaabe put forward at that time. This treaty would need to be revisited in sixty years for Ma-ghe-ga-bo's grandchildren to be able to speak for themselves.

Treaties created relationships among nations. They established relationships of trust. That trust did not end with the completion of a written document; it merely began with it. However, it was the responsibility of all parties involved to maintain the relationships established through treaty making. The sustainability of these agreements was dependent upon each nation adhering to the principles of respect, responsibility, and renewal.

CONCLUSION: CONTEMPORARY APPLICATIONS
OF ANISHINAABE TREATY PRINCIPLES

The story of *The Woman Who Married a Beaver* illustrates Anishinaabe principles of respect, responsibility, and renewal that are critical in treaty making. The Anishinaabe expressed these principles when they negotiated treaties with the United States and Canada. Treaty making was contingent upon trust. Williams has asserted, "By recognizing the central principle of Encounter era Indian diplomacy that a treaty is a relationship of trust, we begin the complex process of rendering a more complete accounting of the importance of Indian ideas and values in protecting Indian rights under U.S. law."

The canons of construction have created a path for a reorientation of federal Indian law by providing an interpretive framework for the courts to expand their interpretations of First Nations' treaty rights. Nonetheless, today federal Indian law in the United States and Canada is primarily rooted in the trust or fiduciary relationship. David Wilkins and K. Tsianina Lomawaima, in their examination of the trust doctrine, note that "common to many, but not all, definitions of 'trust' is the notion of federal *responsibility* to *protect or enhance* tribal assets (including fiscal, natural, human, and cultural resources) through policy decisions and management actions."[70] Although the trust doctrine is critical to the field of federal Indian law and had its inception in treaty making, the courts have not considered Anishinaabe conceptions of trust, as defined in their treaty relations.

Williams states, "The trust doctrine was not the exclusive by-product of the Western legal tradition brought to North America from the Old World. This central protective principle of Indian tribal rights under our law has deep roots in Encounter era Indian visions of law and peace."[71] Therefore, an understanding of the parameters and applications of the trust relationship should require an incorporation of Native peoples' understanding of this important political relationship when it came into existence during the treaty era. Williams's perspective is corroborated by Tsosie and Coffey, who state that "the 'trust doctrine' should reflect our Ancestors' understanding of their relationship to the United States government, including their commitment to having their separate political existence affirmed by the United States, and their belief that the treaties entailed a series of moral duties between two groups that pledge to live in peace with one another and act in good faith."[72] The trust relationship was initially born out of this pledge to live in peace and act in good faith.

Throughout their treaty negotiations with the United States and Canada, the Anishinaabe articulated a notion of trust that infused Anishinaabe treaty principles. An understanding of Anishinaabe interpretations of treaty making, grounded in the three principles of respect, responsibility, and renewal, can shed light on how trust can be put into practice. A return to and recognition of these three foundational principles can provide new directions for federal Indian law that has often constrained indigenous peoples' rights and left them with an ever-shifting status.[73]

The Woman Who Married a Beaver is a powerful story of transformation that sheds light on how the Anishinaabe understood treaty making. The young girl is literally transformed into a beaver. Through this change, she learns how important the principles of respect, responsibility, and renewal are for a healthy and beneficial relationship to continue between the Anishinaabe and the beavers. She brought these lessons back to the Anishinaabe when she returned to her people. These principles were and remain foundational to the development and sustainability of mutually beneficial relationships. Treaty making was about making relationships. They were not mere agreements that ceded one thing in exchange for another. Treaties bound nations to one another. They carried commitments that did not end with the exchange of land for annuities. These agreements connected people. Treaties were a vision for what a multinational society could entail.

The treaty record demonstrates that Anishinaabe understandings of the trust relationship were built upon their foundational treaty principles of respect, responsibility, and renewal. Although these principles were primarily the ideal and were not always the practice, Anishinaabe often saw treaty making as the way to build relationships that worked toward this ideal. In 1873, an Anishinaabe leader in the negotiations for Treaty Three said to Canadian Treaty Commissioner Alexander Morris, "If you give what I ask, the time may come when I will ask you to lend me one of your daughters and one of your sons to live with us; and in return I will lend you one of my daughters and one of my sons for you to teach what is good, and after they have learned, to teach us."[74]

This notion of intertwining families and teachings, of creating shared relationships, echoed time and again by Anishinaabeg in their treaty relationships, can shed light on how various nations can come together to develop long-lasting relationships based on the principles of respect, responsibility, and renewal. These relationships today are often carried out through federal Indian law as Native nations call on the United States and Canada to reaffirm their treaty commitments with First Nations and to continue or revive the treaty process, commitments that carry a relationship of trust. Perhaps this story of the woman who married a beaver can shed light for what a relationship based on trust can look like in practice.

Acknowledgment

I am grateful to David Wilkins and David Chang for their insightful and gracious comments. Participants of the American Indian Studies Workshop at the University of Minnesota also provided generous comments on early drafts. Miigwech!

NOTES

1. Kagige pinasi (Forever Bird) is also referred to as John Pinesi (Penessi, Penassie). For biographical information about this Anishinaabe chief from Fort Williams, ON, see Truman Michelson, ed. and William Jones, comp., *Ojibwa Texts.* Publications of the American Ethnological Society, vol. 7, pt. 1, ed. Franz Boas (New York: E. J. Brill, 1919), xvi–xvii.

2. Frances Densmore and Smithsonian Institution Bureau of American Ethnology, *Chippewa Customs* (1929; repr., St. Paul: Minnesota Historical Society Press, 1979), 70–71; Basil Johnston, *Ojibway Ceremonies* (Lincoln: University of Nebraska Press, 1990), 41–56. For an account of a young Ojibwe woman's fasting experience, see Maude Kegg and John Nichols, *Portage Lake: Memories of an Ojibwe Childhood* (Minneapolis: University of Minnesota Press, 1993), 22–25.

3. Michelson and Jones, *Ojibwa Texts*, 255.

4. There have been a number of names with varied spelling for the people who call themselves Ojibwe. However, as E. S. Rogers notes, "Although the Indian groups now referred to as Chippewa, Ojibwa, and Saulteaux descend from closely related bands that were living in a fairly compact area in the mid-seventeenth century, at no time has there been a single distinctive name for these groups alone" (768). The historical record initially labeled these people as Algonquin, Mississauga, Saulteaux, and Ottawa while contemporary records primarily utilize the modern local band names referencing specific communities and peoples and not the larger group of

the Chippewa/Ojibwe. Chippewa is the English rendering of Ojibwe, and its usage is primarily in the United States and southern Canada. US federal records and treaties label these people as Chippewa. Canadian sources primarily reference these people as Ojibwe (also spelled Ojibwa and Ojibway). Many of the Southeastern Ojibwe were historically referenced as the Mississauga. Saulteaux was primarily found in historical references to the Ojibwe to include the Ojibwe from Sault St. Marie westward, and today is often used to connote the Ojibwe in Manitoba and Saskatchewan. I have chosen to use Anishinaabe as it is the name used by the people and adheres to contemporary scholarly practice. In addition, Anishinaabe connotes a broader group than some of these aforementioned terms are associated with. For a list of the various spellings and meanings associated with the terms used to reference the Ojibwe/Anishinaabe people, see Laura Peers, *The Ojibwa of Western Canada, 1780–1870* (Winnipeg: University of Manitoba Press, 1994); Robert E. Ritzenthaler, "Southwestern Chippewa," in *Handbook of the North American Indians: Northeast*, ed. Bruce G. Trigger (Washington, DC: Smithsonian Institution, 1996), 15:743–59; E. S. Rogers, "Southeastern Ojibwa," in Trigger, ed., *Handbook of the North American Indians: Northeast*, 15:760–71.

5. Michelson and Jones, *Ojibwa Texts*, 257.

6. Bruce White, "The Woman Who Married a Beaver: Trade Patterns and Gender Roles in the Ojibwa Fur Trade," *Ethnohistory* 46, no. 1 (Winter 1999): 109–47.

7. White further notes that "Ojibwa people who hunted, fished or gathered plants had to be aware of their reciprocal obligations with the natural world and give back something to the animals, fish, or plants from which they harvested." Ibid., 111.

8. White notes, "The beaver story shows that reciprocity was necessary to keep the system operating. Without gifts and respect, animals would not be so helpful to humans. They would hold themselves back and would not allow themselves to be used by people. Without gifts and respect, the system would cease to function." Ibid.

9. For further discussion on how gifts function in treaty making, see Cary Miller, "Gifts as Treaties: The Political Use of Received Gifts in Anishinaabeg Communities, 1820–1832," *American Indian Quarterly* 26, no. 2 (2002): 221–45.

10. Robert A. Williams Jr., *Linking Arms Together: American Indian Treaty Visions of Law and Peace, 1600–1800* (New York: Routledge, 1999), 83–84.

11. I utilize the term *band* to refer to the divisions among the Anishinaabe collective. Bands were originally constituted by a number of families that lived together and often became known by their locations, their villages. Today, the Anishinaabe continue to divide along band lines yet maintain a shared identity through common ancestry as Anishinaabe people. These separate bands are primarily recognized as separate nations that maintain their own governments and laws. Many Anishinaabe nations were recognized by their band names in their treaties and continue to employ these names today (e.g., Turtle Mountain Band of Chippewa Indians and Red Lake Band of Chippewa Indians). Some bands were brought together in treaty making and/or vis-à-vis a variety of policies and statutes and are dealt with by the United States as a single nation (e.g., White Earth Nation). In Canada, many Anishinaabe nations maintain names that pertain to their locations. In addition, First Nation is common usage in Canada to refer to Native nations and many Anishinaabe First Nations do not use *band* as part of their official national name. I primarily utilize the term *nation* in place of *band* to reference individual bands because it more accurately recognizes the political autonomy and sovereignty of each band in relation to the Anishinaabe collective.

Historically, the Anishinaabe, an Algonquian-speaking people with origins on the East Coast, migrated west during the course of several centuries. Around the time of arrival at Sault Ste. Marie, distinct linguistic and cultural identities slowly emerged among Ojibwe, Ottawa, and Potawatomi people. The common origins of these three groups are recognized by their shared identity as Anishinaabe people. From Sault Ste. Marie, Ojibwe people continued spreading west along the northern and southern shores of Lake Superior in northwestern Ontario, Upper Michigan, and northern Wisconsin. In the eighteenth century, Ojibwe people began massive expansion into northern Wisconsin and Minnesota. From here, Ojibwe people expanded over a vast area in the plains, establishing communities in North Dakota, Manitoba, Saskatchewan, and Alberta. Plains Ojibwe communities retained distinct woodland cultural institutions, while increasingly drawing on cultural traits of their neighbors on the plains.

12. See Kathy Davis Graves and Elizabeth Ebbott for the League of Women Voters of Minnesota, *Indians in Minnesota*, 5th ed. (Minneapolis: University of Minnesota Press, 2006); William W. Warren, *History of the Ojibway People* (1885; repr., St. Paul: Minnesota Historical Society Press, 1984).

13. Vine Deloria Jr. and Raymond J. DeMallie, eds., *Documents of American Indian Diplomacy: Treaties, Agreements, and Conventions, 1775–1979*, 2 vols. Legal History of North America, vol. 4 (Norman: University of Oklahoma Press, 1999), 6.

14. William N. Fenton, *The Great Law and the Longhouse: A Political History of the Iroquois Confederacy*. The Civilization of the American Indian Series, vol. 223 (Norman: University of Oklahoma Press, 1998); Lewis Henry Morgan and Herbert Marshall Lloyd, *League of the Ho-Dé-No-Sau-Nee or Iroquois* (New York: B. Franklin, 1966); Richard White, *The Middle Ground: Indians, Empires, and Republics in the Great Lakes Region, 1650–1815*. Cambridge Studies in North American Indian History (Cambridge and New York: Cambridge University Press, 1991); Williams, *Linking Arms Together*.

15. Colin G. Calloway, *New Worlds for All: Indians, Europeans, and the Remaking of Early America* (Baltimore, MD: Johns Hopkins University Press, 1998); Williams, *Linking Arms Together*.

16. Nell Jessup Newton et al., *Cohen's Handbook of Federal Indian Law* (Newark, NJ: LexisNexis, 2005), 20.

17. Francis Paul Prucha, *American Indian Treaties: The History of Political Anomaly* (Berkeley: University of California Press, 1994), 26; Alden T. Vaughan, *Early American Indian Documents: Treaties and Laws, 1607–1789* (Washington, DC: University Publications of America, 1979).

18. Brian Slattery, "Making Sense of Aboriginal and Treaty Rights," *Canadian Bar Review* 79 (2000): 208.

19. Prucha, *American Indian Treaties*; Francis Paul Prucha, *The Great Father: The United States Government and the American Indians* (Lincoln: University of Nebraska Press, 1986); Slattery, "Making Sense of Aboriginal and Treaty Rights."

20. Prucha, *American Indian Treaties*, 26.

21. Raymond DeMallie, "Touching the Pen: Plains Indian Treaty Councils in Ethnohistorical Perspective," in *Major Problems in American Indian History*, ed. Albert Hurtado and Peter Iverson (Lexington, MA: D. C. Heath and Company, 1994), 345.

22. Slattery, "Making Sense of Aboriginal and Treaty Rights," 345–46; emphasis in original.

23. Prucha, *American Indian Treaties*, 26.

24. Prucha argues, "The language of the Continental Congress and its contemporaries makes it clear enough from the context which sense of the word it meant. The documents are full of such terminology as 'holding a treaty' with the Indians, 'inviting Indians to a treaty,' providing military support and purchasing presents 'for a treaty,' or greeting Indians as they arrived 'at a treaty.'" Ibid., 25.

25. DeMallie, "Touching the Pen," 346; emphasis in original.

26. The chiefs were often not identified in the negotiation records. Alexander Morris, *The Treaties of Canada with the Indians of Manitoba and the North-West Territories: Including the Negotiations on Which They Were Based, and Other Information Relating Thereto* (Toronto: Prospero Books, 2000), 69; emphasis added. For additional information on Treaty Three, see Wayne E. Daugherty, "Treaty Research Report: Treaty Three (1873)," Treaties and Historical Research Centre, Indian and Northern Affairs Canada, http://www.ainc-inac.gc.ca/pr/trts/hti/t3/index_e.html (accessed 15 August 2008). Originally published in Ottawa by Indian and Northern Affairs Canada, 1986.

27. Although it was recognized that Native people maintained the ability to remember everything stated throughout the negotiations, oral history still has not been given its due weight in the courts. See, e.g., John Borrows, "Listening for a Change: The Courts and Oral Traditions," *Osgoode Hall Law Journal* 39 (1997): 1–38.

28. Olive Patricia Dickason, *Canada's First Nations: A History of Founding Peoples from Earliest Times*. The Civilization of the American Indian Series, vol. 208 (Norman: University of Oklahoma Press, 1992), 276.

29. The United Nation of Ojibwe, Ottawa, and Potawatomi was comprised of Anishinaabe who resided on the western shores of Lake Michigan. In this 1833 treaty, the United Nation ceded these lands for a reservation in western Iowa. See *Ratified Treaty No. 189 Documents Relating to the Negotiation of the Treaty of September 26, 1833, with the United Chippewa, Ottawa, and Potawatomi Indians*, Documents Relating to the Negotiation of Ratified and Unratified Treaties with Various Tribes of Indians, 1801–69, National Archives Microfilm Publications, Record Group 75, Microcopy No. T-494, Roll 3:F66 (hereinafter referred to as NAMP RG 75, M T-494). Records of the Bureau of Indian Affairs, National Archives and Records Services, Washington, DC.

30. Brian Slattery, "Understanding Aboriginal Rights," *The Canadian Bar Review* 66 (1987): 730.

31. *Ratified Treaty No. 247 Documents Relating to the Negotiation of the Treaty of June 5 and 17, 1846, with the Chippewa, Ottawa, and Potawatomi Indians*, NAMP RG 75, M T-494, Roll 4; president's message, 9 July 1846. Also see Morris, *The Treaties of Canada with the Indians of Manitoba and the North-West Territories*.

32. Unlike the 1833 treaty, this treaty consolidated the treaty interests of the United Nation of Ojibwe, Ottawa, and Potawatomi Indians with other Potawatomi bands and referred to the collective as the Potawatomi Nation. See Treaty with the Potawatomi Nation, 1846, June 5 and 17, 1846: 9 *U.S. Statutes at Large* 853; Treaty with the Chippewa, etc., 1833, September 26, 1833: 7 *U.S. Statutes at Large* 431.

33. Dashes in text have been changed to em dashes for readability. *Ratified Treaty No. 247*, NAMP RG 75, M T-494, Roll 4:F300.

34. Ibid., F304. Miamese said, "Our views have been put on paper and will be presented by Mr. Elliot. We have taken time to consider what our great father has said as you told us to do. And what Mr. Elliot will read to you is our reply."

35. Em dash added for readability. Ibid.

36. Many interpreters were not only bilingual but were fluent in multiple languages. The treaty record, however, rarely provides any information on the language skills of the interpreters.

37. *Ratified Treaty No. 247*, NAMP RG 75, M T-494, Roll 4:F333.

38. Also see the records surrounding Treaty Three discussed in the following text and in Morris, *The Treaties of Canada with the Indians of Manitoba and the North-West Territories.*

39. Ibid., 72.

40. Ibid., 71.

41. For additional information on the origin and application of the treaty canons of construction, see "Interpretation of Treaties," in Felix S. Cohen, *Handbook of Federal Indian Law, with Reference Tables and Index* (Washington, DC: Government Printing Office, 1942), 120. Also see Philip P. Frickey, "Marshalling Past and Present: Colonialism, Constitutionalism, and Interpretation in Federal Indian Law," *Harvard Law Review* 107, no. 2 (December 1993): 381–440; David E. Wilkins, *American Indian Sovereignty and the U.S. Supreme Court: The Masking of Justice* (Austin: University of Texas Press, 1997); Charles F. Wilkinson and John M. Volkman, "Judicial Review of Indian Treaty Abrogation: 'As Long as Water Flows, or Grass Grows Upon the Earth'—How Long Is That?" *California Law Review* 63, no. 3 (May 1975): 601–61.

42. Native scholars David E. Wilkins and K. Tsianina Lomawaima point out that "each of these 'canons' theoretically stands for a system of fundamental rules and maxims that the Court agrees to recognize and use in its interpretation of written instruments." However, they find that "this sense of 'canon' as an authoritative rule does not always hold up in the area of Indian law. As we have seen with other doctrines of federal Indian policy and law, each canon has an opposite corollary that may be cited by the courts when it suits the justices' purposes." Wilkins and Lomawaima, *Uneven Ground: American Indian Sovereignty and Federal Law* (Norman: University of Oklahoma Press, 2001), 141.

43. David E. Wilkins, *American Indian Politics and the American Political System* (Lanham, MD: Rowman and Littlefield, 2002), 339.

44. Cohen, *Cohen's Handbook of Federal Indian Law*, 26. Also see *Choctaw Nation v. United States*, 318 U.S. 423 (1943); *Choate v. Trapp*, 224 U.S. 665 (1912); *Worcester v. Georgia*, 31 U.S. (6 Pet) 515 (1832); *U.S. v. Winans*, 198 U.S. 371 (1905); *Choctaw Nation v. Oklahoma*, 397 U.S. 620 (1970); *United States v. Shoshone Tribe*, 304 U.S. 111 (1938); *Jones v. Meehan*, 175 U.S. 1 (1899); and *Winters v. United States*, 207 U.S. 564 (1908).

45. Cohen, *Handbook of Federal Indian Law, with Reference Tables and Index*, 38.

46. Deloria and DeMallie, eds., *Documents of American Indian Diplomacy*, 8.

47. Ibid., 11.

48. Williams, *Linking Arms Together.*

49. Rebecca Tsosie and Wallace Coffey, "Rethinking the Tribal Sovereignty Doctrine: Cultural Sovereignty and the Collective Future of Indian Nations," *Stanford Law and Policy Review* 12, no. 2 (2001): 196.

50. Mervin Huntinghawk, "Since Time Immemorial: Treaty Land Entitlement in Manitoba," in *Sacred Lands: Aboriginal Worldviews, Claims, and Conflicts*, ed. Jill Oakes et al. Canadian Circumpolar Institute Occasional Publications Series No. 32 (Edmonton, AB: Canadian Circumpolar Institute Press, 1998), 41.

51. For numerous examples of Anishinaabe use of the pipe during their treaty practices with the United States see Documents Relating to the Negotiation of Ratified and Unratified Treaties with Various Tribes of Indians, NAMP RG 75, M T-494, Rolls 1–10. Records of the Bureau of Indian Affairs, National Archives and Records Services, Washington, DC. For Canadian treaty records illustrating Anishinaabe use of the pipe, see Morris, *The Treaties of Canada with the Indians of Manitoba and the North-West Territories.* The Anishinaabe also utilized the pipe and other sacred items in their diplomatic practices with other Native nations. See John Tanner, *The Falcon: A Narrative of the Captivity and Adventures of John Tanner* (New York: Penguin Books, 1994); Anton Treuer, *Living Our Language: Ojibwe Tales and Oral Histories, Native Voices* (St. Paul: Minnesota Historical Society Press, 2001); Thomas Vennum, *The Ojibwa Dance Drum: Its History and Construction.* Smithsonian Folklife Studies No. 2 (Washington, DC: Smithsonian Institution Press, 1983); Warren, *History of the Ojibway People.*

52. Huntinghawk, "Since Time Immemorial," 41.

53. Morris, *The Treaties of Canada with the Indians of Manitoba and the North-West Territories,* 63.

54. Em dash added for readability. Ibid., 72–73.

55. Ibid., 73.

56. Ibid., 75.

57. It can be questioned whether the Anishinaabe always upheld their promises. However, I have not found anything in the historical record that suggests otherwise. In addition, it should be noted that the United States and Canada acquired the desired land and resources that they negotiated for. Many treaties carried promises of peace and friendship, and although the Anishinaabe often sought to uphold peace between the nations, unfulfilled treaty promises did often lead to Anishinaabe protest.

58. *Ratified Treaty No. 247,* NAMP RG 75, M T-494, Roll 4:F308.

59. R. David Edmunds, *The Potawatomis: Keepers of the Fire* (Norman: University of Oklahoma Press, 1987).

60. *Ratified Treaty No. 247,* NAMP RG 75, M T-494, Roll 4:F308.

61. Ibid., F306.

62. Principle Chief Ma-we-do-pe-nais likely spoke these words. Chief Powhassan was another principle speaker, however, and the treaty journal only notes that a chief spoke these words; emphasis added.

63. Morris, *The Treaties of Canada with the Indians of Manitoba and the North-West Territories,* 60.

64. President's message, January 7 and 8, 1864; *Treaty of October 2, 1863 with the Red Lake & Pembina Bands of Chippewas*; Indian Treaty Files, SEN 38B-C9, p. 47, RG 46. Also see *Ratified Treaty No. 327 Documents Relating to the Negotiation of the Treaty of October 2, 1863, with the Red Lake and Pembina Chippewa Indians,* NAMP RG 75, M T-494, Roll 6. For biographical information on Chief Hole-in-the-Day (the younger) and his father, see Charles Alexander Eastman (Ohiyesa), *Indian Heroes and Great Chieftains* (Mineola, NY: Dover, 1997). Also see Anton Steven Treuer, "The Assassination of Hole in the Day" (PhD diss., University of Minnesota, 1997).

65. President's message, January 7 and 8, 1864; *Treaty of October 2, 1863 with the Red Lake & Pembina Bands of Chippewas*; Indian Treaty Files, SEN 38B-C9, p. 47, RG 46.

66. *Ratified Treaty No. 247,* NAMP RG 75, M T-494, Roll 4: F311.

67. Ibid.

68. Ibid.

69. *Ratified Treaty No. 223 Documents Relating to the Negotiations of the Treaty of July, 29, 1837, with the Chippewa Indians*, NAMP RG 75, M T-494, Roll 3:F559. Also see president's message, 19 December 1837; *Treaty of July 29, 1837 with the Chippewas*, Indian Treaty Files, SEN 25B-C4, RG 46. For additional information on the 1837 treaty, see James M. McClurken and Charles E. Cleland, *Fish in the Lakes, Wild Rice, and Game in Abundance: Testimony on Behalf of Mille Lacs Ojibwe Hunting and Fishing Rights* (East Lansing: Michigan State University Press, 2000); Ronald N. Satz, *Chippewa Treaty Rights: The Reserved Rights of Wisconsin's Chippewa Indians in Historical Perspective* (Madison: Wisconsin Academy of Sciences, Arts, and Letters, 1991).

70. Wilkins and Lomawaima, *Uneven Ground*, 65; emphasis in original.

71. Williams, *Linking Arms Together*, 133.

72. Tsosie and Coffey, "Rethinking the Tribal Sovereignty Doctrine," 204.

73. David E. Wilkins, "The Manipulation of Indigenous Status: The Federal Government as Shape Shifter," *Stanford Law and Policy Center* 12, no. 2 (Spring 2001): 223–35.

74. Morris, *The Treaties of Canada with the Indians of Manitoba and the North-West Territories*, 63.

REVIEWS

All That Remains: Varieties of Indigenous Expression. By Arnold Krupat. Lincoln: University of Nebraska Press, 2009. 288 pages. $25.00 paper.

Arnold Krupat is one of the earliest, most knowledgeable, and wisest of the historians and critics of Native American literature. He writes elegantly and with admirable lucidity, eschewing whenever feasible the trendy jargon of whatever school of criticism is in vogue for the moment. Any new publication of his is therefore not only an event of interest to students and scholars in the field, but also easily accessible for the general public that may wish to know more about Native American literature. This book is no exception. Rather than an integral text, *All That Remains* is actually a collection of essays, written at different times and for different purposes. An introductory essay offers some overarching themes that serve to hold the disparate parts together, although this device is not always successful. In some ways it would have been better to do without an effort to create artificial unity, for it calls attention to the diverse nature of the collection, raises questions that would not neces- sarily occur otherwise, and sometimes results in seeming contradictions. However, all the individual essays, including the prefatory one, are interesting and contain valuable information and insights.

Krupat begins by reviewing three of the most important theoretical approaches in American Indian literary studies: the "tribal nationalist," the purely esthetic, and the view that modern Indian literature represents "a process of reconstruction, of self-discovery and cultural recovery" (ix). What Krupat quite rightly sees is that these approaches are in reality complemen- tary, and that they are all necessary to come to anything approaching a comprehensive understanding of contemporary American Indian writing. He also quite correctly points out that traditional Native American thought did not feature the binary oppositions so characteristic of Western attitudes but expressed itself in multivalent tropes. It was a mode of thought that recog- nized the existence of both/and rather than limiting itself to the either/or of Euro-American approaches to meaning. For this reason, Krupat maintains not only the appropriateness but also the necessity of using multiple approaches to the study of American Indian literature.

After establishing these "ground rules," Krupat moves on to the essay "Trickster Tales Revisited." Just as the author's preface encapsulated the most important aspects of current theoretical debates about how to interpret Native American literature, this essay provides a nutshell view of the many ways that Indians and white scholars have interpreted the trickster figure of American Indian myth and legend. The multifaceted figure of the trickster exemplifies the necessity of following various avenues of interpretation if one wishes to attain a sound understanding of American Indian literature—which so often features the trickster or trickster-like characters and encounters. If one wishes to do a quick study of the trickster figure, one could probably not find a better text than this relatively short essay.

"Representing Indians in American Literature, 1820–1870" is an examination of how Indians were depicted literarily in America—whether by mainstream writers or Indians—during one rather arbitrarily chosen half-century. The essay concludes with a partially annotated bibliography. This is where the multiple origins of *All That Remains* begin to show through. Krupat explains that what ultimately became this essay was a project on "American history through literature" (31). It reviews well-known stereotypes, such as the noble and the bloodthirsty savage, in connection with the racism of the time—including the "scientific racism" to which fledgling anthropology prostituted itself.

Krupat approaches his discussion of Indian stereotypes in the dominant society's narrative by a quasi-theoretical discussion of comic versus tragic narrative. In this schema, the trope of the "vanishing Indian" exemplifies the tragic narrative. Somewhat surprisingly, the essay does not deal directly with the question of appropriation of voice—mainstream writers representing Indians rather than Indians portraying themselves—since this is an issue of great concern in Native circles. Krupat's catalog of authors and works dealing with Indians is useful, but the rehash of racial attitudes in America adds no new insights to the discussion. One suspects that this particular essay was included just to flesh out an otherwise overly slim volume.

What follows is a fascinating essay, "Resisting Racism: William Apess as Public Intellectual." For those who know about William Apess only from excerpts of his more famous writings sometimes included in anthologies of American literature as token representations of American Indian writing—and more importantly for those completely unacquainted with Apess—this essay is a revelation. Krupat deals not only with Apess's writings but also his persona as a public figure who spoke out on behalf of social justice for Native Americans and deserves to be placed among other impassioned political orators of the early nineteenth century, such as Frederick Douglass and Daniel Webster. Krupat also deftly shows how a study of Apess's life and writings exemplifies several important tenets of postcolonial criticism. The intellectual heat and light this essay generates inspires one to take up the complete works of Apess, which were not easily or fully available until the publication of Barry O'Connell's *On Our Own Ground: The Complete Writings of William Apess, a Pequot* (1992), and to examine the growing body of critical commentary. Krupat's essay, however, does a very satisfying job of presenting a well-rounded picture of Apess in a mere twenty-eight pages.

None of the other essays matches the interest and usefulness of those mentioned, although each of them offers significant information and valuable interpretations of the material they present. The last essay in the collection, "*Atanarjuat, the Fast Runner* and Its Audiences," differs from all the others in that it deals with film, rather than written work. This fairly well-known 2001 Canadian-made adaptation of an Inuit legend has aroused, according to Krupat, the interest of four distinct audiences. The first of these is the Inuit, presenting their self-image to the outside world. The second is comprised not only of other Canadians and Americans but also people from all over the world who are willing to have their preconceptions challenged and to attempt, at least, to see another society as it sees itself. The third, and arguably the largest, audience appreciates the film for its formal beauty (and perhaps for its "exoticism"—although Krupat doesn't exactly come out and say this). For them, it is a work of entertainment that is "consumed" and at best "contemplated" (133). In a note, Krupat hints at the fourth group of viewers, a growing international indigenous audience that is becoming increasingly connected and that presumably would be attracted by the commonalities of their own cultural experience with those portrayed in the film and also by the film's assertion of indigenous identity in a world dominated by modern industrialized societies that all too often ignore their very existence (196). That a work of art, which is also a commercial product, should be subject to the interpretations and uses that its purchasers put it to is not a particularly great revelation, yet Krupat problematizes the multiple meanings the various audiences assign to the film, seeming to ask which is the real one. This seems an odd gambit given his insistence in his author's preface on the multivalent nature of Native thought and art and the necessity of approaching it with a both/and rather than an either/or mentality, of accepting simultaneous different points of view and not seeing them as necessarily opposing. He ends up solving the dilemma by invoking this very directive, thus making the whole essay seem either contrived or, paradoxically, insufficiently conceptualized in advance. The investigation of the multiple responses to the film would have been a worthwhile enough endeavor, without overinterpreting it.

There are some technical issues with the book that perhaps reflect more on its editors than its author. The bibliography often lists the works of Indian writers that have been edited for publication by the name of the editor rather than the author, thus inadvertently (one supposes) "erasing" the Native author and denying his or her agency. In such cases it would have been helpful to have double entries (by editor and by author). This is a supreme irony in a work by an author so committed to combating cultural erasure as Krupat. Then there is the matter of the endnotes—grouped together at the end of the book instead of at the end of the essay to which they pertain. This is presumably a result of putting matters of convenience and economy in publication above the interests of the scholar who reads the book and wishes to follow up on references without the maddening necessity of constantly flipping back and forth and engaging in a hunt for the relevant note.

The bigger issue, however, stems from the book title. It is presumably derived from a Wendy Rose poem about sunset that is used as an epigraph (v):

a line so thin
that it steps through the dark

like a seal slips through water.
And what remains? dissolving
touch
echo of whispers
begun long ago. . . .

Even if this is its source, the title reads like an epitaph. It has resonances of the "vanishing Indian," knowable only through the material culture left behind. This is completely at odds with one of the messages of the book—that the vanishing Indian is a stereotype to be dismantled and discarded. It certainly is also at odds with the vibrancy of many contemporary Native American cultures, including their literary flowering of which Krupat has been one of the chief proponents. Surely the vanishing Indian was not the intended allusion contained in the title, but there it is, nonetheless. In spite of these reservations, Krupat has once again provided a thought-provoking and often informative and enlightening experience to his many admirers: students, teachers, and scholars of Native American culture, and even anyone who may just happen to pick up this book and read it out of intellectual curiosity.

John K. Donaldson
George Washington University

Also Called Sacajawea: Chief Woman's Stolen Identity. By Thomas H. Johnson with Helen S. Johnson. Long Grove, IL: Waveland Press, 2008. 124 pages. $14.50 paper.

Three years after the commemoration of the 200th anniversary of the Lewis and Clark expedition, all things Lewis and Clark—and Sacagawea, the Shoshone woman who traveled with the expedition—are still highly sought after. Thomas H. Johnson's book should be added to the mix. The anthropologist tells readers he started reporting "whatever the Eastern Shoshone wanted to tell," but he ended up doing much more (1).

Scholars generally agree that Sacagawea was captured by the Hidatsa and ended up belonging to the French Canadian trader Toussaint Charbonneau. Lewis and Clark encountered them in 1804 in what is today North Dakota. Charbonneau expressed interest in working as an interpreter, letting it be known that he had two Shoshone women. So Lewis and Clark decided to bring Charbonneau and one of his wives along to interpret the Shoshone language for them. In February 1805, Sacagawea gave birth to her first child, Jean Baptiste Charbonneau. Sacagawea, Charbonneau, and Jean Baptiste joined the expedition on a sixteen-month journey to the Pacific Ocean and back.

Stories about Sacagawea are wrought with myth and debate. At least four different tribal nations claim to be her birthplace. Whether her name has Shoshone or Hidatsa origins is contested. Here Sacagawea refers to the Shoshone who traveled with the expedition, and Sacajawea is Johnson's

Paraivo, Chief Woman, or "Also Called Sacajawea." Dozens of children's books wrongly identify Sacagawea as the expedition guide. Many sources insist that if a romantic relationship did not exist between Sacagawea and Clark, at least a one- or two-way admiration prevailed. Two places claim to be her burial site: one was a fur trading post, Fort Manual, near the Missouri River bordering what is today South Dakota and North Dakota; the other is on the Wind River Reservation in Wyoming, which is where Johnson's story takes place.

For one hundred years after the expedition, Sacagawea was unknown. Americans "discovered" Sacagawea after authors Eva Emery Dye and Grace Raymond Hebard used her to promote the suffrage movement, in the process trading accuracy for legends in epic proportions. Unlike Hebard, who set out to prove that Sacagawea was from the Wind River Reservation, Johnson's patient, inductive approach allowed him to investigate until answers unfolded. Johnson ends up refuting Hebard's claims, and his insights on Hebard's life and career stimulate thought.

Hebard's personal goals led her to minimize Chief Woman's contributions to her people. Johnson, however, quotes John C. Luttig's 20 December 1812 journal entry that "This Evening the Wife of Charbonneau (Sacagawea) a Snake Squaw, died" and William Clark's cash book that "Se-car-ja-weau" was "Dead" as evidence of Sacagawea's importance (34, 13). Hebard may have lied, or perhaps she believed her version so much that she only listened to supporters and dismissed opposing evidence. She would not be the first scholar to make that mistake.

Some Shoshone may feel that Hebard has duped them. Others will not believe Johnson. Some may interpret *Also Called Sacajawea* as a story that refutes Shoshone claims to Sacagawea, but it is much more. Johnson outlines important lessons of oral tradition and its place in scholarly research; negotiated boundaries, especially those involving reservations; stories concerning indigenous survival and success; and evidence of the commodification of Indians. From imposed gravestones on Shoshone land to the story of the model for the Sacagawea coin, Johnson provides a look at how poor research can harm a community. He explains that Reverend John Roberts at first knew the elderly woman only as Bazil's mother, but after Hebard's intervention and subsequent correspondence, Roberts had three names for her.

Traditional historians may be disappointed in Johnson's preference for oral tradition over the Lewis and Clark diaries. However, his study of the subject and the intricacies of Wind River culture and the differences between it and mainstream American culture delivers a strong contribution to the field. But Johnson's even-handed approach is not without minor glitches. Johnson rightfully claims that in-depth knowledge of Sacajawea is unnecessary to comprehend his work; however, prior knowledge of the subject allows for deeper engagement with the book (115). Johnson generally does a good job but does not always substantiate his claims. For example, he writes that French speakers seldom shortened *Jean-Baptiste* to *Baptiste*, but it is unclear if he is referring to French speakers from France or American voyageurs (22).

Tables from appendix A, "The Elements of a Myth," and appendix C, "Under Husband's Other Wives," could use more explanation. A better

Wyoming map and an index would have been helpful, and reorganization may be in order for the next edition. Johnson writes in chapter 6 that he first came to Wind River in 1966. Chapter 7 jumps to his 1980 conversation with Blanche Moore Schroer and Maude Clairmont, and then chapter 8 returns to 1966 and his Sun Dance encounter, which readers may have appreciated knowing earlier.

Although Johnson did not pay Shoshone informants except for language lessons, he does not acknowledge a researcher's influential power: "The information Shoshone have shared with me over the years has been freely and willingly given" (66). He is not without bias, writing "Indians had actually helped *us* win a war. They had fought on *our* side" (48).

Johnson claims Sacagawea was a "token" of peace and writes, "It was clear that Sacagawea and her baby could guarantee safe passage" (46). This is inaccurate. Expedition organizers knew that simply including a woman and a baby would not ensure a safe passage. Instead, a tremendous amount of gun power protected the explorers as they trekked across the continent, and even then there were several close and dangerous encounters.

Also Called Sacajawea has some unique features. "The Wind River Sacajawea Who's Who" is a service for novice Sacagawea scholars as are the eighty-seven references in the bibliography, recommended reading list, and URLs for Shoshone Web sites. Especially useful is Johnson's "Student Study Guide" that explains his ethnographic approach. After a summary for each chapter, "Questions for Discussion" are listed with "Topics for Research and Report Writing." The book would work as a text for a general class on history, anthropology, ethnography, or American studies. Whether readers agree with his conclusion, Johnson's work is also worthy for students and fans of Native American studies and the Lewis and Clark expedition. This book will rank as required Sacagawea reading with Esther Burnett Horne and Sally McBeth's *Essie's Story: The Life and Legacy of a Shoshone Teacher* (1998); Donna J. Kessler's *The Making of Sacajawea: A Euro-American Legend* (1996); Kenneth Thomasma's *The Truth about Sacajawea* (1998) and *Waheenee: An Indian Girl's Story told by herself to Gilbert L. Wilson* (1981); and work on the subject by Irving Anderson and James P. Ronda.

One might interpret Johnson's book as a step away from the Wind River Shoshone culture. Instead, Johnson's research supports the relevance and strength of oral tradition and indigenous storytelling, providing an example of the harm that poor research can do to a community. Many pieces of the Sacagawea puzzle are pulled together and analyzed by someone who has been involved in the Wind River Shoshone culture for more than forty years. Of his experiences Johnson writes, "Everything told the true story of the woman buried in the cemetery, the woman who also came to be called Sacajawea" (3). Johnson delivers relevant and important information from his interpretations and longtime study of the subject matter.

The story of Sacagawea is about more than truths and lies. It is a story of indigenous endurance and survival. Johnson writes, "The Shoshone were in control all the time. Regardless of what the whites tried to impose on them, the most sacred Shoshone beliefs remain intact" (81). Weak scholarship and research can damage, interrupt, and displace a community. Sacagawea scholars now wait for future Shoshone scholars to respond to Johnson, providing even more in-depth answers and personal reflections on the subject.

Selene G. Phillips
University of Louisville

Buffalo Inc.: American Indians and Economic Development. By Sebastian Felix Braun. Norman: University of Oklahoma Press, 2008. 280 pages. $39.95 cloth.

Duane Champagne has suggested the potential for capitalism to take hold in American Indian communities in a way that is significantly different from the way it generally operates in American society as a whole. Calling it "tribal capitalism," Champagne asserts that this particularly indigenous version of economic development is not dedicated to individual accumulation the way capitalism conventionally is, but rather to the collective good of a tribal community. This communal good comes in terms of collectivized financial success to be shared throughout a community, mainly in terms of civic projects and social welfare, and in terms of the support of tribal sovereignty and the sustaining of cultural values. Dean Howard Smith, along with Stephen Cornell and Joseph Kalt, also urge tribal communities to bring indigenous cultural values to the fore of discussions about appropriate and responsible tribal economic development. However, much of the work on tribal capitalism is either theoretical or prescriptive policy suggestions. Few book-length studies exist about how tribal capitalism works in practice in indigenous communities—even fewer that are not based on studies of gaming enterprises.

Braun's *Buffalo Inc.* provides an excellent example of what tribal capitalism looks like on the ground: its practicalities, successes, and challenges. Braun has conducted a highly thorough, ethnography-based case study of the Cheyenne River Sioux tribe's effort to establish a buffalo herd for the joint goals of economic development and cultural revitalization. His analysis of the critical connection between these two goals gives us an opportunity to see how well tribal capitalism can work and what its internal and external impediments are. Braun's main focus is on Pte Hca Ka, Inc., the Cheyenne River Sioux tribally sponsored buffalo-raising operation. He clearly has intimate experience with this operation through extensive fieldwork, ethnographic interviews with Pte Hca Ka's managers and employees, and his work for the operation. However, his book does much more than provide an ethnographic account of the administration of a tribal enterprise. He contextualizes Pte Hca Ka in terms of responsible tribal economic development and the revival of cultural identity in order to consider several issues: the broader economic and ecological challenges facing tribal (and non-Indian rural) communities of the northern plains; the role of cultural revitalization and cultural identity in decolonization efforts; culturally based notions of ecological "sustainability" and "conservation"; and how indigenous communities embroiled in settler colonialism can envision and practice self-sufficiency within dominant capitalist societies.

Broken into fourteen chapters, this book does many things at once, but in the first few chapters Braun provides an historical overview of the Cheyenne River Sioux Reservation and the tribe's political economic history. Throughout these chapters he also considers the ecological history of buffalos in North America and the cultural history of Northern Plains people's interaction with and cultural interpretation of buffalos. Here he provides a detailed understanding of not just the bison's role in northern plain's ecology but also how the growth of industrial farming and cattle ranching affects and compares to the buffalo's ecological relations. Moreover, these early chapters also include an explanation of the centrality of buffalos to Lakota culture and contemporary cultural identity. Perhaps the most valuable part of this discussion is the way that Braun describes the Lakota interpretation of their relationship with buffalos and their belief that buffalos have their own culture, a culture from which the Lakota can learn social values by interacting with the buffalo. Braun does an equally fine job of not essentializing Lakota culture in regards to the buffalo by providing a sophisticated conversation of the way that buffalo play a symbolic role in the contemporary formulations of cultural identity that can serve discrete political goals of decolonization through revitalizing the sociocultural and physical health of Lakota communities.

The middle chapters of *Buffalo Inc.* look more closely at the cultural and administrative foundations of Pte Hca Ka and the eventual political and cultural conflicts that led to the tribal enterprise's dissolution. In these chapters Braun discusses how Pte Hca Ka was explicitly established with the joint goals of economic development and cultural revitalization in mind. Making sure that buffalos were present in the life of the Cheyenne River Sioux people was just as critical, if not more so, to the enterprise's founders as was the goal of turning a profit. In practice this was illustrated through the way that Pte Hca Ka grew and managed the herd. Unlike the non-Indian managers of other nontribal bison herds, Pte Hca Ka used Lakota cultural knowledge in order to determine the way that the buffalo were raised, corralled, and slaughtered. These chapters also detail the way that, through Pte Hca Ka's growth and economic success, it became embroiled in tribal politics. Originally sheltered from the day-to-day administration of the tribal government, Pte Hca Ka came under more direct tribal governmental control when it had trouble financing an expansion of the herd's grazing land. Eventually, internal political forces, a collapse in the national market for bison meat, and some tribal members' desire to separate the buffalo-raising operation from cultural practices—making it a purely economic endeavor—led to the dissolution of Pte Hca Ka through the complete liquidation of the herd.

The final few chapters of the book use the Pte Hca Ka experience to comment on cultural interpretations of sustainability, conservation, and economic development. Like many others before him, Braun reasserts the notion that when analyzing American Indian economic development we must consider the economic and the cultural simultaneously. He reminds us that "because culture is always a system, cultural concerns influence economic relationships and choices and vice versa," and these mutual influences are constantly in flux and negotiation so that trying to consider tribal economic development in "American Indian terms . . . is a function of history and not simply an essentialized revitalization of historic cultural values" (210). Therefore, when we consider tribal economic development projects—like Pte Hca Ka—we must do much more than just consider the financial success and failure. Braun has done just that in his well-thought-out and well-argued book, which is an excellent addition to our understanding of tribal economic development.

David Kamper
San Diego State University

Celebration: Tlingit, Haida, Tsimshian—Dancing on the Land. By Rosita Worl with a foreword by Byron I. Mallott, essays by Maria Williams and Robert Davidson, and photographs by Bill Hess. Edited by Kathy Dye. Juneau, AK, and Seattle: Sealaska Heritage Institute and University of Washington Press, 2008. 152 pages. $40.00 cloth.

This book is a compilation of essays and photographs capturing the early stages of Sealaska Corporation's attempt to "educate the youth about their culture" (16). Worl explains that the newly formed Sealaska Heritage Institute (SHI) began a small regionwide gathering of clans in order to showcase its region's cultures and treasured clan objects known as *at'óow*. The SHI elders soon started to see this event as being similar to a traditional ceremonial *ku.éex'*, or invite. Thus, what began as a celebration of cultures through song and dance would ultimately become a venue to revitalize local interest in the ancestral cultures and languages. With the first three-day event drawing a little more than two hundred attendees, it now boasts more than forty clans and two thousand people from all over Alaska, Washington, Oregon, California, Hawaii, and Canada, and with invited guests from New Zealand, participating in a five-day international celebration.

The foreword, preface, and acknowledgments confirm the power of honoring ancestors for their lives. The commonalties among each serve to recognize the power of preserving traditions and history despite the atrocities encountered through the colonial and current governmental reigns. Singing and dancing serve as foundational elements to the tribes along the Alaska southeast coast and are keys to understanding some of the complex inter- and intratribal expressions of their existence. This book documents some of those who have contributed to the celebration by their presence, pride in their culture, and efforts to maintain cultural continuity and affirm their unending sovereignty.

There are some surprises in this book, and though most of the content—112 pages of 152—is photographs, the accompanying text reveals much about honoring ancestors, coastal tribal art and products, cultural survival and adaptation, masks, and the significance of celebrations. As a historical collection of photographs about the celebration, its significance is evident in the pride manifested in each picture from the very genesis of the event to its most recent moments. Bill Hess's camera vividly captures the elaborate pageantry of the dances and art throughout the celebration. Worl notes that identifying participants becomes difficult when the number of attendees and participants gradually and consistently increase, and some people remained unidentified, but with this publication, there is a hint or hope that others will see those pictures and identify the participants for a later edition (11). As such, some of the pictures only convey basic information about the dance, mask, or regalia. The effort to identify the tribal affiliation also revealed only basic information at times.

The text prepares the reader for the photographs that exemplify the topic. Concerning art and *at'óow*, the discussion presents the intricate history behind each artifact: its ownership and the right of a clan or an individual to display that item. Worl explains that the commissioning of an art object by an individual, family, or clan sets the parameters of ownership and display of that object. The Tlingit word *at'óow* signifies an "owned or purchased object." The object contains natural and supernatural significance and can represent human and nonhuman entities that pertain to tribal geographical consequence. This process of commissioning and then claiming ownership is part of the legacy of each family or clan that, by rights of ownership, brings forth its *at'óow* for public display and alone has ownership and rights to pass the *at'óow* on to its relations.

Williams's chapter on survival and adaptation is specific to the Tlingit Nation, but the content is certainly applicable to all the region's tribes and all the indigenous populations worldwide. The question of how music and dance have adapted to the current geopolitical world receives a multilayered answer. Although a variety of songs and their occasions is acknowledged, it is also noted that songs could be given to other tribes to be adopted as gifts. Traditionally, songs are quite narrow in their ownership, and the venue for their occasion changes as the pattern of habitation changes. These songs are situated in a clan-house setting, but that changes when the clan houses were abandoned in the twentieth century. Thus, the pattern of a single-clan celebration yields to the gathered-clan celebration.

Although the historical precedent of identification and justification of song ownership resided with the celebrating clan, current singers fail to identify whose clan the songs belong to during their performances or fail to follow previously accepted protocols for song identification and ownership. One protocol is particularly apropos to hats, which in some villages have specific songs associated with their creation and ownership. Performing some songs thus becomes contentious and stirs up strife between genera-tions because the elders expect traditional protocol for acknowledging rights and ownership, but the younger generation is often unaware of such protocol and is simply trying to maintain a connection to its culture by dancing and singing. The younger generation often does not know the song's familial or clan significance, history, and, at times, meaning and translation. Williams concludes that new songs and dances must be part of the effort to revitalize the cultures, just as the acceptance of new regalia is also a part of survival and adaption.

The next two chapters about masks contain some insightful vignettes about the coastal songs and dances and the role that a mask has in the performance. Wearing a mask is not simply a concealment of one's identity, but also a complex instantiation of the character portrayed. Worl explains that there is a threefold purpose for the masks—transformation, clan dramatization, and conflict resolution—though conflict resolution no longer occurs (104). Davidson asserts that masks can display one's crests, illustrate a myth, reveal personal or clan history, invoke supernatural beings and their power, and allow transformational capacities (114). He also claims that the power of the mask is such that the artist becomes the mask, becomes that character in the dance or song, and begins to manifest personality qualities that are easily identifiable with the topic of the mask. Although the photographs contain some of the beauty and detail of various masks, they cannot capture the sequence of subtle dance movements that identify and distinguish certain characters, such as Raven on the beach eating oolichans.

The final chapter contains vignettes and photographs about the different celebrations: the parade, Native artist market, juried art show and competition, language and cultural workshops, black seaweed contest, canoe races, and baby regalia review. Notably, the Native artist market is carefully monitored to ensure indigenous authenticity and accuracy. The art show had to break into two categories because the elders staunchly regard traditional art and its design, though it is not necessarily regarded as such by the younger generation. The controversy to maintain strict adherence to traditional forms led to the formation of the contemporary art category, which allows a greater exploration and expression of new and older forms, ostensibly pleasing the elders who strongly preserve traditional forms and the younger artists who want to be innovative. With the role of language in songs and narratives in dances, the language and culture workshops are a natural outcome capturing a need for documentation and revitalization.

Although reading this book is quite easy and fast, its content will require concerted endeavors to appreciate the text and accompanying photographs. The text and pictures will certainly bring greater appreciation for the complexity of Northwest Coast art, culture, and language to the point that the reader will yearn to participate in the next celebration.

Frederick White
Slippery Rock University

Fire Light: The Life of Angel De Cora, Winnebago Artist. By Linda M. Waggoner. Norman: University of Oklahoma Press, 2008. 355 pages. $34.95 cloth.

Angel De Cora (1869–1919), of Winnebago and Métis ancestry, had a brilliant career as a painter, graphic artist, educator, lecturer, and pioneer in the arts and crafts movement in the late 1800s and early twentieth century; a period in American history when only a few women of any race had professional careers. Linda Waggoner's biography of De Cora does more than merely chronicle her life as an artist. Waggoner situates De Cora's life in the midst of America's sociopolitical history, delving into issues of American Indian policies, broken treaties, the forced removal of American Indian children from their homes for transfer to boarding schools, women's rights, segregation, racism, and eugenics. Waggoner's biography of De Cora is contextualized because all of these topics impacted De Cora's personal family life, education, and career as an artist during those tumultuous times.

As a young child De Cora was enrolled at Hampton Institute in Virginia, which was a school initially opened for freedmen (and women) after the Civil War and later made available to American Indian children from western tribes. Conflicting reports exist concerning whether De Cora was kidnapped. Although one of her guardian uncles placed De Cora in the care of officials transporting children to Hampton, neither De Cora nor her mother were informed that De Cora was leaving her home on the Nebraska Winnebago Reservation to be taken by train all the way to Virginia. Nonetheless, despite the initial trauma and culture shock, De Cora flourished academically and artistically at Hampton and was admitted to Smith College after graduation to study art.

For readers not very knowledgeable about art history Waggoner does an excellent job of describing the various art movements taking place in the United States and Europe during De Cora's art training and subsequent career and explaining the competing theories of art education. *Fire Light* contains eighteen illustrations of De Cora's paintings and graphic designs, but unfortunately they are all in black and white. Also included are nine photos of De Cora teaching art, creating art, posing with fellow students, and occasionally dressing in regalia.

Classes that De Cora took at Smith College emphasized good draftsmanship and clearness of the beauty of line, principles pertinent to the aesthetic movement of "art for art's sake." Smith College's instructors also emphasized tonalism, a style distinct from the popular European impressionism. Tonalism emphasized landscapes that were subdued, rarely dealt with historical narrative, and seldom used people as subject matter. If people were present they were painted frozen in time, rapt in thought, and staring into space out on landscapes that were blurred and misty, usually at dusk or dawn. De Cora immersed herself in this technique, winning a prestigious annual prize while at Smith, and received critical acclaim in the *Boston Journal*. Reporters were fascinated that a woman with "very dark skin" and "Indian features" could be so talented (65–66).

This early acclaim led to De Cora being invited to speak at a prestigious Indian gathering, the Lake Mohonk Conference of Friends of the Indian, in 1894. Waggoner details De Cora's meeting of future colleagues and friends at the conference such as Richard Henry Pratt, the founder of Carlisle Indian School; Carlos Montezuma, a Yavapi physician; Senator Henry Dawes of Massachusetts; Charles Eastman, a Dakota physician; and other distinguished participants. Some of these prominent American Indians became the founders of the Society of American Indians, an organization that De Cora participated in as a voting member and invited speaker.

After graduation from Smith, De Cora studied at the Drexel Institute of Art in Philadelphia under the renowned illustrator Howard Pyle. De Cora prepared for a career in Indian illustration at Drexel, encouraged by Pyle to paint "her people" (70). In February 1899 *Harper's Monthly* published De Cora's "The Sick Child," an autobiography with illustrations. The November 1899 *Harper's Monthly* published her "Gray Wolf's Daughter," marketing the illustrated story as a naïve tale of the North American Indian.

Between 1898 and 1899 De Cora opened a studio in Philadelphia and became long-term friends with two women who would later become well-known portrait artists: Cecilia Beaux and Alice Barber Stephens. But despite all of her professional success, the author chronicles how De Cora was still in somewhat demeaning, dependant relationships with her white patrons and benefactors, especially Cora Folsom, a Hampton instructor who helped De Cora financially but also dictated her lifestyle, discouraging her from visiting her relatives on the Winnebago Reservation. Although most readers are familiar with the cliché "caught between two worlds," Waggoner makes the phrase have real meaning as she details how De Cora assimilated into the "white world" on one level but was still treated as a child by some of her instructors and called a "girl" well into adulthood; all the time feeling home-sick for her Indian family, who unfortunately sometimes felt envious of her success and assimilation.

In 1900 De Cora moved to Boston, opened a studio near the Museum of Fine Arts, and began studying at the museum's Cowles School of Drawing and Painting, which was under the direction of Rodefer De Camp, a founding member of "Ten Americans," an offshoot of the Society of American Artists. The school was committed to a modified style of European impressionism and provided drawing from nude models, which was considered risqué for women at that time. De Cora was breaking gender and racial boundaries. During her time in Boston, De Cora published three illustrations in *Harper's* for Mary Catherine Judd's book *Wigwam Stories. Harper's* published books in serial form. De Cora also designed the book cover and provided twelve full-page illustrations for the book *Old Indian Legends.*

In June 1900 De Cora's art was featured in *Atlantic Monthly.* The magazine's publisher and the American Indian writer Francis La Flesche commissioned De Cora to illustrate his book *The Middle Five,* a story about the boarding school experience. De Cora's frontispiece was an alternative to the then-popular Carlisle before-and-after photos of stoic American Indian children with long hair and Indian clothes juxtaposed with images of them wearing school uniforms and short hair cuts. De Cora's painting featured a young boy wearing buckskin with his body open to the viewer but his face hidden in despair while an older boy in uniform tries to comfort him. The book's cover incorporated abstract American Indian motifs using bows and arrows for the border design, arrows on the book's spine, and two tipis decorated with the thunderbird symbols on the bottom half of the cover. The thunderbird, De Cora's clan symbol, was used in her art throughout her career.

Another prominent commission described in the biography was De Cora's interior design work for the 1901 Pan-American Exposition in

Buffalo, New York, where she designed an American Indian–themed living environment with a fireplace mantel and furniture constructed by American Indian students and decorated with Indian artifacts and De Cora's paintings. This model environment reflected De Cora's embrace of the arts and crafts movement with its love of simple lines and handmade construction and its rejection of European intricate Victorian ornamentation. De Cora's painting, *Fire Light*, executed in the tonalist style and depicting her Nebraska rolling prairies at sunset with two lovers beneath clouds, was displayed on the fireplace mantel.

But what really makes this commission so important to American art history is that De Cora's interior design brought American Indian art objects into mainstream American homes. American Indians began to be regarded as a race of artisans similar to the Japanese and the Persians. The widespread acclaim for De Cora's design work highlighted her influence on the arts and crafts style. For that time period, the early twentieth century, it was phenomenal that an American Indian woman was trained in Western art at leading institutions and also able to incorporate her vision of Indian motifs into her designs. According to Waggoner, the Pan-American Exposition marked a shift in the course of De Cora's prominent career toward what De Cora termed "Native Indian Design."

Also influential in popularizing American Indian design were De Cora's 1905 illustrations for *The Indian's Book*, edited by Natalie Curtis, which is a collection of American Indian songs, legends, and lore. De Cora designed the book's cover (a conventionalized eagle), title page, and each chapter's typography and created a different type of lettering for each Indian picture. The form of the letters was composed of motifs from the drawings. The author states that it may be difficult for twenty-first-century readers and art lovers to appreciate the uniqueness of De Cora's designs because her style soon became adopted by popular culture.

By this time De Cora had been appointed the head of Carlisle's art department. Unfortunately this appointment coincided with the American debates about which minority group was the least civilized, the Negro or the Indian. De Cora got caught up in this racial drama. Francis Leupp, the Indian commissioner under President Theodore Roosevelt, and De Cora believed in theories regarding different physical, mental, and moral traits for different races. Pratt believed in universalism and had more liberal views on race and social integration. Leupp believed in race-based education and was adamantly opposed to Indians and Negroes (the term used then) being educated together at Hampton, De Cora's alma mater.

Many American Indians were drawn to Leupp's racist ideology because his administration elevated Indians on the racial hierarchy scale and denigrated people with African ancestry as being Darwinian ape-like. History has shown that most people need to feel superior to someone. De Cora became part of Leupp's circle because of his advocacy of preserving American Indian art, believing its beauty could uplift American society.

In 1904 Pratt resigned from federally funded Carlisle because of the administration's racist views. William Mercer, the new director, created a

School of American Indian Design which utilized Indian cultural traditions that appealed to students' race pride. In 1907 he had a new art studio constructed in the arts and craft style that included one of the best photography studios in the state of Pennsylvania and an equally impressive press and print shop whose students and staff became influential in developing new styles in American typography. Emphasis was placed on industrial training and producing Indian craftsmen as opposed to fine artists.

As the head of Carlisle's art department, De Cora supported the idea of the American Indian craftsperson but still felt committed to the fine arts and developed theories of abstraction as a binding principle of Native Indian art. The year of Carlisle's construction of a new art studio, 1907, was also the year that Picasso painted the now world-famous "Les Demoiselles d' Avignon" by using "primitive" African design elements that invigorated the modern European art world and later led modern artists to total abstraction. For De Cora, this abstraction had already been discovered by American Indians.

Waggoner's book also discusses De Cora's reverence for the traditional American Indian woman and how she felt art making could provide self-sufficiency for Indian women. De Cora believed in a "universal" Indian woman, who she wanted to uplift as well as learn from. In her middle age she sought to reclaim her lost heritage through her design work by using her clan symbol as a symbol of dignity and cultural survival. However, Waggoner's book never discusses the "Cult of True Womanhood," which was a prevalent ideology among American white women, and never mentions the "uplift" strategy used by middle-class African Americans to help their less fortunate community members, especially those uplift programs espoused by the Negro Women's Club Movement. These two prevailing women's ideologies had to have some impact on De Cora's approach to helping American Indian women.

At age thirty-eight De Cora married William Dietz, a twenty-three-year-old football player and art student who was working for the Carlisle Indian Press as the art director of *Indian Craftsmen*, and who would eventually become De Cora's assistant. Dietz and De Cora collaborated in illustrating Elaine Goodale Eastman's novel *Yellow Star: A Story of East and West.* Waggoner's biography chronicles their marriage, providing insights on the many De Cora–Dietz art collaborations, Dietz's dubious claims to American Indian ancestry, their ups and downs that led to divorce, and De Cora's death in 1919, away from her American Indian family and friends.

Waggoner's passions in writing De Cora's biography seem to be many: to acknowledge a little-known American Indian artist whose contributions to American art history have not been adequately recognized by scholars, note the contributions of American Indian design to the mainstream arts and crafts movement, and highlight the value of De Cora's, Dietz's, and other Carlisle staff's art to American typography. Also mentioned but not elaborated is De Cora's attempt to have American Indian sign language's influence on the hand manual for American Sign Language given more recognition. Deeper exploration of this phenomenon needs to be undertaken by scholars in American Indian studies and in deaf and hearing-impaired communication studies.

Lastly, De Cora also needs to be remembered as a pacifist during World War I. She was vociferously opposed to the misappropriation of the thunderbird symbol as the insignia embellishing American and European military uniforms and banners. According to De Cora's research, the thunderbird was a symbol of authority and social rank, representing dignity, arbitration, and peace for the Winnebago and many other tribes. De Cora was quoted in the *Washington Post* as stating, "It is an unfortunate perversion that makes the symbol of arbitration and peace the banner which leads to war and devastation" (227).

These are words that can still resonate today with the current misappropriation of American Indian symbols for sports mascots and fighter jets. Some things never change.

Phoebe Farris (Powhatan-Renape)
Purdue University

The Indians of Iowa. By Lance M. Foster. Iowa City: University of Iowa Press, 2009. 162 pages. $16.95 paper.

Iowa, encompassing the fertile land that is situated between the Mississippi and Missouri rivers, has been the home of diverse Native American peoples during the past nine centuries. Yet the history of most of these populations has been underreported by notable academic publications, and, as a result, the general public knows little about these original inhabitants. Beginning with the ancestral Oneota, Glenwood, Great Oasis, and Mill Creek cultures of the late prehistoric period, Native Americans settled in earth-lodge villages that stretched across the entire span of the future state. Their societies depended upon extensive agriculture, hunting, foraging, and far-flung trade networks. Today's archaeological sites at Blood Run National Historic Landmark near Rock Rapids, Wittrock Indian Village National Historic Landmark near Sutherland, and Hartley Fort in northeastern Iowa provide ample evidence that these early peoples flourished on the Iowa landscape and were the progenitors of some of the later tribes that were contacted by Spanish, French, and English explorers during the historical period.

Of the two-dozen tribes discussed in this book, only the Meskwakis still possess a federally recognized reservation within the state. Often referred to erroneously as the Fox tribe, which originally denoted only one clan of the broader population, they became closely confederated with the Sauk tribe by the early 1700s. French fur traders and their Indian allies drove the two confederated tribes out of the western Great Lakes country, and the beleaguered migrants settled in northeastern Iowa by the 1730s. The US government negotiated pressured treaties with the affiliated peoples during the 1840s, and they were forcibly removed to eastern Kansas. The Meskwakis struggled valiantly to return to their sacred environment along the Iowa River, and, in 1856, they were able to purchase the lands that they remain on today near the community of Tama. Their former confederates, the Sauks, occupy lands in Kansas and Oklahoma, far removed from their once-shared villages in Iowa.

The indigenous people who ultimately provided the state of Iowa with its name also reside outside the state boundaries today. The Iowa tribe traces its ancestry to the prehistoric Oneota culture, and its villages were located along the state's major river systems during the 1700s. An 1836 treaty with the United States prompted their removal to a small reservation that now lies along the Kansas-Nebraska border. Today the relatively small population of Iowas remains divided between those who live on the Kansas-Nebraska Reservation and those who live in Oklahoma.

The Missouri River border of western Iowa and eastern Nebraska became the home of several other tribes during the early and mid-nineteenth century. The Omahas and Winnebagoes briefly lived and hunted in the northwestern sections of Iowa, but by the 1860s were resettled on adjoining reservations across the river in northeastern Nebraska. Further west in Nebraska, at the confluence of the Missouri and Niobrara rivers, the less populous Ponca tribe also had established its villages by 1800 in order to take advantage of the expanding Missouri River fur trade. Although the Poncas no longer have a federally recognized reservation in Nebraska, they still retain a small amount of trust land along the Niobrara River. Meanwhile, the Omahas and Winnebagoes own a few hundred acres in Iowa's Monona and Woodbury counties. Federal courts determined during the 1970s that a mid-nineteenth-century change in the course of the meandering Missouri River left two former reservation areas known as Blackbird Bend and Monona Bend on the Iowa side of the river. These small tracts were returned to the respective tribes, and today they support casinos for the Omaha and Winnebago peoples.

Eighty miles south of the Omaha and Winnebago reservations, along the banks of the Missouri River, three other small but important tribes made their homes during the 1830s and 1840s. Residing at the Council Bluffs (Iowa)-Bellevue (Nebraska) Indian Agency were the Otoes, Missouris, and Potawatomies. Unfortunately, their villages occupied prime real estate that by 1854 was designated as a new jumping-off place for the Oregon, California, and Mormon trails. After resettling on Nebraska's Big Blue River Reservation for thirty years, the Otoes and Missouris were again forced to undertake new lives in Oklahoma. Likewise, the Potawatomies wound up a fragmented people—some in eastern Kansas and some in Oklahoma.

The final two tribal groups addressed at some length in this book are the Santee Sioux and the Yankton Sioux. In the former case, the discussion mostly focuses upon the 1857 Spirit Lake Massacre in northern Iowa and the 1862 Santee Uprising in southern Minnesota. The Yanktons also occupied portions of northwestern Iowa during the 1700s, but they eventually moved into present-day South Dakota where they adopted more of a Plains Indian lifestyle, complete with stereotypical tipis and buffalo hunts.

Many tribes can claim Iowa as their home at particular times during the past, but only one can make that claim today. The Meskwakis at Tama represent an aberration in the unjust legacy of forced removals, and no other tribes can presently claim sovereign lands within the state. Probably most Native Americans who reside within Iowa today do so as "urban Indians" who live in Des Moines and other sizable cities. Thus Iowa may not constitute "Indian country" in the minds of most present-day Americans, but a century and a half ago this was not the case. Native Americans dominated the scene at that time, and their diverse stories are worthy of retelling to modern generations of Indians and non-Indians.

Lance Foster, an enrolled member of the Iowa tribe of Kansas and Nebraska, has prepared this brief book to convey some of the cultural richness of the indigenous peoples who once resided in Iowa. Trained as an anthropologist, most of his focus is understandably directed at topics such as material culture, language, economic pursuits, spirituality, arts and crafts, kinship, and migration patterns. His targeted audience clearly is the group of general readers who have no in-depth knowledge of Iowa's Native past or present. Serious researchers will find little that is not already well-known to them, and the lack of footnotes, extensive bibliography, and fresh analysis will preclude any chance of sparking new intellectual debates about the fascinating topic.

Despite these shortcomings, Foster has achieved what he set out to do. He has provided basic information about two dozen historical tribes and their travails and accomplishments during the last three centuries. His black-and-white sketches of historical and contemporary Indian scenes, inclusion of updated tribal Web sites and postal addresses, addition of a useful reading list, and descriptions of relevant sites to visit today eloquently speak to the needs of the general readers who will profit most from this book.

Michael L. Tate
University of Nebraska at Omaha

Inkpaduta: Dakota Leader. By Paul N. Beck. Norman: University of Oklahoma Press, 2008. 188 pages. $24.95 cloth.

As author Paul Beck notes, the Wahpekute Dakota leader Inkpaduta (Scarlet Point) is an elusive and mysterious figure who played a major role in the events leading up to the Dakota War of 1862 in Minnesota and the subsequent Sioux wars on the plains. Because historians have focused on the Dakota War of 1862 and its aftermath, scholarship on the Wahpekute Dakota band on the Iowa-Minnesota-South Dakota frontier from the 1820s through the 1860s is limited. Beck's stated goal is to counterbalance the overwhelmingly negative image of Inkpaduta as a bloodthirsty, villainous savage in the published accounts by presenting the Dakota view of him as a heroic warrior defending his people.

The Wahpekute Dakota engaged in prolonged warfare with the Sauk and Fox over hunting territory in northwestern Iowa in the 1820s and 1830s. Coupled with smallpox, this resulted in considerable population decline. Among the Dakotas the Wahpekutes were considered to be perpetual wanderers, and some early accounts from the 1800s indicate they were also seen as "lawless." They were not subjected to missionaries, nor were they well documented in the European or American literature of exploration.

The band divided over treaties, resulting in a split between the followers of two leaders and the murder of one of them. Inkpaduta's father was the leader of the Wahpekutes who resisted the treaties. The nonresistant group, under the leadership of the son of the murdered leader, was relocated to the Minnesota River Reservation set aside in the 1851 treaties that ceded the rest of Dakota land in Minnesota Territory.

The resistant Wahpekutes, made up primarily of relatives of Inkpaduta, continued to hunt, camp, and trade within the ceded territory, including northwestern Iowa, which had become a state in 1846. The event that catapulted Inkpaduta into the role of public enemy number one on the western frontier was the so-called Spirit Lake Massacre in 1857. Apparently in retaliation for the murder of a close relative, anger over the authorities' refusal to do anything about it, and their dire circumstances, Inkpaduta and the remaining warriors in his small band attacked and killed a number of settler families living in the headwaters of the Little Sioux River, stealing as much as they could take with them. Four women were also taken captive. These events unleashed the wrath of the state and territorial authorities, as well as terror and hysteria among the settlers.

With word of mouth as the only means of communication, newspapers spread wild stories of Indian atrocities and sightings, demonizing Inkpaduta as evil incarnate. The ever-growing number of settlers on the frontier, including many of less than stellar repute, became increasingly unaccepting of the presence of the thousands of reservation Dakotas who were their neighbors. While soldiers from forts established to protect settlers searched for Inkpaduta, he and his band traveled widely, eluding their military pursuers. Finally, the reservation Dakotas were forced to send out a search party, led by Little Crow, who later spearheaded the 1862 war against white settlers and the military. Their annuities were being withheld until they brought in Inkpaduta and his warriors. A few members of Inkpaduta's band were killed, and several were taken prisoner. Although two of the captive women had died, two were rescued.

When Minnesota attained statehood in 1858, Inkpaduta was still at large. Perhaps more dangerous than the potential threat to settlers, the authorities' inability to punish Inkpaduta and his warriors, including his sons, demonstrated to the reservation Dakotas the ineffectiveness of the military. Inkpaduta moved his followers westward, living among the Yanktons, Yanktonais, and eventually the Lakotas. They took part in the warfare resulting from the military expeditions on the plains following the Dakota War of 1862. Inkpaduta was present in the encampments along the Little Bighorn River in 1876 when Custer was defeated and eventually followed Sitting Bull's people into Canada, where he died, probably in 1879.

Although nominally a biography of Inkpaduta, this book is primarily a chronicle of events in which Inkpaduta played a role, as well as quite a number of events in which he was thought to have been involved but was not. In reality, virtually nothing in Inkpaduta's life is entirely certain. The sources include only a few eyewitness accounts written at the time of the events, memoirs, newspaper accounts, and other historians' works, most of which were written long after the events took place. Only a very small number of the non-Dakota actors in the events ever laid eyes on Inkpaduta. He is best known for his elusiveness and inscrutability, the very qualities that would have been admired by Dakotas and abhorred by Euro-Americans.

This book does not contribute substantially to the existing published literature on the Spirit Lake massacre, the Wahpekutes, or Inkpaduta. It is not a nuanced new historical interpretation that provides contextualized analyses of events or actors. It relies primarily on secondary sources, including those the author criticizes for vilifying Inkpaduta. Like its precursors, this history often strays from fact into supposition and surmise. Works by Dakota authors with elliptical references to Inkpaduta are cited, and the author also cites interviews with several Inkpaduta descendants and other Dakotas. However, the reader is left with a sense that the interviews were quite limited. It is not surprising that the Dakotas should revere Inkpaduta, Little Crow, or the thirty-eight warriors hanged at Mankato in 1862. The Lakotas, for example, similarly revere Crazy Horse, Sitting Bull, and other leaders and warriors who resisted Euro-American imperialism and colonialism.

In this book the author conveys only a superficial understanding of Dakota culture, in references to Dakota kinship and warfare practices, for example. The cultural background information provided relies upon uncritical use of older sources, not more recent ethnological ones (see Raymond J. DeMallie, "Sioux until 1850," in *Handbook of North American Indians*, vol. 13, 718–60, and "The Sioux at the Time of European Contact: An Ethnohistorical Problem," in *New Perspectives on Native North America*, 239–60). Erroneous understandings of Dakota culture are thus perpetuated. Moreover, standard orthography for the Dakota language has existed for more than one hundred and fifty years. Although the name Inkpaduta follows this orthography, nearly all of the other names do not, perpetuating misspellings used in period sources. Perhaps most egregiously, the author does not make reference to any of the considerable published literature about the mythology of the American frontier, including the imagery and symbolism of Indians and Indianness, or the extensive literature on captivity narratives.

Inkpaduta: Dakota Leader provides no new analysis of the role of Inkpaduta and the events in which he was engaged in setting the stage for the Dakota War of 1862 or the Sioux wars on the plains. Nor does it provide a nuanced analysis of Inkpaduta's role in frontier mythology or the eventual vilification of the Dakota as a people deserving of genocide and therefore subjected to the seemingly more humane treatment of imprisonment and exile. Perhaps it will, however, as Beck encourages, lead to further investigation by other scholars.

Carolyn R. Anderson
St. Olaf College

Iroquoian Archaeology and Analytic Scale. Edited by Laurie E. Miroff and Timothy D. Knapp. Knoxville: University of Tennessee Press, 2009. 328 pages. $48.00 cloth.

This edited volume is modeled around concepts of analytic scale in the Haudenosaunee (Iroquois) archaeology of New York, Pennsylvania, and Ontario. Specifically, the editors wish to encourage a research approach that utilizes various scales of time, from momentary activities to long-range culture change, and space, from a single-fire hearth to regional and multiregional models. The authors of the ten chapters slide between scales in their considerations of this archaeology, usually before settling in to focus on either a finer or coarser scale of their own research. The approach manages to tie these chapters loosely together. Each chapter stands on its own and is ample, with space for a detailed theoretical and cultural background and the exposition of detailed data, which is not always the case in edited volumes. The price of this is some redundancy, particularly in ethnographic background. The well-taken primary point is that detailed analysis at any scale or multiple scales can break entrenched stereotypes about the Haudenosaunee and reveal previously unseen cultural variability.

The chapters are in chronological order. Christina B. Rieth discusses the inadequacies of sites as a unit of analysis and the long-standing emphasis on nucleated villages in Haudenosaunee archaeology. Her study of smaller sites like camps, hamlets, and processing stations indicates a shift after AD 900 to the floodplains and terraces of major streams in eastern New York. Douglas J. Perelli examines the archaeological correlates of gender roles and the accompanying village (female) and forest (male) domains. Using artifacts, ecofacts, and features such as hearths, he defines ritual versus domestic activities in order to postulate shifts of activities from the forest to village domain by AD 1450. Peter A. Timmons discusses Tillsonburg Village, Ontario (ca. AD 1400). This stereotype-breaking site was an unusually dispersed village with longhouses separated by twenty to fifty meters, abundant space, and apparently no concern for defense or warfare.

Laurie E. Miroff looks at local analysis of the Thomas/Luckey site in southern New York (ca. AD 1400s), a site that "does not possess traditional expected 15th century Iroquoian site characteristics" (71). Her observations that standard pottery types do not stay within their assigned time periods matches my own experience. The site's "longhouse" does not exhibit the expected redundant artifact combinations of semi-independent nuclear families but is suggestive of a single cooperating group of families. Social organization thus may have varied considerably among the longhouses of the Haudenosaunee lands. Timothy D. Knapp follows with a study of pottery, ethnic identity, and co-occurrence of pottery types within pit and hearth features of the same site. He believes that the intermingling of pottery types from southern New York and central Pennsylvania at the site represents alliance building through intermarriage instead of the stereotyped idea of captured brides.

Tracy S. Michaud-Stutzman considers broad-based community and micro-household contexts at the Parker Farm (Cayuga) site (ca. AD 1450–1650). Her analysis results in the obvious conclusion that food was prepared and consumed within the longhouse while hunting tools are outside. Otherwise this article appears to be a reason for publishing some site data. Kathleen M. Sydoriak Allen uses a microscale approach, the analysis of one stratified trash deposit feature, in order to try and understand large regional issues. She is concerned with the meshing of time and space in different scales and their interface with the archaeological record. What were the relations between the Cayuga located on the eastern and western sides of Cayuga Lake? We are left unsure, except for the assumption that the Cayuga were unified.

William Engelbrecht discusses what he considers a Haudenosaunee preoccupation with defense. He argues that ditch and palisade systems, close longhouse spacing, and specific longhouse alignments were oriented to defense at many villages. This may be true in some regions, but the argument is undercut by several other chapters in which the authors are surprised by the absence of palisades or concerns with defense. Cayuga sites also exist where the ditches and palisades front the vertical cliffs while the level side was left open. Clan mothers have explained to me that this was to protect the children from the cliff edge.

Kimberly Williams-Shuker examines the effects of European interaction at the household level (Rogers Farm site, Cayuga, AD 1660s–1680s). It is a "bottom-up" view of a site associated with the Jesuit mission of St. René. She finds continuity in architectural principles and even Huron influence on the longhouse architecture. (The site has an ossuary that suggests a Huron presence.) The Cayuga seem to have maintained their shared social and economic obligations of longhouse organization despite demographic collapse and participation in a capitalist economy and emerging world markets.

Lastly, Kurt A. Jordan discusses an eighteenth-century Seneca village (Townley-Read site). The Mohawk model of acculturation has been superimposed on other Haudenosaunee peoples by archaeologists in order to understand the contact period, but Jordan views the Seneca as having been much more selective than the Mohawk in adopting the European lifeway. The absence of European plants and domesticated animals, beaver bones, and other indicators suggest that the Seneca had a fundamentally different contact experience than other nations, and that in general there were various levels of assimilation and resistance throughout Indian country.

Because junior scholars dominate this volume it gives us an opportunity to assess the present and near future state of Haudenosaunee archaeology. In terms of technical analysis and theoretical innovation in integrating regional, site, and microlevels of understanding, this archaeology is in fine shape. The book literally represents a flood of new archaeological data and an important bibliography of the extant literature. Also positive is the repeated emphasis on refuting the myths of emptiness and abandonment of particular regions that have been used to deny Native land rights. The presence of villages without palisades at several times and places also negates a long-standing stereotype about endemic warfare and defense in Haudenosaunee territory.

In terms of progressive approaches to collaboration, cooperation, and indigenous archaeology, however, this volume is troubling. There is careful avoidance of any mention of modern Native communities, consultation, or approval. Only one author (Timmins) cites collaborative projects as an interest in the author biographies, and I know of only one New York archaeologist here (Jordan) who communicates with Native leaders. This book has some cringers too, such as the suggestion that the matrilocal residential pattern was a response to European contact and male involvement in the beaver trade (ch. 9). Emic perspectives are sometimes discussed on the basis of how they were reported by white historians like William Fenton (ch. 7), when the works of many Native authors are available.

Site protection takes a hit in this volume. Several chapters show fairly precise maps of site locations, which would not be approved by Native leaders. One site (Rogers Farm, ch. 9) is presented as under the stewardship of the Department of Environmental Conservation. We also learn that this site has been plowed for fifty years and impacted by a road, gravel parking lot, and several farm buildings. No mention is made of conservation for any sites discussed in this volume. They are presented more or less as playgrounds for archaeologists to experiment with multiscalar analysis.

For several years I have encouraged, cajoled, and begged archaeologists working in Iroquoia to contact the Haudenosaunee Standing Committee, clan mothers, and chief councils of the nation homeland where they work. New York archaeologists tend to carry on old-style business as usual because most Haudenosaunee land is dispossessed and under private ownership. The Haudenosaunee are interested in archaeology and have taken a positive approach, selectively approving excavations, particularly when it involves issues that interest them or broadens affiliation within the framework of NAGPRA-based repatriation. They also wish to correlate the archaeological record with oral histories, an issue never mentioned here. I hope that the rise of noncollaborative multiscalar archaeology that emphasizes regional diversity will not harm their ongoing quests to reclaim their history and bring home their ancestors.

Jack Rossen
Ithaca College

Kenneth Milton Chapman: A Life Dedicated to Indian Arts and Artists. By Janet Chapman and Karen Barrie. Albuquerque: University of New Mexico Press, 2008. 344 pages. $34.95 cloth.

This biography of Kenneth Milton Chapman (1875–1968) relates the remarkable life of a quiet, humble man who became an intrinsic part of almost every scholarly institution founded in Santa Fe during the first decades of the twentieth century. He was a founding staff member of the Museum of New Mexico, the School of American Research (now known as the School of Advanced Research), and the Laboratory of Anthropology; cofounded the Indian Arts Fund and the Indian Fair (the forerunner to Santa Fe's annual Indian Art Market); worked on some of the most important archaeological digs in northern New Mexico; wrote some of the first studies of Pueblo pottery; restored old homes; and painted the occasional mural. Born in Indiana, Chapman trained for a short time at the Art Institute of Chicago and worked in Illinois and Indiana as an illustrator before he moved to Las Vegas, New Mexico, in 1899 seeking the healing desert air as an antidote to his long-term health issues. It was in New Mexico that Chapman found his calling, or rather callings, because he worked in a variety of positions, becoming, as he described himself, a "Jack-of-all-trades" (142). Based on his personality, Chapman is an odd choice for a biography. Shy, retiring, modest, and, by all accounts, moral, Chapman possesses none of the drama usually seen in an engaging life story. Based on his experiences, however, Chapman's story merits this scholarly attention.

What is striking about Chapman's life is how it encompassed great society and technological changes and what these changes meant for his life. The authors begin by fleshing out the stories of Chapman's parents living in the Midwest, but, avoiding a common fault in many biographies, they do not linger too long in Chapman's early history. Moving on to his art training and early jobs for various publications as an illustrator, Chapman's life reads as a preamble until he reaches New Mexico. The authors capture the unique quality of life there, rural and multicultural, attracting artists, health seekers, and those interested in life outside of urban settings. All three of these qualities attracted Chapman, an artist by profession and a great lover of the outdoors. It was in Las Vegas that Chapman met the two men who would influence his destiny, the attorney Frank Springer and the archaeologist Edgar Lee Hewett. Chapman formed a deep attachment to Springer, whom he saw as a father figure. Chapman worked for Springer for almost three decades, helping in all the lawyer's plans, from teaching at the Las Vegas Normal School to the illustration of Springer's study of fossil crinoids. With Hewett, Chapman had a complicated relationship; Hewett was sometimes Chapman's mentor and sometimes his adversary, but Chapman's story was inextricably woven with Hewett's.

This book was truly a labor of love. The authors, Janet Chapman and Karen Barrie, are freelance writers, and they worked together to create this well-researched and well-written volume about the extraordinary life of Chapman's great uncle and Barrie's great uncle by marriage. Chapman and Barrie created an intimate portrait of their mutual relative but never neglect the bigger picture of his life and works. The authors used various sources, secondary and primary, including notes Chapman left for an auto-biography that he never completed; the notes were a collection of unrelated events. Although he remembered many specific moments in great detail, the memoirs lacked a narrative. His writers provided this by organizing the events chronologically and pulling together different moments into a story. The results are compelling, slowly drawing the reader into the rich landscape of Chapman's life. What emerges is a picture of a man with an ad hoc art education and a jumbled collection of jobs, including work in various trades such as selling postcards, watercolors, and paintings; working on archaeological digs;

teaching art; and becoming one of the world's foremost authorities on Native American art, particularly Southwestern pottery.

The authors use Chapman's own words effectively; when they quote from Chapman's memoirs or other writings, they integrate the quotes into their own prose but distinguish the words by italicizing them. This editorial choice works well to create a cohesive text while also giving voice to their subject whenever possible. One problem not addressed by the writers is the veracity of Chapman's memoirs. Though they were written in the 1950s when Chapman was in his seventies, most address events that took place before the 1920s, some as early as the 1880s. Although Chapman's recollections of the events, as noted in the quotations from his unpublished memoirs, are quite precise and detailed, they were written much later and the intervening years must have colored his memories.

The genuine affection Chapman and Barrie feel for their mutual relative is infectious; reading their biography it is impossible not to root for Chapman as his life meanders between his various professions, his health is challenged, he looks for love, and he works to help Pueblo potters. He had a restless mind and pursued various interests including, but not limited to, illustration, painting, architectural restoration, furniture making, collecting, administration, and archaeology. In addition to showing the story of Chapman's life and its impact, the book retells many anecdotes, such as Chapman's planting a false *tuxtla* (a small Olmec statuette found in 1902 with human and animal characteristics) at the dig site for archaeologist Sylvanus Morley to "discover" or relating the dangers of driving with Jesse Nusbaum. These moments give flavor to life in New Mexico during the early twentieth century.

Perhaps Chapman's greatest legacy is his work in the field of twentieth-century Pueblo pottery. Chapman's love of Native art came about organically, beginning with a childhood fascination with Native cultures and growing into a full-fledged interest while he worked at archaeological digs in what used to be known as the Rito de los Frijoles, now part of Bandelier National Monument. He spent many hours mending pots and classifying potsherds. He got to know the potters personally, especially the great potters from San Ildefonso, Maria Martinez and Tonith Roybal. He shared the designs found on older Ancestral Pueblo (Anazasi) and Mogollon pots with contemporary potters by copying the images onto paper and taking the pattern books to the potters. He used the Indian Fair to encourage potters to continue creating quality pieces. His articles in *Art and Archaeology* and *El Palacio* attempted to organize the potsherds found at the dig sites into a chronological history. His research into Native art and culture offers some of the earliest studies of pottery as a true art form, and he wrote some of the first in-depth studies of Pueblo pottery.

Chapman and Barrie's biography adds to the growing number of works about Chapman, including several articles and a recent book. It serves as an excellent counterpoint to Marit Munson's annotated anthology *Kenneth Chapman's Santa Fe: Artists and Archaeologist, 1907–1931* (2009). Munson edited a selection of Chapman's original writings from his unpublished memoirs, his articles, and other sources, which were compiled into one volume along with Munson's observations on the texts. Although Munson's volume offers researchers the information in a concise, clear format, Chapman and Barrie's biography provides a richer, more readable version of Chapman's life. This biography fleshes out many elements of Chapman's life, although, given his large body of work as a painter, more color images of his paintings, particularly the murals he painted for the St. Francis Auditorium at the Museum of New Mexico, would have been helpful. As it is, the book is an enjoyable read for anyone interested in the history of this unique part of the country, and scholars from various fields, from Native American cultures to archaeology and art history, will find much to recommend it.

Suzanne Newman Fricke
University of New Mexico

Kennewick Man: Perspectives on the Ancient One. Edited by Heather Burke, Claire Smith, Dorothy Lippert, Joe Watkins, and Larry Zimmerman. Walnut Creek, CA: Left Coast Press, 2008. 298 pages. $65.00 cloth; $29.95 paper.

This book makes an important contribution to ongoing conversations about the social ethics of archaeology and the path toward collaborative working relationships with indigenous communities. It does so by focusing on the controversy over Kennewick Man, also known as the Ancient One, and compiling a diverse array of perspectives on this complicated issue. The book is comprised of forty-one short chapters; authors range from tribal elders and cultural resource managers to museum curators and junior and senior archaeologists and anthropologists. Originally intended to be two volumes, the editors decided to combine the collection so as to reveal the overlapping concerns and perspectives that exist between Native communities and scholarly interests. As an anthology, it is distinct from other books on the subject that tend to present a single author's interpretation of the controversy, its history, and its implications.

Kennewick Man is a 9,600-year-old body discovered in the eroding banks of the Columbia River in 1996. Following the Native American Graves Protection and Repatriation Act (NAGPRA), the Army Corps of Engineers determined to repatriate the remains to local tribal communities for reburial. A group of scientists sued to halt the reburial and gain control of the remains for study. After years of legal proceedings, the courts found for the scientists. The remains are currently housed in the Burke Museum in Seattle, Washington.

A variety of common themes can be traced throughout the diverse contributions to this volume: media coverage of the controversy, traditional Native perspectives regarding the remains, damage to working relationships as a result of the controversy, what archaeologists and tribes can learn from the conflict, and a critique of NAGPRA as it currently stands.

Media coverage of the case has been problematic. Coverage emphasizes artificially polarized positions, pitting "science" against "religion," and

"Natives" against "archaeologists" when, as this text demonstrates, such binaries are far from clear. Much of the media storm has focused upon initial descriptions of the body as having Caucasoid characteristics. Journalists and members of the public were quick to misinterpret the descriptor as implying that the Ancient One was of European descent. As one piece in this volume notes, the repercussions of this can still be seen on white supremacist Web sites that point to Kennewick Man as evidence that white Americans are the only true Americans.

Numerous chapters highlight Native perspectives on the Ancient One that emphasize their responsibility to care for the earth and the dead. Native authors locate the conflict in terms of the continuing sacred connection they hold with their past, the natural world, and their ancestors. They argue that they have inherent responsibilities and rights to protect and care for the deceased. Authors also critique the scientists seeking control of the remains, seeing them as driven by "pure selfishness," pursuing "their own personal gain" and "prestige," and having an agenda intent on undermining the legitimacy of indigenous identity (151, 48, 99, 225). The court's decision to allow scientists access to the remains is seen as undermining indigenous sovereignty and a tribal community's right to care for and rebury its dead.

Indigenous and nonindigenous authors express concern that the Kennewick Man controversy has irrevocably damaged working relationships between tribes and archaeologists. For Native authors, the heart of the conflict stems from the failure of scientists to show tribes "common decent respect" (99), and several authors point out that such conflicts could have been avoided from the beginning if tribes had been properly consulted. As one author argued, "respect and empathy are huge components that need to be interjected into this whole process" (101). Archaeologists mirror this concern, fearing that the plaintiff scientists acted inappropriately, showed disrespect, and intentionally sought to undermine NAGPRA. Several authors express fears that in so doing the plaintiffs have damaged working relationships for the future.

Archaeologists here also offer critiques of archaeology, pointing to its foundations within a colonial, racist, and patriarchal past. Authors argue that this case provides an opportunity for archaeologists to reform their tradition despite the risks it may pose to their existing authority. Such reform, authors argue, would provide opportunities to make archaeology more relevant and useful to the communities it purports to study. As one author put it, the controversy provides an opportunity to challenge "undisguised attempts to limit the effects of NAGPRA" and the "fraud, folly and ineptitude" that characterized the initial approach to Kennewick Man (215).

Rather than marginalizing indigenous voices from their own histories, virtually all of the academic voices in the book embrace the inclusion of indigenous knowledges within their work, and many chapters call for the creation of collaborative projects. Existing models for collaborative work are discussed here, despite the fact that they are generally overlooked within the media. As chapters call for more respectful relationships built on cooperation and engagement, they also provide suggestions for how compromise could be (or could have been) achieved. One author argues that the Ancient One's remains should be studied under the supervision of advisers selected by the Native communities concerned, so as to ensure proper standards of care and that analysis of the remains pursues questions relevant to the tribes. Another argues that shifting from a paradigm of "ownership" to one of "stewardship" in regard to ancient human remains would provide "an opportunity for accommodating multiple claims of affiliation by opening the door to the possibility of joint or collaborative stewardship" (189). If archaeologists can achieve a shift toward building respectful relationships between all concerned parties, another author argues, it will become evident that the best caretakers of human remains will be teams comprised of archaeologists and Native Americans. Native voices within the text make their own case for increased engagement with the archaeological field, pointing out the need for tribes to take an active role in providing cultural sensitivity training for the next generation of archaeologists. By doing so, tribes will be able to ensure that they have a hand in writing their own histories and managing their own cultural resources.

The book also offers an important critique of NAGPRA, demonstrating its inability to protect or ensure the repatriation of indigenous human remains adequately. Authors point out that NAGPRA applies only to public lands and problematically defines human remains as "property." As one author argues, the point of such legislation should be "not to respect the rights of their descendants, but to respect *the ancestors themselves*" (138, emphasis in original). NAGPRA also stumbles over the definition of what it means to be "indigenous," illustrating the complicated nature of indigenous identity, particularly given the relatively recent construction of "tribes" as we know them today and the artificial (and modern) construction of race. Essays point out how this case has put the responsibility upon indigenous people to prove their identities, while discounting their own methods for demonstrating their history. One possible solution to this conundrum suggests that scholars move away from notions of "affiliation" toward "patrimony," which would allow for an understanding of identity that is more fluid and in-process, enabling archaeology to affirm multiple cultural perspectives and thus be more politically engaged and responsible.

Overall, the book is an extremely valuable contribution, both because of the diversity of opinions presented here and the efforts made to overcome the artificial polarization of positions as they have been presented in the media. It demonstrates that tribes and archaeologists share common concerns and can build respectful working relationships. Within the undergraduate classroom, the book provides helpful resources and pedagogical challenges. A detailed timeline of events and legal proceedings is quite helpful, as is the inclusion of such a wide array of diverse authors. Although the organization of the selections is fine for a general reader, it might have been done more thoughtfully for the educational context. The editors do not explicitly frame the contributions or arrange them according to overlapping themes. Although the book includes a short introduction, it is primarily up to the reader to find common themes among the chapters and bring them into conversation with each other. If educators are willing to do this, the book provides a wealth of learning opportunities. Educators can challenge students to read these chapters as primary texts, encouraging them to interpret various positions, examine them, and compare them with each other. Although a more helpful organization and framing of the selections might have made the text more easily translatable into the classroom, it remains a valuable tool. *Kennewick Man: Perspectives on the Ancient One* is recommended for readers interested in indigenous legal rights, repatriation, anthropological and archaeological ethics, and indigenous care for the dead.

Suzanne J. Crawford O'Brien
Pacific Lutheran University

The Monacan Indian Nation of Virginia: The Drums of Life. By Rosemary Clark Whitlock. Tuscaloosa: University of Alabama Press, 2008. 248 pages. $46.50 cloth; $24.95 paper.

Perhaps the most contentious debate in the social sciences and humanities today, particularly where indigenous peoples are concerned, is the question of representation and authority. Does the researcher's critical training privilege her or his interpretation of culture and community over the understandings of those who live the experiences in question? In *The Monacan Indian Nation of Virginia: The Drums of Life*, Rosemary Clark Whitlock seemingly confronts this question head on, paradoxically, by sidestepping it. Whitlock, a member of the Monacan Nation who did not grow up in the tribe's core community, but who has made every effort to embrace and be embraced by her people, offers a meticulously honest account of the Monacan Indian tribe of Virginia through a series of oral histories juxtaposed with critical historical documents that explicate the tribe's unique and turbulent colonial experience.

One of the binding themes of this work is the Monacan people's collective experience with eugenic policies in the state of Virginia during the first half of the twentieth century. From 1914 to 1946, state registrar Walter A. Plecker coordinated a virtual witch hunt designed to erase Indians from the documentary record. Convinced that all Indians in Virginia were heavily intermixed with other races, Plecker authored and saw the successful passage of the 1924 Virginia Race Integrity Act, which essentially declared that the state would thereafter acknowledge only two races existing in Virginia—white and "colored." Accordingly, he devised a pseudoscientific system for determining the race of individuals based on surnames listed as anything other than "white" in years past. For Indians, this meant persecution for simply self-identifying as such, and it uniformly prevented all tribes in Virginia from gaining access to public schools until the early 1960s. Interestingly Plecker seems to have devoted a disproportionate amount of attention to chastising Monacans in Amherst County and surrounding areas, thereby impacting their historic identity in profound ways. Virtually every oral history presented herein illuminates Plecker's stamp on the Monacan psyche.

The first of such interviews, for instance, is with Monacan Chief Kenneth Branham, who has held that office since 1995. As one of the first Monacans to be integrated into Amherst public schools in 1964, his words recount an experience that bridged generations but still carry the dark weight of exclusion and persecution. Branham not only recounts how he and his peers were shunned, but also how they frequently penciled in the word *white* on forms requiring racial designation, realizing that if they used the term *Indian* teachers would replace it with the word *colored.* He also admits to harboring bitterness over his and other Monacans' experiences vis-à-vis the eugenic legacy in Virginia. Yet it is such open and honest statements that make this book remarkable, for Branham's recounting is also of a process of reconciliation and perseverance.

The manifestations of such perseverance are seen in interviews with tribal members such as Diane Johns Shields and Karenne Wood, both of whom grew up outside of the community with limited knowledge of their heritage, but who arrived in the 1990s to become stalwart actors in tribal governance and community organizing. At the time these interviews were collected in the late 1990s both women were actively involved in the process of compiling data to help the tribe secure federal recognition (as of this writing legislation is matriculating through Congress). Shields and Wood reflect the sentiments of other so-called newcomers that have grown up away from the community at a time when the specter of race integrity laws loomed heavy; they feel compelled to use skills and resources not available to earlier generations in order to empower the contemporary community.

What of the elder generations? Whitlock provides an impressive range of interviews with older Monacans who lived through the peak of eugenic policies intended to erase them from the record. Lucian Branham, age eighty-seven at the time of his interview in 1997, recounted his disappointment at being denied access to public education and described the dynamics of community that distinguished the Monacans from other people in the area. This includes a rare description of midwives, who also served as doctors, and the networks of reciprocity that enabled Monacans to endure decades of debt peonage as tenant farmers on local orchards. One of the shortest but most intriguing interviews is with Dena Branham, who for many years had a reputation for self-sufficiency. In her late eighties at the time of her interview, Dena recounted in detail how her family produced virtually everything they needed, and she provides a formidable inventory of goods and pharmacopeia.

It is the diversity of interviews that constitutes one of the strengths of this book. One of the boldest interviews is with William Sandidge, who served as clerk of court in Amherst County during the heyday of racial integrity policies. In his nineties at the time of the interview, Sandidge expressed great remorse at having classified Monacans as "colored" on vital records, while recounting in detail the moments when Plecker threatened the clerk with jail time if he caught him acknowledging Monacans as Indians. In some ways, however ironic, this interview constitutes the thematic focal point for this volume. The impact of Virginia's eugenic policies on Indians cannot be understated; where the Monacans are concerned, this collection makes it clear that the experience has become another chapter in their sacred history—comprising yet another designator of tribal identity—and that Plecker is regarded as a historic antagonist.

In the preface to this volume, J. Anthony Paredes states, "This is not the usual book from an academic press. It makes no pretense of scholarly analysis, intellectual discourse, or defense of a thesis" (ix). Yet as a cultural anthropologist who has worked with the Monacans for fifteen years, this book inspires me. Whitlock's forthright and honest approach, in writing and in securing interviews, has produced a rare corpus of timeless oral historical material. Significantly, she includes a list of questions used to guide semistructured interviews, as well as her personal advice as a novice (but, in my opinion, highly skilled) interviewer that would provide a valuable supplement to courses on qualitative methods. These interviews are accompanied by eleven appendices filled with primary documents contextualizing the Monacan experience during the Plecker years, including letters from the registrar; birth, death, and marriage records; and letters written by Monacans protesting the racial integrity policies.

Although Whitlock makes no claim to being a historian or anthropologist, she has produced an engaging and extremely accessible compendium of Monacan life that appeals to scholarly and general audiences equally. From her vantage point as a tribal member who grew up and was educated on the margins of the community, she is able to deliver a frank observation in her own autobiographical statement that makes explicit what postmodernist and critical race theorists have struggled with for years: "All Americans are triads [triracial] or at least duos [biracial]. . . . Why is it that some of us refuse to accept that fact? We can't pigeonhole people as much as some people would like to" (160). Such a statement not only calls into question the social construction of race but also beckons a consideration of cultural adaptation and configurations in a global age. Although this book may not be uniformly embraced as critical theoretical literature, it does provide a potential model for indigenous challenges to the Western academic canon and interpretive praxis.

Samuel R. Cook
Virginia Tech

A Nation of Women: Gender and Colonial Encounters among the Delaware Indians. By Gunlög Fur. Philadelphia: University of Pennsylvania Press, 2009. 264 pages. $39.95 cloth.

In 1742, the Onondaga Speaker Canasatego lambasted a Delaware delegation in Philadelphia by proclaiming, "We Conquer'd You, we made Women of you, you know you are Women" (163). Scholars have long debated the extent to which this pronouncement of the Delaware as women defined their relationship with the Iroquois Confederacy. Gunlög Fur, professor of history at Växjö University in Sweden, argues that scholars have, for too long, debated whether the appellation was pejorative or one of admiration.

Instead, she attempts to contextualize the encounter within the morphing gender structures of Delaware society and larger colonial America. *A Nation of Women: Gender and Colonial Encounters among the Delaware Indians* certainly sheds light on the context of the 1742 meeting between Delaware leaders and Canasatego, but it also does much more. Using a variety of fresh source material, including Swedish records, Pennsylvania colonial materials, Moravian missionary accounts, private letters, images, and travel journals, Fur reveals how Delaware or Lenape society initially attempted to maintain gender roles amid pressures from missionaries and colonial officials to conform to European gender-types. Decades of contact and trade, Fur argues, eventually altered how gender functioned within Lenape society to produce new meanings for what it meant to be labeled "a nation of women."

In a powerful opening chapter, Fur attempts to reconstruct Delaware society prior to contact by focusing on European accounts from the earliest moments of European and Delaware encounters. She outlines how gender roles functioned in precontact Lenape society to regulate the roles of men and women, as well as how the Delaware were a matrilineal- and agricultural-based society in which women played a vital role in maintaining peace and stability within the nation. Fur argues that this is why the earliest accounts of Europeans included references to Lenape men and women, because women participated in the early encounters and performed significant roles in tribal leadership. The Delaware divided labor based on gender; women were responsible for the planting, cultivation, and harvesting of agricultural foodstuffs, while men were responsible for hunting and providing villages with sources of protein. This division often led to physical divisions of space, as women tended to the fields while men left the villages to hunt. Gender roles became blurred along the Atlantic Coast, as male and female work complemented one another in skills necessary to harvest and catch the products of the sea. "For instance," Fur surmises, "women sometimes hunted (particularly small game) and fished, and men helped in the fields" (19). Fur concludes that the division of labor led to a fairly egalitarian Delaware society and demonstrates how this "basic egalitarian structure also manifested itself in the Lenape mode of clothing," as an early image of a Delaware family depicts a male and female couple dressed in similar garments (25).

Fur also examines how Lenape gender roles functioned within the context of a single Delaware community, Meniolagomekah, and chronicles the spatial orientation of everyday life by demonstrating how the arrival of Moravian missionaries often meant the restructuring of gendered divisions. She demonstrates how the expectations contrived by Europeans eventually clashed with the structures of Lenape society. Moravian missionaries increasingly viewed their understanding of good and evil through a gendered lens, associating evil with the female gender. For missionaries, Fur concludes, "women presented a threat to the orderly Christian community" (121). Regardless, Delaware women often welcomed missionaries into their community. Fur demonstrates that women were more likely than men to approach missionaries about conversion, because the missions initially maintained significant and powerful roles for women with mission and village life. Unlike European officials, who assumed that only men within Delaware society held power, missionaries, at first, offered an alternative that more closely resembled precontact Lenape social structures. The choice of Lenape women to join the missions might also be explained by the better living conditions of Christian towns, as they offered healthier environments in which families could raise children.

Only after outlining changes within Lenape social structures from precontact to the eighteenth century does Fur attempt to give meaning to the appellation of the Delaware Nation as a "nation of women." What is striking in this late chapter is Fur's ability to distinguish both the difference between European and Lenape gender structures and the stark discrepancy in terminology as Europeans and multiple Native communities employed it. In examining the deployment of gendered metaphors, she successfully traces shiftiness in language that morphed the metaphor of a "nation of women" from one of respect and obligation to one of denunciation. She discovers that the Delaware Nation "in general persisted in arguing that theirs was a position of honor" by claiming "that the female role was one that involved responsibilities as peacekeepers or broker of peace in the complicated relations between different Native and European peoples in the Pennsylvania colony" (169). However, the language of councils convinced many indigenous nations, including the Iroquois, to adopt a different meaning for the description of the Delaware as women. For European officials, onlookers, and other Native communities, being called a woman became a derogatory and shameful act.

Ultimately, contact altered the role of women and men within Lenape society and shifted the way that indigenous peoples spoke about gender roles. In the end, Fur concludes, "A century of contact had led to the erosion of the Lenape land base, that vital link between women and land, and to the adoption of certain European habits" (200). It also colored the way that subsequent Europeans and present-day historians have interpreted Canasatego's denouncement of the Delaware as a "nation of women." It might appear that a study of gender among an indigenous nation labeled as *women* would center almost solely on deconstructing that phrase, but Fur uncovers far more about Delaware life than one might suspect. She fleshes out an amazing analysis of men and women within Lenape society and chronicles how decades of contact between the Delaware and Europeans meant changes for both sexes. Yet her bigger challenge involved uncovering the lives of women from the relatively silent colonial sources.

The scarcity of general source material on indigenous people in the early contact period makes the role of recovering the stories of Delaware women extremely challenging, and Fur demonstrates how the gendered bias of European observers often had the effect of underplaying the role of women in Lenape politics and economic survival. So how does one lift the lives of Delaware women from relative obscurity? In one case that demonstrates Fur's creative use of sources, she examines the Delaware woman Notike by using the only three documents that chronicle her life. Here Fur is at her best as she couples generalizations about Lenape gender structures with intimate narratives of individual Delaware lives. In order to demonstrate the role that women played in politics and property management, Fur discusses Notike's role in a heated disagreement between Dutch and Swedish colonists who fought over a valuable tract of land. The Dutch colonists claimed that the Delaware had donated the land to them, while the Swedes produced a signed statement from Notike, the widow of the former sachem, declaring that the Delaware leader who claimed to represent the nation had no right to donate it to the Dutch. The account leaves Fur with more questions than answers, as she deconstructs this little-known case and demonstrates the important role of Lenape women in property holdings and the part of historical sources in obscuring women's roles in Delaware politics.

A Nation of Women demonstrates how excellent historical detective work and thick description of cultural practices might lead scholars of American Indian studies to new interpretations of old debates. Fur provides readers with a detailed account of Lenape life that is well worth reading.

James J. Buss
Oklahoma City University

Native Activism in Cold War America: The Struggle for Sovereignty. By Daniel M. Cobb. Lawrence: University Press of Kansas, 2008. 336 pages. $34.95 cloth.

Most studies of American Indian activism have focused on the Red Power movement of the 1970s. In particular, scholars have looked at the national protests that began with the occupation of Alcatraz Island in late 1969 and were carried on into the next decade by the American Indian Movement. With *Native Activism in Cold War America*, Daniel M. Cobb works to relocate to an earlier period and redefine what constitutes American Indian activism. At the same time, Cobb bridges larger conversations about the war on poverty, the 1960s, and post-1945 politics and social movements.

Cobb concentrates on the 1950s and 1960s, showing how "writing grants, holding community meetings, convening summer workshops for college students, organizing youth councils, giving testimony at congressional hearings, authoring books and editorials, and manipulating the system from within were means [for Native people] of exercising power and acting in politically purposeful ways . . . no less invested with meaning than takeovers and occupations" (2). The book's narrative begins in the early 1950s, with Native activist D'Arcy McNickle's efforts to apply the language of the cold war to issues affecting American Indian tribes. Over the next several years, the National Congress of American Indians (NCAI) and individual Native intellectuals adopted this tactic, working to embrace the language of international development for the purpose of making the situation of American Indians analogous to Third World development, a cold war priority. Meanwhile, a younger generation of Native activists was emerging to challenge what they saw as the submissive, conciliatory attitudes of their elders. During the early 1960s, through a series of meetings, workshops, and organizations that included the American Indian Chicago Conference, Workshops on American Indian Affairs, and National Indian Youth Council (NIYC), Indian youth developed an aggressive, national agenda. Impatient with the NCAI's patriotism, they were more inclined to critique the Kennedy administration's emphasis on modernization theory and make connections between colonialism at home and abroad. In the end, older and younger generations of Native activists sought self-determination for tribal peoples and a repudiation of the disastrous federal policies of assimilation and termination. Wrapping these arguments in the language of the cold war appealed to established organizations and activists, while younger Native people chose to define modern tribalism on their own terms.

The activism of this period, including the debates that they produced, positioned Native people to take advantage of the War on Poverty when it was instituted by the Johnson administration in 1964. For the remainder of the decade, Native people were involved in the war on poverty, and they struggled over how to use its language to serve their needs and concerns. A primary figure in this effort was Dr. James Wilson, head of the Indian Division of the federal Office of Economic Opportunity (OEO). Calling himself a "manipulator" rather than an "activist," Wilson saw the programs of the OEO as an opportunity to train Native people to take over their own affairs. Along with the NCAI, the newly created Task Force on American Indian Poverty, and numerous community activists, the Indian Division concentrated on developing and implementing tribal Community Action Programs (CAPs) at various reservations. These programs, with their insistence on Native control and freedom from the dictates of the Bureau of Indian Affairs, made real progress toward furthering the principles of Native self-determination in a relatively short period of time. Over the next few years, as political conservatives attacked the OEO, Native activists like Vine Deloria Jr. worked to build support for tribal CAPs by positioning American Indians as moderates in a period of increasing urban unrest and more radical demands for racial justice. Despite dwindling federal expenditures for the War on Poverty, the NCAI and established reservation leadership continued this strategy of framing themselves as a less controversial minority group, garnering government support that led to the Johnson administration's National Council on Indian Opportunity, among other gains. The NIYC, meanwhile, critiqued the pace of change brought by the OEO and the CAP and began to consider more radical protest, culminating in Native participation during the 1968 Poor People's Campaign in Washington, D.C.

These rich accounts of advocacy by Native people throughout the 1950s and 1960s fulfill Cobb's goal of reframing American Indian activism. Although some scholars may previously have seen a handful of reservation-based protests and the fish-ins of the 1960s as precursors to the Red Power movement, this book adds several layers of complexity to a Native activist movement that must now be considered to have begun in the years immediately following World War II. In doing so, *Native Activism* fits into a broader effort to rethink fundamentally the movements for racial and social justice in postwar America. During the past decade and a half, historians have emphasized a "Long Civil Right Movement" that extended from the 1930s through the 1970s and included not just African Americans but also other aggrieved groups. Furthermore, such studies have worked to deemphasize national protests and focused on the less flashy work of organizing, educating, and managing bureaucracy at the grassroots level and within the structures of government. Cobb deftly shows that Native people were also engaged in these broader trends yet took particular avenues based on their unique needs and historical experiences. Scholars in American Indian studies will especially appreciate Cobb's exploration of the ways that Native people used the language and priorities of the cold war and War on Poverty to advance their concerns; the well-crafted biographies of Native intellectual and activists; and the examination of the generational tensions that at times took Native activism in multiple directions. Despite Cobb's obvious fondness for his subject and the individuals that drive the narrative, the book avoids overly romanticizing the activism of the period and the gains that it made. Although Cobb does not make the claim, there is much for contemporary activists to ponder as they continue their struggles to advance the causes of Native people.

Stronger linkages might have further advanced a broader rewriting of the history of Native activism. The book's conclusion, "A Struggle Just Beginning," argues that the events of the period under study combined with the actions of Native people allowed American Indians entry into the political arena. Native activists continued their struggles through the end of the 1960s and beyond, as the young people featured in this book became leaders within tribal communities and as they and others continued to work with the federal government to develop programs to advance self-determination. Standing somewhat outside this narrative, however, is the Red Power movement. Cobb argues that the events associated with the rising militancy of the late 1960s and early 1970s "were not direct extensions of what happened during the 1960s . . . but they were not complete departures either" (203). Without further explanation, some readers will go away wondering how the Red Power movement was more specifically linked to the activism of the 1950s and 1960s or seeking to understand better how Cobb envisions the Red Power movement "resituate[d] . . . within a larger context of Native political action" (2). Such connections, however, might very well be the starting point for an entirely new project that traces Native activism through the 1970s and into subsequent decades. Any scholar taking on such a study will be required to begin with Cobb's crucial work, for its narrative of Native activism in the period before the Red Power movement and its reconceptualization of what it means to advocate for Native people.

Nicolas G. Rosenthal
Loyola Marymount University

Native People of Southern New England, 1650–1775. By Kathleen J. Bragdon. Norman: University of Oklahoma Press, 2009. 312 pages. $32.95 cloth.

Kathleen J. Bragdon's *Native People of Southern New England, 1650–1775* is a worthy companion to her earlier volume documenting the Native people of the same region, *Native People of Southern New England, 1500–1650* (1996). As a scholar who lives and researches in this geographic and cultural area, her new work is a welcome addition to the literature. This newest work has the advantage of building off her earlier research and successfully adopts a new approach to examining the topic and era by placing "an emphasis on the linguistic and cultural premises that underlay Native life in the region, as enacted within community settings" (xi). This approach is clear in its goal to provide a Native voice to this era and locale through an analysis of the use of language, whether it was Native dialects or English, spoken or written. As such, it seeks to avoid the pitfalls of scholars who either directly or implicitly adopt an acculturation model that marches Native peoples steadily down the road of culture loss and marginalization, overlooking the sophisticated negotiation of the new political, economic, and cultural landscapes that confronted them.

The numerous charts and tables make it easier to follow linguistic comparisons and geographic connections between Native communities. This visual representation is useful in keeping track of the complex interrelationships between communities and dialects, and underscore just how interwoven Native societies of the region still were at the time period being studied, in spite of the subsequent land and population loss and dislocations of Native peoples following catastrophic events such as the Pequot War and King Philip's War. The careful analysis and identification of Native communities of this era also reminds contemporary scholars how much more diverse the Native community was in terms of language and Native political units.

The role of women receives careful analysis among these Native peoples during this time period. Although other scholars have all too frequently focused on the male sachems and viewed the female sachems as anomalies, Bragdon's review of numerous deeds and other land transactions clearly identify a female role in the holding and transfer of land, while political titles usually were handed down to males of the same lineage. Along with the role of women and land, the discussion of land, its utilization by lineages, and its distribution of the foundation of Native economy does much to explain how land loss contributed to the portrayal of the wandering Indians of the late colonial era. Her description of how Natives took up a mobile way of life communally runs counter to the depictions of lone itinerant Indians wandering across the landscape as laborers, Indian doctors, or sailors. This mobility was a response to their inability to settle due to land loss and an unwillingness to abandon their relatives and homeland. This mobility also reflected something of their traditional seasonal shifts in subsistence.

Perhaps one of Bragdon's most interesting descriptions is how southern New England Native communities adapted some of the very forces of acculturation in order to increase community cohesion. Christianity, long viewed as a primary factor in the loss of Native culture and land, as well as the justification of European colonization, had a much more nuanced role in the region. Although Native conversion did remake alliances between Native peoples and led to the creation of new Native polities in the form of praying towns, Native people from sachems' lineages led these same towns. Additionally, Christianity in this region had two other important contributions to Native cultural persistence and political autonomy. First, literacy was viewed as a key part of the Puritan understanding of a good Christian. Therefore, to be good Christians, the Algonquians of this region had to be able to read. Interestingly, this missionary endeavor led not only to Native literacy but also literacy in Native languages. John Elliot and other missionaries translated the Bible and authored numerous tracts in a variety of the regional dialects. Natives owned copies of these documents, handed them down for multiple generations, and used them as part of community life. This newfound literacy also set the stage for Native-language wills, land deeds, and even some business records. These Native-language documents provided glimpses into the Native perspective of themselves and their surrounding world that were instrumental to the author's latest work.

As a side effect of Christian conversion, the minister replaced the *powwaw* as the public center of religious life in the community. In another region-specific adaptation, these ministers spoke the Native dialects as well as trained Native ministers who often taught Native students (adults and children), and connected Christian Indian communities. Like the *powwaws* before them, they were community leaders of what became an enduring social institution among many Native communities: churches. Churches were places to gather to discuss politics, community events, and speak the Native language in a sanc-tioned setting. Old ways combined with the new as Native men smoked pipes, combining indigenous tobacco offerings with Christianity, following the services. What could be seen as an institution representing the European colo-nizers had been co-opted to become a safe place for Natives to gather, over which they exercised control. *Powwaws* or festivals that represented the earlier traditions of first-fruit gatherings found their home on the church grounds. As leaders, these Native ministers also advocated for their communities' rights and equitable treatment. Initially a source of change, the Indian church became an institution of conservatism, particularly in the area of language.

Although much of the volume and argument is for ongoing Native resistance and mitigation of the forces of colonization, Bragdon does not downplay the deleterious effect on Native people of becoming the marginal-ized other. The very diagrams that show relationships between colonial Native communities also underscore, for those scholars of contemporary Native peoples of the region, just how many are no longer extant as distinct peoples. Adaptations to a decreasing land base led to the restructuring of Native societies in an effort to cope with long-term absences of members of family groups, whether it was men on whaling ships or various military campaigns. Loss of resources, and increasing incursions by non-Natives, led to a growing record of criminal complaints against individual Natives. Ultimately, these communities, although still connected through kinship and culture, became more like islands in the English colonial sea. An increasing localization of language reflected this shift and could have contributed to the decreasing use of Native languages by Natives and English colonists.

As a scholarly work looking at colonial Native peoples, *Native People of Southern New England, 1650–1775* creates a context in which colonial-era writings by Natives of the region can be better understood. In particular, the works by New England Native ministers Joseph Johnson, Samson Occum, and even the later William Apess would be greatly enhanced by first reading this book. Bragdon clearly sets the stage on which these Native actors emerge, as Christian Indian leaders, writers, and political advocates. It is an important work bridging the time between King Philip's War and the emergence of the early American nation state and ably documents Native people of the region who, "on their journey to becoming modern Americans, . . . continued to take a different path" (234). It is accessible for the general reader of American Indian history and is an important tool for scholars seeking to understand this period and region better.

James Cedric Woods (Lumbee)
University of Massachusetts–Boston

A New Deal for Native Art: Indian Arts and Federal Policy, 1933–1943. By Jennifer McLerran. Tucson: University of Arizona Press, 2009. 320 pages. $59.95 cloth.

Federal Indian policy and its effects on Native Americans has long been one of the most significant areas of Native American/First Nation studies. Law and policy scholarship was a key area highlighted at the 1961 Chicago conference that called for the new discipline, and its absence was one of the central critiques of anthropological investigation. Law and policy publications constituted some of the first scholarship using a Native American studies paradigm, and this hallmark continues to the present. By its nature, research in the law and policy arena is interdisciplinary, multicultural, and comparative, and the resulting studies on land, education, religion, identity and membership, economics, government and politics, and a wealth of other topics has added new dimensions to the study of Native cultures and societies as well as necessary historical contextualizations. These studies have also taught us a great deal about American society; the country's changing philosophies, feelings, conundrums; and its governmental responses, because in many ways this subspecialty of Native American studies is as much about general American society and government as it is about Native American groups.

A New Deal for Native Art falls squarely into this corpus of law and policy studies. It focuses on the desire of the federal government to create sustainable markets for Indian artists during a period of national economic crisis. However, the work deals with the intersection of policy areas rarely considered by legal and public policy experts (for example, arts, economic development, identity, and consumer protection). A handful of excellent books and articles that deal with laws affecting the production and sale of art by those who can claim to be American Indian artists exist. (Native American artists are the only group in the United States that have to prove membership in a marked social group—federally recognized tribes—before they can label themselves *Native artists*.) Most authors have focused on the 1935 Indian Arts and Crafts Act, which established the Indian Arts and Crafts Board (IACB), or the 1990 revised Indian Arts and Crafts Act (P.L. 101-644), a truth-in-advertising law that led to several lawsuits over Indian identity. These excellent works have been written by lawyers, sociologists, or anthropologists who have looked solely at these important pieces of legislation and their ramifications. Other authors have analyzed the aesthetic and political influences of René d'Harnoncourt, the influential first director of the IACB, and his museological agenda and educational programs. Absent has been a comprehensive approach that documents how federal policies about Indian art based on romanticism, nostalgia, and hierarchical primitivism were interwoven in a number of coordinated (and uncoordinated) federal programs and how these programs did or did not implement a uniform policy. Also missing, until now, has been an analysis using a combined legal, policy, folklore, cultural studies, and art history perspective that focuses on the theoretical concepts of the Other, colonization, tourism, and conflicting American social thought that led to another round of federal paternalism without consultation with Native peoples.

Jennifer McLerran produces such an informative analysis by concentrating on policy creation, philosophy, and implementation as the result of the romanticization of indigenous artists as individuals predisposed to produce preindustrial forms, that is, as peoples who lived outside modernity, a perspective utilized by the American government to further the goals of the Roosevelt administration. These programs were designed to alter federal Indian policy radically and reverse devastating assimilationist policies while helping to preserve traditional Native cultures and revitalize Native art, which was held to have been corrupted by tourism. Federal players also designed programs to increase individual and community self-sufficiency and generate income. McLerran documents how the expansion and upgrading of Native arts for the fine arts and decorative arts markets became an important cog in these initiatives; however, it was one that "actually propagated a binary [hierarchical] construction of tradition and modern" that was not always beneficial but served the agenda of the romantic primitivist reformers working to energize art revivals (2). It is a perspective that contemporary Native artists still have to deal with, one that has hindered their ability to compete successfully in the fine art market and produce a thriving ethnically marked arts market.

McLerran is an art historian and folklorist who uses an American studies approach to her topic, as well as an aesthetic analysis of the art produced. She has previously published on Navajo textiles, focusing on the collections of a famous Southwestern arts trader. A well-informed and meticulous archival and collections-based researcher who has mined heretofore unused documents, McLerran has long been interested in the New Deal programs designed for Indian artists and consumers. In *A New Deal for Native Art* she describes these programs as part of a single, multi-pronged effort to improve the market for American Indian art based on the models of Indian reform and assistance associations and the successes of d'Harnoncourt to promote indigenous cultures, art, and tourism in Mexico. She argues successfully that Indian art marketed under these auspices must be seen as a commodity that is controlled by law, a component of the US economy, part of national political trends and reform efforts, and a continuation of colonization. She does this convincingly while documenting the different meanings these projects had for Native artists, Native communities, collectors, institutions, and government personnel.

One of the major contributions of this work is that the author looks at New Deal Indian arts programs across various federal agencies—something that no one has attempted before. She illustrates that these initiatives were extensive and diverse. McLerran focuses on the IACB, the Civilian Conservation Corps (CCC), the Works Projects Administration (WPA), and the Home Extension Division and the Education Division of the Indian Service. In surveying these agencies and specific projects, McLerran has broadened the context of the IACB programs that are usually discussed as if they were the only federal New Deal initiative. She emphasizes the importance of Commissioner of Indian Affairs John Collier and Secretary of the Interior Harold Ickes ensuring that there was an Indian division in all of the major New Deal arts programs developed by the Department of the Interior.

McLerran begins her study of the transcultural dynamics of policy, production, and consumption with a fascinating example, Gerald Nailor's eight-panel mural project, *The History and Progress of the Navajo People*, which adorns the Native Nation Council House. This example is one of my favorite parts of the book because I have often seen the art but never knew its history. The construction of these magnificent paintings and the building illustrates the goals of all Indian New Deal policies well, emphasizing an unproblematic story of survival as continuity with change that would be read differently by federal Bureau of Indian Affairs (BIA)/WPA agents and the Navajo people.

McLerran continues her narrative by providing the reader with important background information on the New Deal Indian arts programs, beginning with identifying the social, aesthetic, and economic problems they were designed to solve. The excellent analysis of the art recommendations in the Meriam Report is a contribution to the literature and places the New Deal initiatives in historic and social context. Special attention is paid to two key players, Collier and d'Harnoncourt, and how their philosophies, past experiences, and humanistic agendas shaped the development and implementation of New Deal Indian arts programs.

McLerran next focuses on case studies in order to illustrate her points about why public works projects, schools, community centers, and workshops were built and how they became the centers of arts and crafts production and marketing. She includes chapters based on types of initiatives such as traditional and nontraditional arts and crafts produced in community-run, rural cooperatives; exhibits in metropolitan museums; murals painted in state and federal buildings; monumental wood carvings; and architectural reconstructions on public lands. Exceptionally informative are the sections on the IACB's Seneca Arts Project and the rural cooperatives, the WPA mural projects, and the CCC's archaeological restoration and totem pole projects, none of which has ever been analyzed before. Because of this approach, McLerran minimizes the work of the Soil Conservation Service in which much interesting work with art and economic development was done and the BIA's programs on sheep reduction and the education of artists about raw materials. I hope that she will publish more in the future about these programs, so we can learn more about American society and policy and the opportunities and barriers it created for Native American artists.

For those new to this topic, what is most important about this creatively illustrated book is the compilation of information about the different programs and how it fits together to reinforce government policy. For all readers interested in Native studies, this historical analysis about federal Indian art policy and political philosophy will be a valuable addition to our libraries.

Nancy J. Parezo
University of Arizona

The Nez Perces in the Indian Territory: Nimiipuu Survival. By J. Diane Pearson with a foreword by Patricia Penn Hilden. Norman: University of Oklahoma Press, 2008. 383 pages. $34.95 cloth.

I conducted anthropological research on the Colville Indian Reservation in the late 1980s and subsequent research on the Indian powwow circuit in the Northwest through much of the 1990s. The former brought me in touch with some of the Washington descendants of the survivors of the Nez Perce War, and it was commonplace to hear references to Chief Joseph, his place of burial, and so forth. The latter research included attendance at the Chief Joseph and Warriors powwow held every June at Lapwai, Idaho, on the Nez Perce Reservation. Throughout those years, the events that resulted in the geographical division between these two groups of descendants, who both assert a claim on Chief Joseph, were a mystery to me. Numerous works devoted to traditional Nimiipuu society and to the 1877 campaign exist, but almost nothing in any detail can be found about the years of imprisonment and exile following the war and the eventual return of the survivors to two different reservations. At last we have this enlightening text by J. Diane Pearson to enhance our understanding of those sad and tumultuous years.

Only a chapter or two at the beginning is devoted to the Nez Perce War. The remainder of the text examines various events, government policies, Native interpretations and actions, and religious and educational developments that affected or were initiated by the Nimiipuu people in the years after the war. The text follows the geographical progression of the people—nearly four hundred men, women, and children at the time of surrender in 1877—as they were transferred from the final battlefield at the Bear's Paw to the Indian Territory (Oklahoma) on foot, in Army wagons, on flatboats on the upper Missouri, and by train. It was a journey of much suffering and some mortality, which passed through numerous military encampments and forts and took about ten months, including a lengthy stay at Fort Leavenworth. The people arrived at their assigned territory in north-central Oklahoma in July of 1878.

As indicated in the subtitle, Pearson frames the Nez Perce story as one of survival. Although beset with many deaths from disease and harsh conditions, the Nimiipuu (and some members of the Palus and Cayuse tribes who had fought and been captured with the Nez Perce) sustained themselves to the degree possible on the expectation that they would be able to return in the near future to Idaho and even the Wallowa River area of northeastern Oregon. They organized and conducted themselves in such a way as to keep this dream alive and thus did survive under horrendous living conditions.

Pearson presents some really amazing material seldom, if ever, included in works about the Nez Perce. She provides detailed and well-documented accounts of daily life in the encampments, the inevitable attempts of the government and missionaries to "civilize" and "Christianize" the people, and the specific impacts on tribes and individuals of institutions like the Carlisle Indian School in Pennsylvania, where some of the young people were sent. Even less common in previously published accounts is information about media coverage of Native issues at that time and the steady parade of tourists and rubberneckers who waited along roadways and at train stations to catch a glimpse of Native captives in transit, or who milled about in the military encampments and Indian settlements to watch horse races, religious ceremonies, and gambling games or just to gawk. One of the many illustrations that Pearson includes shows a drawing (from *Leslie's Illustrated Newspaper*, 20 June 1885) of a group of Nez Perce men playing cards while white Victorian tourists peer over their shoulders.

Of special interest to me was a discussion of the impact that Christianity (generally Presbyterianism) had on the cohesiveness of the group, or rather, the role it played in dividing them. Although most of the Nimiipuu maintained some connection to traditional religious beliefs and rituals, the faction that came to be known as the Chief Joseph band remained the most traditional and least Christianized, a status that made their situation more problematic in the eyes of government officials and non-Native religious leaders. The latter wanted to keep the non-Christian Indians in Oklahoma and let only the converts return. A split developed between the Joseph band and the people who converted more thoroughly to Christianity, although they resisted at first and asked that they all be kept together. Eventually the group was divided largely along religious lines between the Nez Perce and Colville reservations. (The division was also influenced by vindictive criminal indictments in Idaho filed against some of the warriors.) I had known about the religious dimension of this divide only vaguely before and am grateful for the new information in this text. It remains a difficult topic, however, especially when Native groups nowadays (and their non-Native supporters) understandably would rather emphasize solidarities than disparities.

The last part of the book details the return of the two groups of Nez Perce to their Northwest destinations, a controversial and complicated undertaking. The non-Indians in Idaho and Washington were against resettlement of what they perceived to be "dangerous renegades," and the tribes on the Colville Reservation were also against the idea of receiving the Chief Joseph band—who spoke a different language and had different beliefs and practices—among them, especially as prisoners of war and exiles from their own tribe. The book includes a short epilogue describing how the Nez Perce settlers in Washington eventually rebuilt their lives and adapted to the other tribes and they to them.

Present throughout the text is the haunting figure of Chief Joseph, who was only one of several Nimiipuu leaders before and during the Nez Perce War, but who of necessity became a key individual at the surrender and in the years that followed. After his resettlement in Washington, he tried for many years to recover and return to his homeland in the Wallowa Valley but was forever disappointed in his efforts. He died (as his physician famously said, of a broken heart) in Nespelem in 1904 and was buried on the Colville Reservation, but to this day he is also honored at Lapwai and, increasingly, in Oregon. This text has given me a greater respect and admiration for the man and for his role in helping his people survive their eight-year ordeal and beyond.

The book includes copious endnotes, numerous historic photographs and illustrations, an invaluable bibliography, and an index. There is one map showing the almost absurdly convoluted path the Nimiipuu had to follow to get from their homeland to the Indian Territory and back again. My one quibble with the book is that it could contain a few more maps and diagrams showing in more detail the many places where the Nez Perce were stationed. But that is a minor quibble. Pearson has written a moving and well-documented account of the Nimiipuu imprisonment and return that can take its place alongside our narratives of the other trails of tears and long walks all over this land that Native Americans have suffered—and survived.

Kathleen A. Dahl
Eastern Oregon University

Pushing the Bear: After the Trail of Tears. By Diane Glancy. Norman: University of Oklahoma Press, 2009. 176 pages. $14.95 paper.

American history books usually allocate two pages or fewer to the Indian Removal Act of 1830, President Andrew Jackson's ruthless push of the Cherokees to Oklahoma in order to open up land to settlers. Colin G. Calloway in *First Peoples: A Documentary Survey of American Indian History* references Jackson's propaganda. Cherokees were deemed an "unhappy race," lacking intelligence and suffering from moral turpitude (1999, 250). The term *Trail of Tears* is so familiar to the collective mind of America that it has lost its potency to enrage or move us emotionally. Diane Glancy, the prolific, award-winning author, recreates the human suffering of this forced relocation.

This work is a sequel to *Pushing the Bear: A Novel of the Trail of Tears.* Glancy was intrigued by the idea of starting life over from nothing. Indian Removal was based on Thomas Jefferson's notion that Indians would resist "civiliza-tion" if they had too much land, but agriculture played a role in the Eastern Woodlands, and the Cherokee had a tribal government, a constitutional republic modeled after that of the United States.

Of Cherokee and German-English ancestry, Glancy traveled from New Echota, Georgia, to Fort Gibson, Oklahoma, to imagine the relocation. The Cherokees were forced to walk ten miles a day; the line of exiles was ten miles long at times. One-quarter of the Cherokee perished, and the use of the $500,000 promised by the US government for resettlement remains unclear.

In the afterword Glancy describes the work as "fictional, historical non-fiction" (188). The documentation for the book came from *The Nineteenth Annual Report of the Bureau of American Ethnology to the Secretary of the Smithsonian Institution, Part I, 1897–1898* by J. W. Powell. The book, published in 1900, came into Glancy's life serendipitously and inspired her reconstruction of the events.

The daughter of an undocumented Cherokee; Glancy animates the nine-hundred-mile forced removal through descriptions of the "spirit, the emotional journey, the heartbeat during the march" (189). Glancy describes the exiles looking back every other step to the green hills, forests, and streams, the prime land appropriated by the US government. In her attempt to present the collective point of view, Glancy has not engaged in conventional techniques of "characterization." Reverend Bushyhead and Maritole are exceptions. Reverend Bushyhead leads his people forward with his evangelical fervor, alluding to the exile of the Jews to Canaan: "We work each day to drive away our discouragement. We work each day to plow our unmanageable land" (81).

The community had to depend on Bushyhead to put in orders to the government for all the necessities: bed cords, dishes, knives, forks, candlesticks, scissors, salt, and sugar. Bushyhead is also occupied with his translation of the English Bible into Cherokee. "Bushyhead found the old language buck under the yoke of translation. Some times the old words did not want to carry the new message of Christianity. But despite the tedious work of bending and stretching the old language—despite the rain, hardship, and uncertainty of everything, Bushyhead had a cabin and a log church with hewn seats and pulpit" (128–29).

The preacher is adamant in his conviction that Christianity and "conjuring" cannot coexist; his followers must leave the old ways aside. At night he could hear the groans of people. The struggle to remove rocks from the soil, to convert the hard Oklahoma dirt into farmland, was formidable. Bushyhead also listens with consternation to conjurers singing in the woods at night.

Maritole grieves over the death of her child and longs for a pregnancy. When Anna Sco-so-tah, who offers to cast a spell, approaches her, Maritole demurs. Glancy includes chants from Alan Kilpatrick's book *The Night Has a Naked Soul: Witchcraft and Sorcery among the Western Cherokee* (1998). The exiles agree that if they can once again grow their corn, they will reclaim their spirit. "The plow was the holy stick they followed. The bear was their determination to continue" (78). The conditions were brutal and some of the people succumb to torpor, despair, and madness.

The oral history of the Cherokee people predicted the Removal trail. The Nunnehi, the immortals, lived underwater: they counseled the people to stand on a mound and wait for the immortals to take them away. The ground shook and thunder was heard; the people screamed in fear; and the Nunnehi dropped part of the earth. That mound is known as Setsi in present time. The people became immortal and invisible as they were transported away.

The tragedy of *Pushing the Bear* is relentlessly depicted: reading the fifty-nine short chapters became as onerous as digging rocks out of the stubborn Oklahoma soil. A foreshadowing of hope arrives with the first green shoots of corn. At Fort Gibson the people are given shovels to dig for wells. For the first time Maritole allows a conjurer in her field. The conjurer took his rattle and drum to the field; in the cabin the people could feel the old power. "Something old broke loose in Maritole and she cried at the table." They could smell the earth from the dig, and it was not only the smell of a grave and death but also a source of water on their new land. "Out of it their lives would return" (185).

Glancy integrates passages from *The Baptist Ministry Magazine* published in the 1840s; the magazine documents the subjugation of the Cherokees in baptismal ceremonies—month by month, year by year. The officious tone mirrors government policy—this was business. Included in *Pushing the Bear* are photographs from the Cherokee Nation papers and lists of slaves, lost animals, reclamation, and spoliation claims. The dialogue in the book is contrived:

> "I feel sometimes we have walked to the moon," Maritole said.
> "There is nothing but work lined up for the rest of our lives," O-ga-na-ya said. "We won't make a dent."
> "We will all plow fields," Knobowtee said. "We will hold them in common."
> "There is already talk of taking care of the field nearest to the cabin we will build," O-ga-na-ya said (12).

The impossibility of rebuilding was a bear—the enormous task of starting over, the weight of discouragement.

The short sentences and repetitive structuring give the prose a wearisome, staccato rhythm. The pastiche of episodes, historical documents, and occasional myth were reminiscent of N. Scott Momaday's *The Way to Rainy Mountain*, but Glancy's prose does not have the same eloquence. In recounting the shameful brutality of the US policies during the nineteenth century, it is appropriate that we turn to the human, earthy prose of writers such as Glancy because the matter-of-fact tone of panoramic history books flattens and eviscerates the trauma of the displacement of Native people.

Gloria Dyc
The University of New Mexico—Gallup

Searching for Yellowstone: Race, Gender, Family, and Memory in the Postmodern West. By Norman K. Denzin. Walnut Creek, CA: Left Coast Press, 2008. 240 pages. $89.00 cloth; $29.95 paper.

Sometimes a book comes along that is so muddled and derivative, it is a wonder that it ever was published. *Searching for Yellowstone* is such a book. Overly earnest, broad in scope, and carelessly compiled, Denzin's multi-genre study offers very little that is new or interesting to Native American studies or American studies. The sections containing his personal memoirs, however, are appealing highlights of the book. Skimming the surface of stereotype and received ideas, Denzin's approach is overly impressionistic and speculative and lacks consistent intellectual rigor. Although Denzin criticizes representations of Native Americans manufactured by the Euro-American imagination, he is guilty of the same vices of romanticization and lack of tribal specificity. Denzin writes of American Indians and creates Native voices in his fictional and historical dramas as though indigenous voices were monolithic, ignoring regional and tribal specificity. He also does so seemingly without being terribly familiar with Native American literature or critical theory. Ultimately, *Searching for Yellowstone* is a sentimentalist hodgepodge that barely earns the descriptor *bricolage* and cannot justifiably be called postmodern. It's more just a mess.

The book has problems beginning with the title. First of all, a book titled *Searching for Yellowstone* was already published back in 1997. If I were the author of that book, Paul Shullery, I would be slightly annoyed that someone had the chutzpah to recycle my title a little more than a decade later. Next, examine the subtitle. Denzin's kind of taking on a lot, isn't he? Race, gender, family, memory, the postmodern West—the subtitle reveals right away the overly wide scope and lack of focus that mars this book. If Denzin bit off more than he could chew, he is more satisfying with regard to the last two elements of the subtitle. Denzin's sensitive autobiographical writings dealing with his family in the cold war period are by far the strongest material here. With race he makes some headway, if only in terms of Euro-American imaginings of Native Americans and how these aid in constructing whiteness; with gender, not so much, beyond some reflections on Euro-American masculinity and non-Native constructions of Native American femininity.

Then there's the "postmodern" part of the subtitle. In the past, the once-trendy term *postmodern* has been used to cover a multitude of sins including imprecision and vacuity, but it has lost some of its power. Befitting Denzin's subject of the "postmodern West," he purports to deploy postmodern literary and critical strategies in his book, blending multiple genres including auto-ethnography, drama, and cultural criticism. Although the bringing together of eclectic materials and quotations may be considered as meeting one oft-cited criterion of the postmodern style, Denzin's tone and politics do not mesh with most definitions of *postmodernism*. To be specific, Denzin's book and his authorial voice are not ironic, free-floating, fragmented, or archly self-aware. Rather, Denzin follows a pointed political agenda of lamenting Euro-American aggression and racism and romanticizing and idealizing Native Americans. He is earnest and sentimental about Indians; his tone and persona are far removed from the postmodern. D. H. Lawrence once wrote that "white people always, or nearly always, write sentimentally about Indians. . . . The highbrow invariably lapses into sentimentalism like the smell of bad eggs." Denzin's authorial voice, plainly stoked by "white guilt," is consistent throughout the book, and despite the fact that Denzin dramatizes heteroglossic voices and historical sources, what we hear all along is solely his own.

Denzin seeks to address everything that he can think of that is iconic or representative of Native Americans as they have been treated in American mythology and popular culture. An armload of ingredients is tossed in the stew, their flavor diminished by too much handling: "Indian" sports team mascots, Lewis and Clark and Sacagawea, Pocahontas, infected blankets, and most of all, Yellowstone. The problem is, Denzin does little that is novel with these subjects; rather he chooses to cherry-pick quotations and excerpts from a multitude of sources, allowing their sheer juxtaposition to imply a critique of Euro-American attitudes or practices. These juxtapositions, however, are rarely as incisive as their author presumes them to be. What's worse, Denzin sometimes makes implications that are not grounded in historical fact. His method involves "inventing scenes, foregoing claims to exact truth or factual accuracy, searching instead for emotional truth, for deep meaning" (18). Going for subjective "emotional truth" in a work of scholarly nonfiction could be risky business.

Looking again at the title, ostensibly this book is about Yellowstone National Park. Denzin asks us to link Yellowstone rhetorically with indigenous peoples and practices and asks us to lament the ways in which the land was stolen by Euro-Americans in order to construct a national park (America's Best Idea, if we are to believe Ken Burns). He wants Yellowstone to operate as a powerful symbol of "Indian land" and the basest form of white expropriation. Good, but Denzin fails to make the case in a persuasive way; we are simply asked to accept his premise. Denzin fails to show us how Yellowstone was integral to any particular tribe; moreover, he presents counterarguments that, against his intentions, begin to cast some doubt on his premise. We are told about tribes that traveled through Yellowstone, but no case is made to show how the land that today comprises Yellowstone is profoundly linked or claimed by any particular tribe or nation, excepting a band of Shoshones called Sheepeaters. Along with this, Denzin also acts as though the reader will find it shocking that the early motives of many planners of Yellowstone Park were commercial in origin.

Another problem with Denzin's text is that as a non-Native he opts to speak on behalf of Native Americans and create fictional Native American voices in a clumsy, romanticizing way that evinces no value of tribal specificity. For example, in one of his many dramas, Denzin quotes from a historical source that states that Native Americans lacked knowledge of Yellowstone. Then a "Native American" speaks. He or she has no name and no tribe and speaks for all indigenous people. "This is nonsense," the "Native American" intones. "We knew the region intimately" (47). All Native Americans? Who is speaking? Can we be a mite more specific?

Although Denzin presents information on the history of contact between Native Americans and Euro-Americans, he also doesn't seem overly familiar with Native American literature, culture, or theory. Few Native writers populate his bibliography. He finds the idea that Indians could also be cowboys striking (and postmodern), in spite of the fact that this figure has long been present in Western American history—he refers to Indians "playing cowboys." We might assign part of the blame to a fatuous quotation from Ward Churchill that Denzin uses as an epigraph: "White domination is so complete that even American Indian children want to be cowboys" (25).

More importantly, although his project is concerned with simulation and simulacra—and the postmodern Indian—Denzin ignores the theory of Gerald Vizenor, the preeminent Anishinaabe crossblood critic who draws from postmodernism and poststructuralism. Unbelievably, Jean Baudrillard is ignored as well. Vizenor's innovative theories on the post-Indian, post-Indian warriors of simulation, the autoposer, and other subjects, might have helped Denzin to articulate his perceptions of the postmodern West and performative Indianness better. The critical works of Louis Owens, Craig S. Womack, Jace Weaver, and others are notably absent, although Elizabeth Cook-Lynn and Paula Gunn Allen are cited. Regarding his choice of critics and his quotations from the pop-prose of Sherman Alexie, it appears that Denzin likes his Indians indignant, with essentialist tendencies.

Along with speaking of indigenes as undifferentiated, he also commits the same error in discussing Euro-Americans. He frequently speaks of the "white community" and "white America," and he implies (or states) that only "white people" make use of the Yellowstone National Park or are entertained by "Indian" sports mascots. Denzin even has a "Native American" state, "Whites don't know how to play anything other than Indian." What, not even polo? What is "whiteness"? What is this "white community"? It is taken for granted that we know the answer, and that these "whites" are all the same. That there might be differences in temperament, religion, and treatment of Native Americans among various groups of Euro-Americans over history in various regions never seems to occur to Denzin.

Besides neglecting crucial indigenous critical voices, Denzin frequently makes missteps with the writers that he regards as Indian. Churchill is quoted without qualifying him or pondering his habits of dishonesty and plagiarism, much less his morphing and challenged claims of having Native American ancestry. Moreover, Denzin is under the impression that William Least Heat-Moon is a widely accepted Native American writer, for he quotes him under the heading "A Native American Responds." Geary Hobson has baldly stated that Least Heat-Moon "is not an Indian writer, at least in the very important cultural sense of the term." Vizenor writes that Least Heat-Moon "is another cause of manifest manners and simulations in the literature of dominance . . . [he] assumes a surname and embraces pronouns that would undermine his own intented identities as a postindian author."

With his Yellowstone-area vacation property, Denzin wants to have things both ways. He wants to enjoy the park and all that it offers fully, impacting the environment (though less than his polluting neighbors whom he criticizes) by supporting the growing tourist and leisure industry. But he also wants to lament how the "white man" stole the land away from Native peoples and defaced the landscape to make the national park and its tourist environs that he consumes. With regard to Yellowstone, his overarching argument is nebulous. It is never even made clear why Yellowstone in particular was chosen to symbolize expropriated tribal land. He clearly has no qualms about taking advantage of the resources of the park nor is he calling for the park to be given "back to the Indians." So does he just want all "white people" to feel guilty about doing the same? Words such as *hand-wringing, self-righteous, sanctimonious*, and *navel-gazing* come frequently to mind when traversing this work, which reads as though it were held together with pieces of chewing gum, frayed duct tape, and baling wire but with precious little logic or solid argument. Apparently we are to dream of Yellowstone as a new utopian space where people of all races can join together as one in harmony. That's a great thought, and a nice dream, but where does such sentimentalism take us? Without a clear proposal, at what point does a fantasy go beyond a pleasant dream of unity into action?

Michael Snyder
University of Oklahoma

Spain, Europe and the Wider World, 1500–1800. By J. H. Elliot. New Haven, CT: Yale University Press, 2009. 352 pages. $38.00 cloth.

Few historians of Spain and the larger Spanish empire rival J. H. Elliot in terms of developing broad conceptual frameworks that seek to identify and explain the major periods of the early modern Spanish world. Scores of graduate students and professional historians have read Elliot's work with an eye toward dissecting his use of evidence, which he gathers from multiple sources, mainly in print form rather than archival-based, and the way he integrates the latest contributions to the historiography. Elliot is part of a cadre of British scholars who have shaped the field of Spanish and Spanish American history through a careful reading of an extensive range of printed matter and secondary materials. The works of David Brading, John Lynch, Anthony Pagden, and Hugh Thomas share shelf space with those written by J. H. Elliot. One would be hard-pressed to find a graduate research seminar about colonial Latin American history at a public or private research university in the United States or Canada that failed to assign at minimum one reading written by these British scholars (or, at the very least, readings that were shaped in part by the scholars' research and interpretations).

Elliot's latest contribution to the literature is a sequel of sorts to *Spain and Its World, 1500–1700* (1989), which tried to bring rhyme and reason to the field of Spanish historical writing. Elliot established a unity to early modern Spain by situating its politics, diplomacy, economy, and diverse society within a larger European context. Much of Elliot's scholarship has sought to link the Iberian Peninsula with the major patterns and personalities of European history, not to mention with the difficulties of maintaining such a vast and far-flung empire. Whether he makes analytical comparisons between the Count-Duke of Olivares and Cardinal Richelieu or the colonial projects of Spain and Great Britain, Elliot has done much to show his fellow Europeanists just how interconnected the historical experiences of Spain and Europe have been.

Often film critics express disappointment in Hollywood sequels. Historians will not have this problem with Elliot's sequel. As a series of lectures, articles, and conference papers, *Spain, Europe and the Wider World* elucidates a number of themes that Elliot sees as key to understanding Spain's role in the early modern world, including the symmetries in European overseas expansion, the asymmetries in conquest and colonization, and the reconfigurations that took place in the late eighteenth and early nineteenth centuries as former European colonies made the uneasy transition to nation-states.

In particular, Elliot employs the methodology of comparative history in order to establish a network of connections among Spain, Europe, and the Atlantic world, with Asia and Africa also added to the mix when circumstances call for it (for example, the African slave trade or trade with South Asia). In many ways, the above-mentioned themes that Elliot finds so compelling are case studies for the comparativist. Eschewing the nation-state or civilization as the natural unit of study, practitioners of comparative history employ case studies of either contiguous or analogical relations to test a hypothesis, which in turn relies on the development of explanatory variables and the use of evidence to confirm, alter, modify, or reject a previous hypothesis regarding the subject matter. Elliot does not quite articulate his approach to comparative history in this way, but the research questions that he asks of his evidence mirror quite nicely those posited by comparativists, including Laura Benton, Micol Seigel, and Philip Curtain, among others.

Elliot also provides keen insight into the evolution of Spanish historical writing since the end of the Franco dictatorship in 1975. Setting aside the traditional preoccupation with the "Spanish problem" or the "Spanish question," which tried to explain why Spain was so different, that is, backward and in decay, from the rest of western Europe, a new generation of Spanish historians began to travel abroad; digest and assess the major trends in international historiography; and, finally, question the suppositions of the previous generation. The result of this long intellectual exercise has been the end of the *hispanista*, or the foreign scholar who had to fill the gaps in the historical literature or develop new interpretations of the Spanish past by utilizing the theoretical frameworks most influential in the historiography. According to Elliot, with democratization in full bloom in Spain, "there is no longer any need to look to foreign researchers . . . Spanish scholars are perfectly capable of doing this for themselves" (xv).

Historians and graduate students alike will profit from reading J. H. Elliot's sequel to his 1989 work, especially the author's solid application of the comparative method to early modern history. When we take the long view of Elliot's professional career as a historian and as a member of the British cadre of *hispanistas*, we cannot help but wonder if a third installment is forthcoming, one that would transform the first two books into a trilogy worthy of any academic or research library.

Michael M. Brescia
University of Arizona

The Texture of Contact: European and Indian Settler Communities on the Frontiers of Iroquoia, 1667–1783. By David L. Preston. Lincoln: University of Nebraska Press, 2009. 408 pages. $45.00 cloth.

David Preston's fantastic new book, *The Texture of Contact*, is a wonderful addition to the existing literature on the Iroquois that historians with a more general interest in Early America will want to read. Focusing upon a series of *Iroquoian borderlands* or *Iroquoian frontiers*, Preston examines in close compass the nature of the relationships that developed between Native peoples and settlers not solely on battlefields or in council houses but also at "frontier farms, forts, churches, mills, taverns, and towns." In these small-scale encounters, he argues, "ordinary people powerfully shaped the larger social, economic, and diplomatic patterns of cultural contact through their routine negotiations." These local relationships, the substance of everyday life along these early American frontiers, he adds, "were as important in maintaining peace as the formal alliances orchestrated by British, French, and Iroquois diplomats" (5).

Preston prefers to employ terms like *Iroquoian borderlands* to older concepts like, for example, the New York Frontier, because the Five and later the Six Nations "did not operate in nebulous and boundaryless borderlands but with definite senses of boundaries among themselves and with other nations." Settlers living along the Iroquois frontier "operated in a distinctly Indian context and landscape" (14). Settlers found themselves quite often conforming to Iroquois expectations and accommodating themselves to what the Haudenosaunee expected from their neighbors and kin. The Iroquois expanded during the colonial period, establishing frontiers in the St. Lawrence, Ohio, and Susquehanna river valleys. They defy and complicate the stereotype of Native peoples retreating consistently in the face of expanding colonial settlements. The Laurentian Iroquois towns, Preston correctly points out, were not mere dumping grounds for Catholic refugees but were "towns that flourished both spiritually and materially." Sidestepping, in a sense, the historiographical debate over the role of Catholicism in the founding of Kahnawake and other settlements in the region, Preston asserts that the growing and significant population of these Christian Iroquois communities, as well as "their importance as trading partners and military allies of the French, gave the settled Indians the ability to assert their autonomy and independence" (28). For the Mohawk Valley, Preston describes how Palatine, Dutch, English, Irish, and African colonists lived in close order with Mohawks, Oneidas, and Mahicans. At Schoharie, Tiononderoge, and Canajoharie, Indians and non-Indians lived lives "often characterized by mutually beneficial social, economic, and religious relationships" (70). The material existence of the Mohawks and their neighbors closely resembled each other, and they derived their living from the land in remarkably similar ways. Though New Yorkers steadily pressed upon Iroquois lands in the Mohawk Valley, the "Mohawks accommodated the New York colonists and lived a peaceful, if increasingly tense, coexistence" (115).

Despite this mounting tension, the Mohawk Valley remained at peace during the colonial era, but this was not so for Iroquoian frontiers in the

Susquehanna River valley. Settlers who moved into this region sought land and independence, and for them, peaceful relationships with the local Indians were literally a necessity for survival. They coexisted, Preston argues, and "communicated, and crafted mutually beneficial relationships through such routine encounters as the small-scale trading of corn, alcohol, tobacco, and wild game" (118). Still, with some considerable understatement, Preston points out that at times and in places an "undercurrent of disagreement" existed. Preston does not ignore the violence that so many historians have found characteristic of these frontiers. Natives and newcomers, after all, competed for control of finite frontier resources—hunting grounds, springs, and fertile soil—which in the end they used in incompatible ways. Out of these incompatibilities came conflict. Furthermore, "different cultural beliefs about alcohol, land use, property, and reciprocity made settler-Indian encounters prone to break down into fights, brawls, and, more infrequently, murders" (130). Thus in Preston's retelling, the source of the bloodshed that came to the region in the middle of the eighteenth century stemmed less from disease, systemic abuses in trade, or the failure of diplomacy conducted by imperial officials than it did from "the mistreatment, misunderstanding, and violence that arose in the context of ordinary colonial farmers and Indians' everyday encounters" (155). Preston emphasizes the primacy of local relationships gone bad and finds in the texture of everyday life the roots of racial violence.

Yet throughout the book, Preston argues that too many historians have characterized "all white settlers as racist killers" (222–23) or have viewed colonists only as "land-hungry, violent and ethnocentric catalysts of conflict with Indians" (6). In the Ohio River valley, he argues, even after the violence of the Great War for Empire, "Indians and settlers continued to interact in nonviolent ways, establish mutually satisfactory trading relationships, and negotiate over land just as they had before the wars" (211). Preston concedes, however, that new ingredients "in these encounters were the mutual distrust, hatred, and vengeful feelings that some—but not all—Indians and colonists held" (233).

But how many colonists hated Indians? And vice versa? Certainly Preston's criticism of previous historians is a touch overstated: many scholars have examined these early frontiers and none of them have depicted "*all* white settlers as racist killers" (202). In an effort to distance himself from the work of earlier scholars who have emphasized the violence of the early American frontier, Preston may in places go too far in the other direction, setting up something of a straw man. Clearly, enough colonists and Indians hated each other to immerse parts of the Ohio and Susquehanna valleys in blood during the second half of the eighteenth century, and it does not hurt Preston's argument at all to say so.

Despite the manifold horrors of intercultural warfare in the Ohio country, described so well by so many historians, peace returned in some measure at its conclusion. The responsibility for the violence that reignited there in the 1760s, Preston asserts, cannot justly be placed upon frontier settlers. Rather, it was the British Army "more so than the squatters, with whom Natives often peacefully dealt" that "was the touchstone of conflict because of its military colonization of the Ohio Valley" (223). Like revolutionary-era American colonists, Native peoples in the Ohio Valley "experienced the British presence as an unwanted standing army that threatened to destroy their basic liberties" (227). Perhaps so, but as historians like James Merrell have pointed out, the viciousness of groups like the Paxton Boys—and other Indian killers—can also be understood through examining closely the texture of contact between colonial settlers and Native men and women. Fear and hatred existed uneasily beside the manifold encounters that characterized everyday life.

Preston carries his discussion of intercultural relations along these borderlands through to the end of the revolution. At the outset of the war between rebels and redcoats, the Six Nations found themselves caught "between two hells" with both the colonists and the British demanding their loyalty (283). Even here, however, the texture of earlier contacts influenced the decisions that Iroquois people made. The close ties between Palatine settlers and their Oneida neighbors, for instance, informed the choices of many Oneidas to side with the Americans during the Revolutionary War. That conflict rapidly became a race war characterized by a level of hostility that justified horrid atrocities. Many Iroquois fled the homelands where they had lived in close contact with their non-Indian neighbors. Iroquois people who remained behind understood well that the victorious Americans coveted their lands, hoped to dispossess them, and wished to drive them into the West.

David Preston, in his first book, has offered an important addition to the literature of the Iroquois and Native peoples in Early America more generally. Although a number of important and well-received books on the Iroquois have been published in the past few years, and still more important work is in press, none of these works do quite what Preston has aimed to do. He looks, as much as his imaginative use of the sources allows, at the lives of ordinary colonists and Native peoples. He looks at how they interacted, how Native peoples accommodated Europeans and assimilated them into their world, and how colonists of the empire and citizens of the American state failed to live up to what their neighbors expected of them. Although in places Preston downplays the genuine hatred that developed out of frontier encounters, few recent books demonstrate as effectively the tenuous possibility for intercultural peace and the enormous forces that denied this accommodation a chance to be anything but a short-lived phenomenon.

Michael Leroy Oberg
University of Houston

FIRST PEOPLES
New Directions in Indigenous Studies

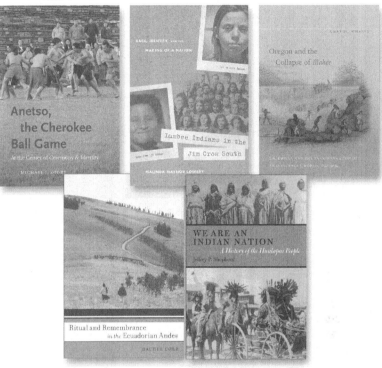

COLLABORATING PRESSES

UNIVERSITY OF ARIZONA PRESS

UNIVERSITY OF MINNESOTA PRESS

UNIVERSITY OF NORTH CAROLINA PRESS

OREGON STATE UNIVERSITY PRESS

First Peoples: New Directions in Indigenous Studies is a four-press initiative that publishes books exemplifying contemporary trends in Indigenous studies. The participating university presses share a collaborative grant from the Andrew W. Mellon Foundation that supports the publication of 40 books over four years and creates the means for the presses to further their commitment to scholarly communication in the field of Indigenous studies.

The initiative seeks the best and most robust research by scholars whose publications will contribute to the development of the field. First Peoples also provides extensive marketing, which will help initiative presses attend to the growing dialogue among Native and non-Native scholars, communities, and publishers.

www.firstpeoplesnewdirections.org

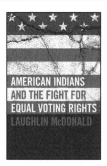
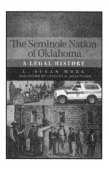

AMERICAN INDIANS AND THE FIGHT FOR EQUAL VOTING RIGHTS

By Laughlin McDonald

$55.00 HARDCOVER · 360 PAGES

The struggle for voting rights was not limited to African Americans in the South. American Indians also faced discrimination at the polls and still do today. This book explores their fight for equal voting rights and carefully documents how non-Indian officials have tried to maintain dominance over Native peoples despite the rights they are guaranteed as American citizens.

THE SEMINOLE NATION OF OKLAHOMA

A Legal History

By L. Susan Work

$45.00 HARDCOVER · 376 PAGES, 10 B&W ILLUS

When it adopted a new constitution in 1969, the Seminole Nation was the first of the Five Tribes in Oklahoma to formally reorganize its government. In the face of an American legal system that sought either to destroy its nationhood or to impede its self-government, the Seminole Nation tenaciously retained its internal autonomy, cultural vitality, and economic subsistence. Here, L. Susan Work draws on her experience as a tribal attorney to present the first legal history of the twentieth-century Seminole Nation.

BEYOND BEAR'S PAW

The Nez Perce Indians in Canada

By Jerome A. Greene

$24.95 HARDCOVER · 264 PAGES, 18 B&W ILLUS.

In the fall of 1877, Nez Perce Indians were desperately fleeing U.S. Army troops. After a 1,700-mile journey across Idaho, Wyoming, and Montana, the Nez Perces headed for the Canadian border. But the army caught up with them at the Bear's Paw Mountains in northern Montana, and following a devastating battle, Chief Joseph and most of his people surrendered. *Beyond Bear's Paw* is the first book to explore the fate of these "non-treaty" Indians. It offers new perspectives on the Nez Perces' struggle for freedom, their hapless rejection, and their ultimate cultural renewal.

UNIVERSITY OF
OKLAHOMA PRESS

2800 VENTURE DRIVE
NORMAN, OK 73069
TEL 800 627 7377

OUPRESS.COM

facebook.COM/OUPRESS
You Tube.COM/OUPRESS

Editing Eden
A Reconsideration of Identity,
Politics, and Place in Amazonia
EDITED BY FRANK HUTCHINS
AND PATRICK C. WILSON
$35.00 paperback

A Doctor among
the Oglala Sioux Tribe
The Letters of Robert H. Ruby,
1953–1954
ROBERT H. RUBY
Edited and with an introduction
by Cary C. Collins and
Charles V. Mutschler
$45.00 hardcover

The Oglala Sioux
Warriors in Transition
ROBERT H. RUBY
Foreword by Glenn L. Emmons
New introduction by
Cary C. Collins
$14.95 paperback

A BISON ORIGINAL
The Fast Runner
Filming the Legend of Atanarjuat
MICHAEL ROBERT EVANS
$19.95 paperback
INDIGENOUS FILMS SERIES

Journeys West
Jane and Julian Steward
and Their Guides
VIRGINIA KERNS
$55.00 hardcover

Natalie Curtis Burlin
A Life in Native and
African American Music
MICHELLE WICK PATTERSON
$45.00 hardcover

NOW IN PAPER
Chief Bender's Burden
The Silent Struggle
of a Baseball Star
TOM SWIFT
$19.95 paperback

*For complete descriptions
and to order, visit us online!

UNIVERSITY OF
NEBRASKA PRESS

WWW.NEBRASKAPRESS.UNL.EDU
800-848-6224 · publishers of Bison Books

"EXPLORING THE RED ATLANTIC".

The Institute of Native American Studies ("INAS") at the University of Georgia ("UGA") invites submissions of paper proposals for the conference "Exploring the Red Atlantic" to be held at the University of Georgia November 12–13, 2010.

In a forthcoming article in *American Indian Culture and Research Journal*, Jace Weaver defines the Red Atlantic as the movement of western hemisphere indigenes and indigenous wealth, ideas, and technology around the Atlantic basin from 1000 C.E. to 1800. From the earliest moments of European/Native contact in the Americas to 1800 and beyond, Indians were central to the Atlantic experience. Native resources, ideas, and peoples traveled the Atlantic with regularity and became among the most basic components of Atlantic cultural exchange. Moreover, Europeans and colonists defined themselves by comparison with and in opposition to Natives. They even sought indigeneity in hybridized identities, as reflected in works of literature like *The Female American* and Susanna Rowson's *Reuben and Rachel*.

We invite submissions on any aspect of the Red Atlantic from its beginnings to 1900. Submissions may reflect any disciplinary perspective. A small amount of funds is available to support travel. Funds will be awarded competitively, and preference will be given to graduate students. Abstracts should be typed double-spaced and be no more than 250 words. They should be sent to INAS@uga.edu before September 17, 2010. Notifications will be made before October 1.

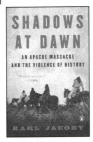

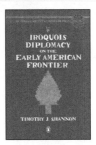